PREACHING WITH
Variety

Other books in the Preaching With series:

Preaching with Conviction, by Kenton C. Anderson
Preaching with Freshness, by Bruce Mawhinney
Preaching with Integrity, by Kenton C. Anderson
Preaching with Passion, by Alex Montoya
Preaching with Relevance, by Keith Willhite

PREACHING WITH
Variety

*How to Re-create the Dynamics
of Biblical Genres*

JEFFREY D. ARTHURS

Kregel
Ministry

Preaching with Variety: How to Re-create the Dynamics of Biblical Genres

© 2007 by Jeffrey D. Arthurs

Published by Kregel Publications, a division of Kregel, Inc., 2450 Oak Industrial Dr. NE, Grand Rapids, MI 49505.

Library of Congress Cataloging-in-Publication Data
Arthurs, Jeffrey D.
Preaching with variety : how to re-create the dynamics of biblical genres / by Jeffrey D. Arthurs.
   p. cm.
   Includes bibliographical references.
   1. Preaching—Biblical teaching. I. Title.
BV4221.A78 2007
251-dc22   2006103429

ISBN: 978-0-8254-2019-1

To my wife:
My proofreader,
a student of the Word,
and the most delightful person I know.

Contents

Illustrations

Foreword

Preachers sometimes get bored with their own preaching. It's the regularity that dulls us. On some Sundays we speak because we are expected to say something and not because we have something to say. In addition, we get bored with preaching the Bible because we treat the Bible as an assortment of texts from which to build sermons. To actually preach with variety and excitement, we must treat the Scriptures as they are—a library of different types of great literature.

Some of the theologians who wrote the Bible communicated their message through stories as gripping as a John Grisham novel. The Bible is inhabited by saints who lived very messy lives. Their family values included polygamy, adultery, incest, lust, rape, even murder. Yet these same people also reflected enormous courage and faith. It is through those very human, sometimes shocking, stories that the holy God revealed himself to us.

Another section of the library contains poetry. The psalmists reflected through their poetry the whole palette of human emotions. The prophets, stern as they were, often presented their messages through poetry. Some realities can only be communicated with images. Because God loves poetry, the preacher must try to appreciate it. The poetry in the Bible can both ignite your spirit and comfort, as well as confront and encourage, your people.

You'll find a collection of proverbs in the Bible that promise to make us wise. Few preachers ever preach from Proverbs, though. We know more about "wise guys" than wise men. It's a shame. Preaching from the literature of Proverbs can change the "worldview" of your people. We need a handle on how to do it.

We also have the parables that Jesus told. They are simple stories that take genius to create. Parables are not illustrations throwing light on some abstract truth. The parable is the truth. A preacher or listener has to work to understand them. It took the disciples years to get the hang of them. If we don't make the effort, Jesus warned, "Hearing they will not hear them." How would you approach a parable? If Jesus used them, shouldn't we?

Then there is "apocalyptic" literature. Even the name of the genre unsettles us. But to begin to appreciate the meaning of Daniel or Revelation, we have to understand the literary form. The heroes and the villains in "apocalyptic" literature seem like creatures that escaped out of a bad nightmare or a horror movie. Yet, we must preach these books. We would welcome some guidance on how to understand and apply them.

Jeff Arthurs introduces us to a variety of literary forms in the Bible and also offers us guidance on how to read and preach them effectively. What he has written, you will find helpful and encouraging. If you invest a few dollars and about five hours of your time to read this book, it may shape you for life and make you better able to preach the Bible—as it is for women and men as they are.

—Haddon W. Robinson

Introduction

Plant a carrot, get a carrot,
Not a Brussels sprout.
That's why I like vegetables:
You know what you're about.
                    —*The Fantasticks* (a musical)

It's comforting to know what you'll reap when you plant a garden.
It's also comforting to know what you're in for when you begin a book,
so allow me to give you a quick tour of the garden in your hands. This
book is about biblical preaching. I believe that a sermon's *content*
should explain and apply the Word of God as it is found in a biblical
text, and a sermon's *form* should unleash the impact of that text. The
second part of that declaration is the special province of this book. We
should be biblical in how we preach, not just what we preach. To that
end, this book describes the rhetorical dynamics of biblical genres and
suggests how preachers can reproduce some of those dynamics in their
sermons. These descriptions and suggestions help to equip preachers
to declare the unchanging Word in ways that are engaging and suited
to modern audiences, and to do so by remaining faithful to the text.

To accomplish this goal, chapters 1 and 2 defend my basic theory—
that variety in preaching is, indeed, biblical, and it can enhance
receptivity. Chapters 3 through 9 then flesh out the application of
the theory to the biblical text. Each of these chapters first discusses
interpretive concerns, examining the techniques that each genre uses
to do what it does. Then, in the "Try This" section, the chapters explore ways to apply the techniques of the biblical text to homiletics.
The genres covered are psalm, narrative, parable, proverb, epistle, and
apocalyptic.

With deference to brother Martin, allow me to declare 9.5 theses
to further clarify the presuppositions of this book.

Thesis 1: A Sermon Must Herald God's Word or Else It Isn't a Sermon

In John Stott's model, preaching is "standing between two
worlds"—the world of the text and the world of the listeners. As
such, preaching is a bridge that carries the Word into the twenty-first
century. The metaphor seems to capture well the essential nature of
preaching.

> Now a bridge is a means of communication between two
> places which would otherwise be cut off from one another
> by a river or a ravine. It makes possible a flow of traffic. . . .
> Our task is to enable God's revealed truth to flow out of the
> Scriptures into the lives of men and women of today.[1]

If a sermon doesn't facilitate this flow, I'm not interested in it. I've
taught public speaking for years and value a well-crafted speech, but
a speech isn't a sermon. Preachers are heralds who speak on behalf of
the King, and their job is to faithfully and skillfully recommunicate
what has already been communicated. Thus, when I advocate variety,
I propose variety of form, not of subject matter.

Thesis 1 raises the question of definition—what is a sermon? The
dynamics of human communication, to say nothing of the dynamics of
the impartation of spiritual life, are difficult to capture in definitions.[2]
Thus we often turn to metaphors like *heralding* and *bridge building.*

Nevertheless, what metaphor offers in breadth it loses in precision, so until someone finds a better way to summarize and transmit the concept of preaching, we're stuck with definitions.[3] In this garden, preaching looks like this: *Accurately heralding the Word of God to a particular audience for a particular purpose by explaining, applying, and embodying that message.*

Thesis 2: Some Issues Are More Important than the Topic of This Book

Preaching with variety can add much to your ministry, but without other components, you have no ministry. One of those components is ethos—the persuasive impact of character. Isocrates, the ancient rhetorician, stated, "Who does not know that words carry greater conviction when spoken by men of good repute than when spoken by men who live under a cloud, and that the argument which is made by a man's life is more weight than that which is furnished by words?"[4]

If you are dishonest, lazy, insincere, volatile, or lecherous, preaching with all the variety in the world will not ensure successful ministry. Our Lord says to us, "Watch your life and doctrine closely, because in doing so you will save both yourself and your hearers" (1 Tim. 4:16). He does not say, "Watch your sermon forms closely, because in them you find life." An observer asked Charles Spurgeon's brother the basis of the great pulpiteer's success. The brother replied, "I think it lies in the fact that he loves Jesus of Nazareth and Jesus of Nazareth loves him."[5]

Since words flow out of the overflow of the heart, a clean heart is ten times more important than using a variety of forms to arrange those words. To borrow a phrase from empirical research, preaching with variety is *necessary*, but not *sufficient.* To accurately herald the Word, variety is necessary, but by itself variety is not sufficient to produce spiritual growth.

Another component that overshadows the need for variety is the end, or *telos*, of preaching. To use John Piper's phrase, the goal of our preaching must be the "supremacy of God."[6] Contrast this goal with less noble goals such as growing a church, giving pleasure to listeners, and increasing knowledge of facts. Magnifying God does not, of course, demand that we ignore people (in fact, it demands the opposite), but the preacher who magnifies God will view all topics, means, and preaching occasions as opportunities to spread his glory. If honorable, yet secondary, ends become idols, we no longer have a ministry worth perpetuating.

Thesis 3: The Topic of This Book Is Still Important

Having argued that some things are more important than variety, I don't want you to throw this book away! Variety is important too. The first two chapters fully present my case, but in brief, how we say something influences how listeners receive it.

Thesis 4: There Is No Such Thing as the Sermon Form

If the use of testimony, music, or parable helps us fulfill our calling to stand between two worlds, we're free to use such forms. If the use of question and answer, story, or object lesson techniques help us glorify God and minister to the listeners, we should feel free to preach with a variety of forms, just as Jesus and other biblical preachers did. The defining essence of an expository sermon lies primarily in its content, not its form.[7]

But thesis 4 needs to be qualified. Some people disagree with it. They believe that preaching *is* marked by a certain form, and they should know! After all, they've heard sermons since they were kids, and they know what preaching sounds like. For some of these folk, a sermon must have three points; for others, the sermon must follow the text verse-by-verse; for others, the sermon must end with an invitation. To these folk, a change of form seems like a change of content. They believe sermons must be delivered within a narrow range of decibels (whether loud or soft), minutes (whether long or short), tone of voice (whether conversational or oratorical), and pulpit style (whether wood or Plexiglas).

So if you drive your homiletical car down a new road, you may be in for a bumpy ride. Davies observes that for many people, preaching is like church bells—an easily recognized and comforting sound that will be tolerated so long as it does not disturb early morning sleep.[8] Howard adds,

Ruts become routines. Routine, carried on in the local church, tends to become "righteous." Righteous routine becomes unassailably, uncritically rigid—the best and only way to do things. Along come those who want to make a change in this rigidly righteous routine. They may find out that what they propose to change is something that others are deeply attached to and not about to change. . . . Fierce defenders of the established faith are also often fierce defenders of the established format.[9]

The solution to entrenched taste is neither to brush it off nor allow it to ruffle your feathers. We must patiently help people distinguish between biblical doctrine and communicative procedure,[10] and in the midst of that patient instruction, we can find encouragement in the fact that most North Americans in the twenty-first century have been socialized to expect variety and multiple perspectives. Preachers who would expand their creativity will generally find receptive attitudes. More on that in chapter 2.

Thesis 5: Preaching with Variety Is Not a Fad

Ample warrant for preaching with variety can be found in both the literature of the Bible and the preaching of Jesus. Chapter 1 will expand this thesis. Suffice it here to say that the Bible is a cornucopia of genres and forms and so was Jesus' preaching. The Bible offers the careful reader more clues for the forms of heralding than most of us will ever be able to employ: dialogues, debates, doxologies, letters, lists, laws, parables, proverbs, prayers, hymns, taunts, baptismal formulas, analogies, symbols, visions, mnemonic devices, and more. God has poured out a profusion of rhetorical forms. When we borrow some of those forms to recommunicate the text, we are faithful heralds.

Thesis 6: Variety Should Not Wag the Dog

No gimmicks allowed. Achtemeier warns that "no preacher can show forth simultaneously his or her own cleverness and the lordship of Jesus Christ."[11] As you read this book, remember thesis 2 and the supremacy of God, and remember thesis 1—our goal is to be biblical.

We use variety because the text does. The form of the sermon should reproduce some impact of the form of the text. You fill your quiver with different kinds of arrows to hit different kinds of targets, not to display your prowess as an archer.

Thesis 7: Listeners Could Use Some Variety

Having emphasized the proper role of variety—the glory of God through the communication of the text—I now urge you not to forget the listeners. Preachers bring glory to God by prompting the glad submission of the human heart. At times, though, "listening to an exposition of Scripture is about as exciting as watching house paint dry."[12] Our listeners deserve better. As they gather to feed on the Word, let us serve our best recipes. Variety can add some zip, spice, and zing to our preaching. Spurgeon said it well: "[Our listeners] must be awake, understanding what we are saying, and feeling its force, or else we may as well go to sleep too."[13]

Thesis 8: Preachers Could Use Some Variety Too!

Sundays roll around with amazing regularity, don't they? You may feel like a worker on an assembly line, cranking out sermon after sermon. One survey discovered that pastors preach an average of sixty-four sermons a year and speak 3.4 times per week.[14] Ministerial burnout lurks in those statistics, especially when coupled with the other stresses of the pastorate. As we crank out sermons week after week, year after year, each sermon sounding just like the others, we begin to feel that nothing different ever happens. Once that attitude forms in our hearts (remember that Jesus said we speak out of the fullness of our hearts), dullness creeps into our words. The mode and mood of our speaking becomes dry. A self-perpetuating cycle forms: our preaching is monotonous, monotonous preaching sours our attitude, a sour attitude leads to monotonous preaching, and the cycle continues. Get off the treadmill! It's time to preach with variety. It could revolutionize your attitude toward your own preaching.

Thesis 9: Preachers Should Minister with Their Strengths

This book will stretch you, but it should not put you on the rack of false guilt. I want this book to unleash you, not unhinge you. I want this book to help you find your stride, go with your pitch, get in a groove, and play within yourself (add your own sports metaphor here). This book gives tools to unleash your gifts; it does not heap on false guilt for failing to use all the latest homiletical bells and whistles. Working from the conviction that preaching is "truth through personality," I believe that the person of the preacher is indispensable in the process of transmitting God's Word. Thus, we should feel empowered to allow God to use our personalities, perspectives, and strengths. If you're a humorous person, be humorous. If you're organized, be organized. If you're erudite, be erudite. If you're quiet, be quiet. God wants to spread His Word through *you.* This book has tools for the warm and pastoral, the imaginative and literary, and the simple and homespun. It will help you communicate from your heart.

It goes without saying that we should not let our strengths become weaknesses (you can be so quiet that no one can hear you), and it goes without saying that preaching is not ultimately about us (see theses 1 and 2), but these caveats do not change the fact that God uses humans to reveal himself. We should joyfully yield to that fact and not put on airs, trying to become something we're not. If you're a shepherd boy, don't try to fight in Saul's armor. Too many preachers fight against themselves in the pulpit. Be yourself, and find some sermon forms that free you to do that.

Thesis 9.5: Preaching with Variety Is an Attainable Goal

My final half thesis is a self-conscious but sincere pep talk: You can do it! Preaching with variety is not hard. True, you may feel awkward the first time you implement question and answer in your sermon, or open up with self-disclosure, or preach with images more than points, but I think you'll find the experience freeing and enjoyable. This has been my experience and the experience of my students. Happy are the preachers who look into the eyes of their listeners and see interest and participation. Preaching with variety helps us communicate. Remember that the root of *communication* is *commune.*

The formation of *community* increases when we *communi*cate with imagination, feedback, affection, and holistic involvement. This book provides down-to-earth instruction and examples for *communi*cating with the souls whom God has appointed us to watch. By God's grace, you can do it.

1

The Great Communicator

There is a . . . sense in which the Bible, since it is after all literature, cannot properly be read except as literature; and the different parts of it as the different sorts of literature they are.

—C. S. Lewis, *Reflections on the Psalms*

I am persuaded that without knowledge of literature pure theology cannot at all endure. . . . Certainly it is my desire that there shall be as many poets and rhetoricians as possible, because I see that by these studies, as by no other means, people are wonderfully fitted for the grasping of sacred truth and for handling it skillfully and happily.

—Martin Luther, quoted in Clines, "Story and Poem"

Here is the Son of God using anecdotes, stories, paradoxes, contradictions, humor, irony, question and answer. Is that the stuff of revelation from on high? It is not the performance that gains tenure or renews contracts. Jesus laid himself open to

criticism from even the sophomore class in a rabbinic school, criticism as to scholarship, logic, and systematic consistency. Why did he do it?
                              —Fred B. Craddock, *Overhearing the Gospel*

Why should we preach with variety? Because God himself is the Great Communicator, and part of that greatness is seen in his freshness and creativity. Consider, for instance, the variety of his special revelation, the written Word. The Bible is a cornucopia of literary forms—poetry, law, parable, and story, to name a few. Because God has "taken the trouble" of communicating with such variety, careful exegetes should sit up and take notice. We rejoice in, respond to, and learn from our Lord's creativity. Chapters 3–9 discuss how we can do that, so I won't belabor the point here except to say that because the Great Communicator communicates with variety in the Bible, it seems natural that we would mirror that variety in our sermons.

Think, too, about the Lord's communication through general revelation. Echoing Psalm 19, Calvin called the universe "a dazzling theater," "a most glorious theater," and "this magnificent theater of heaven and earth."[1] The more I learn about nature, the more amazed I am at God's seemingly infinite demonstration of creativity and variety. Just the other night, as I was studying with my seventh grade son, I learned that the Amazon rainforest hosts 20 million species of insects![2] That's *species*, not individual bugs. This world bursts with an inventive, wise, sometimes wry display of God's power and glory, and variety is part of that glory. As the poet Gerard Manly Hopkins said, "Glory be to God for dappled things":

> All things counter, original, spare, strange;
>   Whatever is fickle, freckled (who knows how?)
>   With swift, slow, sweet, sour, adazzle, dim;
> He fathers-forth whose beauty is past change:
>   Praise him.[3]

While preaching with variety is not the only homiletical value, not even the primary value, it certainly has sanction when we consider the variety the Great Communicator employs.

We also know that God's preachers—that is, the prophets and wit-nesses—employed variety. In some cases, they did so under direct orders from their Master, as when God ordered Isaiah to go around barefoot for three years to communicate that Sargon would take Egypt and Cush captive (Isa. 20:1–6). God ordered Jeremiah to use a clay pot and a yoke (Jer. 19; 27–28), and he ordered Ezekiel to use object lessons such as miniature siege works, body positions, bread, and a shaved head (Ezek. 4–5). Nathan's use of parable is well known (2 Sam. 12:1–12), as is Stephen's use of narrative history (Acts 7). While these examples are not *normative* for all preachers in all times (we are not commanded to shave our heads or use parables), they are *suggestive* of how God's preachers then and now can respond to various exigen-cies. Remember, there is no such thing as *the* sermon form. We have freedom, and the variety that biblical preachers used suggests that we should use that freedom.

God the Son certainly communicated with variety. Dialogue, story, visuals, and "lecture" were common in his teaching, which was par-ticipatory and image laden. He defined concepts by example more than by creed. Lewis and Lewis have counted 19 questions[4] and 142 comparisons just in the Sermon on the Mount.[5] They state, "These metaphors, figures, and likenesses keep stabbing His listeners' minds and memories into constant alertness."[6]

It is self-evident, then, that God uses great variety in his commu-nication. The question arises, *Why?* Why does God use poetry and proverbs, stories and visions? Why did the Son of God use parable and objects, monologue and dialogue?

The answer is twofold: because God is both an artist and a per-suader. He expresses himself with skill, and he moves audiences with purpose.

God "fathers-forth" beauty because he is beautiful. This attribute is reflected in the artistry of the Bible. Under the inspiration of the Holy Spirit, the writer of Ecclesiastes speaks for all the writers of the Bible: "The Teacher searched to find just the right [or 'pleasing'] words" (12:10). While individual biblical texts can be placed along a continuum from more aesthetic to less aesthetic, there is in general, as Leland Ryken observes, "a preoccupation among biblical writers with artistry, verbal craftsmanship, and aesthetic beauty."[7] Their writings tend to be affective, concrete, and experiential, showing the truth more than stating the truth in propositional or abstract form. Verbal artistry reflects the Artist, and it creates delight and enjoyment for the reader.

Such artistry also intensifies impact. God's purposes flow out of his character just as artistry does. He is active as well as beautiful. He is building his kingdom, so the verbal artistry of the Bible is not simply art for art's sake; it is art that accomplishes his purposes. Rhetorical goals, not just aesthetic goals, lie behind the beauty and variety of the Bible. John's statements capture, perhaps, the mind-set of all the writers of the Bible: "These are written that you may believe that Jesus is the Christ, the Son of God, and that by believing you may have life in his name" (John 20:31); "We proclaim to you what we have seen and heard, so that you also may have fellowship with us. And our fellowship is with the Father and with his Son, Jesus Christ" (1 John 1:3).

While C. S. Lewis certainly valued the artistry of the Bible, he made it clear that the Bible is more than art for art's sake: "The Bible is so remorselessly and continuously sacred that it does not invite, it excludes or repels, the merely aesthetic approach.[8] Ramm makes a similar argument when he claims that the Bible is "not a theoretical book or a book of theological abstractions, but a book that intends to have a mighty influence on the lives of its readers."[9] The Bible is well viewed, then, as art and as rhetoric. The chapters that follow in this current book will unpack the dynamics of six genres—psalm, narrative, parable, proverb, epistle, and apocalyptic. These literary forms will be viewed as a means of managing a relationship with readers and listeners, moving them toward predetermined beliefs, values, or actions.

Jesus certainly moved his listeners toward these destinations. Rhetorical sensibilities, in fact, permeate Jesus' communication. When asked by an expert in the law to define "neighbor," Jesus told a story (Luke 10:25–37). Why? To accomplish something that would have been difficult to accomplish with another form. He wanted to reframe the discussion, gradually reveal the truth, instruct the lawyer, engage him holistically, lead him to understand his own heart, convince him of his need, convict him of his values, cause him to ponder the truth, and lead him to faith and repentance. The form of Jesus' communication (parable) was an indispensable component in achieving those goals. For the Great Communicator, form is not simply the husk surrounding the seed, superfluous and cumbersome; it is more like the architectural design of the Vietnam Memorial, inseparable from meaning and impact.

We know intuitively, of course, that form and content go together. Instead of sending an e-mail, for instance, send a singing telegram, and you'll see a difference in how the receiver responds. Instead of shouting at your kids, whisper. The content may be identical, but the impact will be different. Leaf through your mail. Pick up the glossy brochure for a Hawaiian cruise. It shows happy, toned people in crystal blue oceans. The message is packaged as a shimmering vision. Imagine the same ideational content packaged as a one-page business letter, or drawn with crayon.[10] You don't need the artistic sensibilities of Van Gogh to realize that form and content are a unit.

Rhetorician Kenneth Burke explains one way that form functions. It does so by creating and guiding listener experience. Burke defines *form* as "the creation of an appetite in the mind of the auditor and the adequate satisfying of that appetite."[11] Perhaps the clearest example of creating and satisfying an appetite can be heard in music. Imagine a simple progression of chords—C, F, C, G, C. Because you've heard that progression in a thousand country, rock, and pop songs (not to mention gospel hymns!), you expect the sequence to move that direction and end on the tonal C chord. When it does, you feel resolution. Now imagine the progression ends on G. The sequence is unresolved. This leaves you hovering or feeling hollow. Your desire/expectation was not fulfilled. Now imagine the conclusion of a classical symphony. Previous experience tells you that symphonies end with "Tum, Tum, ta TUM!" but say you're listening to one that ends with an abrupt "Tum, Tum." It leaves you emotionally suspended, hovering two feet over the earth. You desire *terra firma*—"ta TUM!"—because the music has aroused an "appetite" that craves fulfillment. When composers provide "ta TUM!" they satisfy the very appetite they aroused.

Form functions the same way in literature. Burke says, "A work has form in so far as one part of it leads a reader to anticipate another part, to be gratified by the sequence."[12] Instead of using musical chords, literature uses a different set of formal features. The later chapters of this book closely examine the features of six genres; here it's enough to argue that the rhythm of a poem or the plot structure of a story creates expectation in the reader. We desire the rhythm to pulse and the plot to climax.[13] From the jigging cadence of a limerick to the classic reversal in Greek drama, audiences expect certain things to happen and are gratified when those things occur. Sometimes the opening line is enough to point the arrows of our expectations: "Once upon a time . . ."; "A priest, a rabbi, and a minister went into a bar"; "I, being of sound mind, do hereby . . ."; "And it came to pass that a certain man went on a journey." From the opening line, you know what's coming, and literature with formal excellence will capitalize on that desire.

Form is one of the factors that determines the level of participation demanded of the listener. Riddles and parables induce thought—their brevity, use of metaphor, and laconic quality cause us to ponder. The sports page, on the other hand, with its endless statistics, multiple stories, and breezy style lends itself to scanning. Advertising jingles work almost subliminally, sticking in our minds like superglue because they hypnotically repeat simple tunes and simple words. Puritan sermons demand concentration lest they numb us by their length and complexity. Readers are sometimes unaware that form prompts their participation, but participate they do, and often without realizing it. Form's influence may, in fact, be most powerful when it is subtle.

When form prompts participation, we are more likely to accept the ideas associated with the form. Burke explains: "Yielding to the form prepares for assent to the matter identified with it. . . . And this attitude of assent may then be transferred to the matter which happens to be associated with the form."[14]

"For instance," Burke continues, "imagine a passage built about a set of oppositions ('*we* do this, but they . . . do that; *we* stay *here*, but *they* go *there*; *we* look *up*, but they look *down*,' etc.). Once you grasp the trend of the form, it invites participation regardless of the subject matter. Formally, you will find yourself swinging along with the succession of antitheses, even though you may not agree with the proposition that is being presented in this form."[15]

I found this to be true for myself with that old Burger King jingle:

Hold the pickles, hold the lettuce,
Special orders don't upset us,
All we ask is that you let us
Serve it your way.

As I swung along with the regular rhythm, clever rhyme, childish tune, and staccato words, I transferred my "attitude of assent" to the proposition—Burger King is looking out for me. They want to serve me. They love me! I participated in my own persuasion, prompted in part by the form of the jingle.[16]

When it comes to advertising jingles, form helps shape our attitudes. When it comes to sermons, form helps shape our faith. Craddock explains:

> Ministers who, week after week, frame their sermons as arguments, syllogisms armed for debate, tend to give that form to the faith perspective of regular listeners. Being a Christian is proving you are right. . . . Sermons which invariably place before the congregation the "either/or" format . . . contribute to oversimplification, inflexibility, and the notion that faith is always an urgent decision. In contrast, "both/and" sermons tend to broaden horizons and sympathies but never confront the listener with a crisp decision. . . . Regardless of the subjects being treated, a preacher can thereby nourish rigidity or openness, legalism or graciousness, inclusiveness or exclusiveness, adversarial or conciliating mentality, willingness to discuss or demand immediate answers.[17]

Later chapters suggest how to expand your repertoire of forms to help your congregation conceive, process, and live out their understanding of God.

Now that I've argued that the form of the biblical text is part of how God, as artist and persuader, expresses himself, and now that I've implied that preachers should pay attention to form, I want to make clear that I'm not a "form fundamentalist." I do not assert that we must slavishly and minutely copy the exact genre of the text. Besides being impossible—for no single sermon can replicate all the dynamics of a text—it might also be ill advised, because we stand between two worlds. We communicate with a different audience than the original audience, and sermons must take into account the needs of the current listeners. The key to genre sensitive preaching is to replicate the impact of the text, not its exact techniques, although technique is the best place to start. A narrative text naturally lends itself to a narrative sermon; a poetic text structured with parallelism naturally lends itself to restatement. But no law tells us that we must use narrative or restatement. We have freedom.

Each chapter in this book contains concrete suggestions for replicating the impact of the text. As preachers, we want to say what the text says and do what the text does. We want to communicate with variety because the Great Communicator did so originally. A quotation from Lubeck, a scholar of biblical interpretation and communication, summarizes my beliefs about genre sensitive preaching:

> Genres provide us with different models for seeing reality. A poetic description of life is qualitatively different from narrative or discourse (compare Exodus 14 with Exodus 15). As preachers and teachers, we only relate the whole counsel of God to others when we accurately represent *all* of these complementary modes of knowing inherent in the diverse literary forms of the Bible. Our preaching thus must reflect sensitivity and fidelity to the *kinds* of truth that may be found in the full range of biblical genres.[18]

This chapter has given one reason that we should preach with variety, that is, because the text uses variety. The next chapter gives a second reason—the listeners.

2

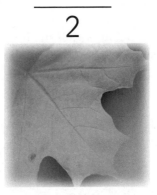

Speaking Bantu to Channel Surfers

The ratio of illiterates to literates is unchanged from a century ago, but now the illiterates can read and write.
> —Alberto Moravia, Italian novelist,
> cited in Sweet, *Soul Tsunami*

There is no good in arguing with the inevitable. The only argument available with an east wind is to put on your overcoat.
> —James Russell Lowell,
> *Democracy and Other Addresses,*
> cited in Sweet, *Soul Tsunami*

It will take all our learning to make things plain.
> —Archbishop Ussher, quoted in Larsen,
> *Telling the Old, Old Story*

More people have been bored out of the Christian faith than have been reasoned out of it. Dull, insipid sermons not only cause drooping eyes and nodding heads, they destroy life and hope.

—H. W. Robinson and T. W. Robinson,
It's All in How You Tell It

The only kind of learning which significantly influences behavior is self-discovered or self-appropriated learning—truth that has been assimilated in experience.
—Carl Rogers, quoted in Miller, *Experiential Storytelling*

The art of teaching is the art of assisting discovery.
—Mark Van Doren, quoted in Miller,
Experiential Storytelling

Why preach with variety? The primary reason, covered in the previous chapter, is because God, the Great Communicator, uses variety. A second reason arises from an incarnational theology of preaching, or as C. S. Lewis says, our need to speak Bantu: "It is absolutely disgraceful that we expect missionaries to the Bantus to learn Bantu but never ask whether our missionaries to the Americans or English can speak American or English."[1] Lewis points out, "If you were sent to the Bantus you would be taught their language and traditions. You need similar teaching about the language and mental habits of your own uneducated and unbelieving fellow countrymen."[2] Martyn Lloyd-Jones, one of the finest expositors of the twentieth century in the Reformed tradition, echoes Lewis:

We are not going to fight this modern battle successfully by repeating the sermons of the Puritans verbatim, or adopting their classifications and sub-divisions, and their manner of preaching. That would be futile. We must learn to hold on to the old principles but we must apply them, and use them, in a manner that is up-to-date. . . . The moment we become slaves to any system—I do not care how good it was in its age and generation—we are already defeated, because we have missed the whole principle of adaptability.[3]

What does the principle of adaptability mean for us? It means we must learn to speak Bantu. The following five factors influence how contemporary listeners listen, and so should influence how contemporary speakers speak.

Visual

Electronic communication media have shifted what Walter Ong calls the "sensorium," the complex of senses used to perceive the world.[4] In the ancient, pretypographic world, the human mind was conditioned to learn through the ear, particularly through the sound of one person speaking to another. After Gutenberg, the sensorium shifted to sight, with words being conceived of as abstract marks on a page (like the ones you are reading now), and no longer as aural encounters with persons. Today the sensorium remains strongly visual, but now pictures have trumped abstract marks. The year 1985 was the first year when more videos were checked out of public libraries than books.[5] In 2006, 80 percent of the cell phones sold in the U.S. included a camera.[6] Consider these statistics about the use of TV in the average U.S. home:

- The television is on for 7 hours and 40 minutes each day.
- Individuals watch more than 4 hours of TV a day.
- Fifty-six percent of children ages 8–16 have a TV in their bedrooms.
- Thirty-seven percent of children age 6 and under have a TV in their bedrooms.
- The average child spends 900 hours a year in school.
- The average child spends 1,023 hours a year watching TV.[7]

The place where the printed word has mostly become a mere annex to the image is probably in the advertising industry. Here's how advertising used to be done in the days of typography: Paul Revere wrote in the *Boston Gazette*, "Whereas many persons are so unfortunate as to lose their Foreteeth by Accident, and otherways, to their great Detriment, not only in Looks, but Speaking both in Public and Private:—This is to inform all such, that they may have them re-placed with false Ones, that look as well as the Natural, and Answers the

End of Speaking to all Intents, by Paul Revere, Goldsmith, near the Head of Dr. Clarke's Wharf, Boston."[8]

Notice the literate style of the communication—long sentences, complex grammar, straightforward reasoning. It strikes us as quaint, or perhaps confusing or boring. What would the same content look like in the hands of today's advertisers? Images would dominate, and words would simply caption the images. If, for example, the ad were created for a magazine, a large picture of pearly white teeth might fill the page. Beneath the picture the caption might read, "Got teeth? If you're missing any, come see Paul Revere." If the ad were created for television, it might show a young man playing basketball. An errant pass might strike him in the mouth. A jump cut might take us to the emergency room to see the basketball player being wheeled in. Then another jump cut might show him walking out of the hospital with a girl on his arm, teeth gleaming. Then the voiceover would state, "Need teeth? Come see Paul Revere."

This visual form of communication seems more immediate and intense than the print ad from the 1700s. It maximizes impact and minimizes logic. Moving images capture involuntary attention, whereas typographic communication demands voluntary attention. Thus, in the electronic age when children see hundreds of thousands of commercials on television alone,[9] repeated exposure to visual communication conditions how we process information. Today, most people are less skillful than Paul Revere's audience was in receiving communication transmitted through abstract marks on a page. Most people prefer to receive communication transmitted through pictures. McDonald's knows this. Their "menu" is a series of pictures.

One response the church can make to media saturation is to throw up our hands in despair, lament that preaching can never compete with television, and resign ourselves to boring sermons. Another response is to raise the drawbridge, hunker down for siege, fling firebrands and millstones over the fortress walls, and pray that the pagan hordes will not break in. People who choose this option sometimes sneer at the shorter attention spans of the electronic world, but their observation needs to be qualified. People today are quite capable of sustained attention—observe a crowd at a movie—but they no longer easily give their attention to, as Hamlet would say, "words, words, words." The siege option can be tempting because, as people of the Book, we rightly value literacy; but to criticize listeners for not being literate and to offer the truth of God's Word only through typographically biased forms (unlike the genres discussed in this book) is like a missionary to the Bantus who refuses to speak Bantu. A researcher in communicating with oral cultures, Grant Lovejoy argues, insisting that people leave their image-oriented minds outside the church door creates an unbiblical stumbling block.[10] In New Testament times most people were illiterate, yet the gospel spread like prairie fire.

Another response to today's visual sensorium is to preach with variety like the Great Communicator. The Bible itself guides us in creating sermon forms suited to today's listeners. We will never lose our love of words, so crucial to communication and to Christianity. For as Andy Crouch says, "The more powerful the image, whether tragic or triumphant, the more we need words to make sense of it."[11] But when ministering to Bantus we need to augment the verbal with a strong visual component.

Speed

The advent of electronic communication, which began in 1840 with Morse and the telegraph, has obliterated time and space in communication. We now communicate around the globe at the speed of light. An unfortunate side effect of the electronic revolution is information overload, for we can now transmit so much information so quickly, as well as store that information, that no one can absorb even 1 percent of what is available. Information (but not necessarily understanding) is fed to us as factoids. For example, the average sound bite of presidential candidates on network news in 2004 was less than eight seconds. The HCSB Light Speed Bible promises to, "in an exhilarating sweep of 24 hours, expose your mind and heart to every word and teaching of the Old and New Testaments." If the Light Speed Bible is too slow for you, try the 100-Minute Bible, a sixty-four-page paperback that the publisher claims is the principal "stories of the life and ministry of its central character, Jesus Christ."[12]

How shall we communicate to this hasty generation, this society overfed with information but undernourished with understanding?

One response, but not the only one, is by employing variety, for it helps maintain and focus attention, so precious in our fragmented world. Variety also helps us communicate holistically, touching the heart as well as the mind, so that biblical truth is perceived as more than factoids. When preaching with variety, we are likely to slow the rapid flow of information typical of expository sermons, yet that slowing will not bore the nanosecond generation, for the sermon shifts perspective often.

Participation and Experience

Information overload has created a gulf between most of the knowledge we receive and most of our daily activities. Henry David Thoreau foresaw this even in the days of telegraphy: "We are in a great haste to construct a magnetic telegraph from Maine to Texas; but Maine and Texas, it may be, have nothing important to communicate. . . . We are eager to tunnel under the Atlantic and bring the old world some weeks nearer to the new; but perchance the first news that will leak through into the broad flapping American ear will be that Princess Adelaide has the whooping cough."[13]

One result of the bifurcation of information and praxis is that people today crave experiential knowledge. They want "real life" to be the seedbed of knowledge. Reading facts from books, or even hearing facts spouted on the evening news, seems increasingly distant and irrelevant because it is mediated and secondhand. Modern listeners have been socialized to participate in their own education and entertainment even with one-way media like radio and television.[14] Radio uses call-in shows, and television programs like Monday Night Football and so-called reality TV shows increasingly invite viewer participation in live polls. Part of the reason television has been forced to become more participatory is because video games have created the expectation that we should be able to manipulate the screen and contribute to our own entertainment. The video game industry is so large that it frequently beats the earnings of TV and movies—and, by the way, the average age of gamers in 2006 was thirty, with 17 percent older than fifty, so don't think that kids are the only ones who speak Bantu today.[15]

The news industry, too, feels the need to shift toward participation. Robert Murdoch, founder and chair of News Corporation, which includes Fox News, commented in a speech to the American Society of Newspaper Editors,

> What is happening right now before us is, in short, a revolution in the way young people are accessing news. They don't want to rely on the morning paper for their up-to-date information. They don't want to rely on a godlike figure from above to tell them what's important. And to carry the religion analogy a bit further, they certainly don't want news presented as gospel. Instead, they want their news on demand, when it works for them. They want control over their media, instead of being controlled by it. They want to question, to probe, to offer a different angle.[16]

Another venue, the museum, is also becoming highly participatory. For decades, children's museums have used interactive learning, but that is now becoming the norm for adult museums as well. The old exhibits with a display and a plaque are fading. Now the norm is more like the Holocaust Museum in Washington, D.C. When you enter the building, you are given some documents—an ID card, background, and story of an actual holocaust victim. As you progress through the permanent exhibits, which are arranged chronologically, you refer to your documents to see what was happening to the victim. The goal is to help you identify with the victim for a few hours, vicariously experiencing the somber events. The impact is enormous, much greater than would be felt from a merely analytical, detached point of view.

How, though, do we speak Bantu to modern Westerners? In the following chapters you'll get some ideas for using variety to heighten participation. Preachers, remember, have freedom to do so, and as homiletician David Buttrick states, "Homiletical form is usually experimental, because preachers are developing rhetoric to match the shape of a new, forming human consciousness."[17]

Participatory education has actually been around for thousands of years. It is part of the genius behind the Jewish seder service as well as Christian rites such as baptism, the Lord's Supper, and anointing with oil. Even in 1884, well before the winds of the electronic revolution reached gale force, John Milton Gregory wrote "Law Two" in *The Seven Laws of Teaching*, which states that "the Learner must attend with interest to the material to be learned":[18]

> One may as well talk to the deaf or to the dead as to attempt to teach a child who is wholly inattentive. . . . Knowledge cannot be passed like a material substance from one mind to another, for thoughts are not objects which may be held and handled. Ideas can be communicated only by inducing in the receiving mind processes corresponding to those by which these ideas were first conceived. Ideas must be rethought, experience must be re-experienced. It is obvious, therefore, that something more is required than a mere presentation; the pupil must think.[19]

Preaching with variety can help us help others to think. This kind of preaching does not dumb down the truth; it offers it in accordance with the best principles of audience analysis and adaptation.

Authority

Modern listeners tend to locate authority in personal experience. They are eager to listen to those who have "been there," and they are skeptical of those who wield authority that comes only from position or "book learning." Furthermore, they tend to believe that truth for a community is best discerned in community. Like the other factors above, authority in experience has strengths and weaknesses. A strength is that the faith is conceived of in terms of lifestyle and the Lord's active working in our lives. A weakness is that authority becomes overly subjective. The church must be taught that God grants spiritual authority to elders and leaders. Furthermore, the church must maintain the legitimacy of reason, not just intuition, as a means of knowing God.

But the question this book addresses is how we can teach such things. Preaching with variety offers some promise. Many of the homiletical suggestions in the following chapters show how to employ communal and experiential forms of communication like dialogue, self-disclosure, induction, and working in concert with the entire service. For the Bantus, these forms tend to soften the brassy trumpet of authority even while effectively teaching the Word.

Types of Learners and Thinkers

One hundred listeners will translate a single sermon into one hundred more or less correlated messages. The dynamics that cause this phenomenon are enormously complex, but the theories of learning styles from the fields of education and psychology help us grasp some of those dynamics.[20] This body of literature includes the Myers-Briggs Personality Types (introvert/extrovert, sensor/intuitive, thinker/feeler, judger/perceiver),[21] Ned Hermann's Brain Dominance model (right-brain, left-brain),[22] Howard Gardner's theory of Multiple Intelligences (linguistic, logical-mathematical, spatial, bodily kinesthetic, etc.),[23] and Deborah Tannen's theory of gender and communication (male and female sociolinguistics).[24] The evidence given to support these theories seems conclusive—people use different senses, abilities, and perspectives when they listen to sermons. Preaching with variety helps us connect with the sampler of listeners. For many of these listeners, Pascal's famous maxim holds true—"The heart has its reasons which reason does not know,"[25]—as does Macneile Dixon's statement, "The human mind is not . . . a debating hall, but a picture gallery."[26] Kent Edwards says simply that "those preachers who want the largest number of people to learn from their sermons should utilize what Gardner refers to as 'multiple entry points.'"[27]

Why preach with variety? Not because we're trying to exalt self, but because we want to exalt God; not because we call the shots, but because God sets the pattern as the Great Communicator; not because we want to manipulate listeners, but because they speak Bantu. Let's get on with it!

3

Psalms

THE SOUND OF MUSIC

[Poetry] has the virtue of being able to say twice as much as prose in half the time, and the drawback, if you do not give it your full attention, of seeming to say half as much in twice the time.

—Christopher Frye, quoted in Wiersbe,
Teaching and Preaching with Imagination

The poet's trade is not to talk about experience, but to make it happen.

—John Ciardi, *How Does a Poem Mean?*

[Poetry is] the art of uniting pleasure with truth, by calling imagination to the help of reason.

—Samuel Johnson, quoted in Wiersbe,
Preaching and Teaching with Imagination

He mobilized the English language and sent it into battle.
—JFK's tribute to Churchill, quoted in Wiersbe,
Preaching and Teaching with Imagination

The psalms were accompanied by music. Are we supposed to sing our sermons? The psalms are personal. But how can we turn subjective experience into public address? The psalms are lyrical—full of emotion and image. How, though, can we translate highly artistic language into vernacular? You can see why some preachers avoid the psalms. Their intuition tells them that we murder when we dissect.

I affirm that intuition. It reminds me of the time a student from Korea overheard me talking on the phone to my wife. The student asked me why I called my wife "dumpling." (I rarely call her that; it's an inside joke.) I explained to the student that the term is a nickname of endearment. She wondered why being called a "dough ball" was endearing? I guess something got lost in the translation.

"Translating" poetry can be equally tricky. Translating epistles into sermons is relatively easy because both use direct address, argument, and illustration. Translating narratives is more challenging but still doable because all of us grew up telling, hearing, and watching stories. But poetry! How do you preach poetry?

What *Is* Poetry?

The term *poetry* covers everything from Dr. Seuss to Shakespeare, greeting cards to epics. Even those who make their living from poetry struggle to define their art:

The intolerable wrestle with words and meanings.
—T. S. Eliot, poet and critic

Poetry is the revelation of a feeling that the poet believes to be interior and personal, [but] the reader recognizes as his own.
—Salvatore Quasimodo, winner 1959 Nobel Prize

The poem . . . is a little myth of man's capacity for making life meaningful. And in the end, the poem is not a thing we see—it is, rather, a light by which we may see.
—Robert Penn Warren, poet and critic

> The journal of a sea animal
> living on land
> wanting to fly in the air.

> —Carl Sandburg, poet

We can be thankful biblical scholars are able to describe the psalms with more precision than these literati, although in the final analysis everyone agrees that it's easier to illustrate poetry than to define it. The difference between poetry and prose is a matter of degree. A screen door, not a brick wall separates the two, but poetry is marked by greater emphasis on form and reified language.

How Does a Poem Mean?

How texts communicate cannot be divorced from what they communicate. That is why poet John Ciardi asks *how* does a poem mean?[1] Does it communicate with a jigging, sing-song rhythm? That form suggests silliness or childishness: "Roses are red, violets are blue. . . ." Does it use unusual punctuation as in this stanza from e. e. cummings?

> and eddieandbill come
> running from marbles and
> piracies and it's
> spring
> when the world is puddle-wonderful[2]

The form as well as the content creates the picture of two inseparable friends galloping pell-mell. Does the poem swell to a thousand pages? The epic form suggests grandeur and dramatic action as with the *Iliad, The Divine Comedy,* and *Paradise Lost.* Big poems for big themes.

When exegeting a psalm, we must ask *how* the poem means as well as *what* the poem means. As Robert Alter states, "An understanding of the poetic system is always a precondition to reading the poem well."[3] C. S. Lewis agrees, arguing that the Bible "cannot properly be read except as literature; and the different parts of it as the different sorts of literature they are. Most emphatically the psalms must be read as poems; as lyrics, with all the licenses and all the formalities, the hyperboles, the emotional rather than logical connections, which are proper to lyric poetry."[4]

The goal of this chapter is to describe the literary and rhetorical dynamics of the genre and then suggest how preachers can re-create the impact of those dynamics.

How the Text Communicates, What the Text Does

As lyric poetry, the psalms display the following features: brevity, intricate structure, concrete images, and intense emotion.

Brevity

Lyric poems like the psalms tend to be short. If they were movies, they would present one scene, perhaps in slow motion, rather than reel after reel of an entire drama. This doesn't mean that a psalm lacks movement. As will be seen below, psalms are intricately structured and tend to progress from disequilibrium to resolution, but the movement is compressed.

Since most psalms are short, they do not usually provide complete answers to questions. Like proverbs, the psalms may flirt with heresy. "My God, my God, why have you forsaken me?" (Ps. 22:1) is the cry of a believer when surrounded by enemies, not a textbook on the problem of evil. David felt abandoned, and he distilled that experience in a poem. While a single lyric does not express the whole truth on a given subject, collections of poems such as the book of Psalms capture all the hues and tones of a theme. They are like snapshots that become a montage.

One reason the psalms are often short is that they were originally accompanied by music. The ancient Hebrews were music-loving people. The Bible alludes to a number of secular songs such as work songs for digging (Num. 21:17–18) and making wine (Isa. 16:10; Jer. 48:33). Music was integral to ceremonies such as marriages (Jer. 7:34) and funerals, at which laments were sung or chanted (2 Sam. 1:19–27). In his works *The Hobbit* and *The Lord of the Rings*, Tolkien captures the way that ancient oral cultures used music. Notice how often and with what lack of self-consciousness the characters sing in Tolkien's works—they sing as they bathe, drink, walk, work, lament, and commemorate.

If music was plentiful in the secular lives of ancient Hebrews, it was even more integral to their public worship (see 1 Chron. 25). Psalms were used like hymns, and while we can experience much of the rhetorical impact of hymns by the words alone, we mustn't forget that much of their power lies in their music—in the *sound*. The rise of the melody line, the tempo of different sections, or the silence of a rest helped make the psalms potent. As brief, musical prayers the psalms combined form and content into powerful emotive and spiritual experiences.

Intricate Structure

Like nearly all poetry, the psalms possess intricate structure. The chief feature of that structure is, of course, parallelism. First recognized by Robert Lowth in 1753, the details of parallelism are often disputed because the Hebrew poets were not slaves to convention. They didn't shape their poems with cookie cutters. Just as Shakespeare used iambic pentameter as his standard rhythm, yet violated it as his genius directed, so the psalmists employed variety within the convention of parallelism.[5]

The main types of parallelism are well known:

Synonymous (second line restates the first)

> The sea looked and fled,
>   the Jordan turned back;
> The mountains skipped like rams,
>   the hills like lambs.
>
> (Ps. 114:3)

Antithetic (second line contrasts with the first)

> The LORD is King for ever and ever;
>   the nations will perish from his land.
> (Ps. 10:16)

Synthetic (second line completes the first)

> He set the earth on its foundations;
>> it can never be moved.
>>> (Ps. 104:5)

While commentators note the presence of parallelism in Hebrew poetry, and sometimes admire its artistry, they do not often discuss its impact—its rhetorical effect. They describe the parallelism but do not dig deeper to discuss its implications.

One rhetorical effect parallelism prompts is meditation. When we read the psalms well—when we read according to the cues the literature itself provides—the structure of Hebrew poetry prompts us to slow down. Hebrew poetry is a prism that turns this way and that so that we catch the different hues of a single idea, image, or emotion. While modern literary conventions discourage this sort of refraction, the psalms delight in it. Thus, Hebrew poetry is written not for speed readers or skimmers.

Even as parallelism prompts us to slow down, it also intensifies the reading and listening experience. Lines of Hebrew poetry do not simply repeat or contrast ideas; they almost always intensify ideas. There is a "focusing, a heightening, a concretization of the original material."[6] Long gives this helpful example: "My son is thirteen; he's a teenager."[7] The first statement is factual and introduces the theme. The second statement intensifies the theme by connoting the world of male adolescence with its music, dress, attitudes, and so forth. With the second statement the speaker begins to prompt identification. Perhaps the speaker intends us to feel sympathy, humor, or worry.

Notice how these synonymous lines intensify:

> Cleanse me with hyssop, and I will be clean;
>> wash me, and I will be whiter than snow.
> Let me hear joy and gladness;
>> let the bones you have crushed rejoice.
>>> (Ps. 51:7–8)

The lines above move from "mere" cleanliness to absolute purity, from external joy (a sound) to internal joy (a feeling). Thus, the psalmist does not merely repeat ideas, because "poets understand more subtly than linguists that there are no true synonyms."[8]

What is true of poetic structure on the microscale is also true on the macroscale. The structures of entire poems often intensify. The pressure mounts, the problem becomes intolerable, and then a sharp reversal takes place. As Alter states, "The structure that predominates in all genres of biblical poetry is one in which a kind of semantic pressure is built from verset to verset and line to line, finally reaching a climax or a climax and reversal."[9] This structure is a powerful vehicle to carry intense experiences from speaker to listener. Thus, it is clear why the psalms have for millennia ministered to the hearts of believers.

As a structural feature, intensification is present in most of the subgenres of psalms, such as confession, thanksgiving, and enthronement, but it is most clearly seen in the largest subgenre, lament. Just as stories are structured by conflict, rising action, climax, and denouement (see chap. 4), so do laments announce and intensify a complaint but typically then hinge to conclude with an affirmation of faith. Psalm 77 provides a case study:

- Verse 1 announces the theme—a feeling of abandonment:

  > I cried out to God for help. . . .

- Verses 2–9 intensifies that theme:

  > I stretched out untiring hands. . . .
  > I groaned. . . .
  > I was too troubled to speak. . . .
  > Has his unfailing love vanished forever?

- Verses 10–15 serves as the hinge:

  > Then I thought. . . .
  > I will remember. . . .
  > Your mighty arm . . . redeemed your people. . . .
  > *Selah.*

- Verses 16–20 affirm faith by remembering God's deliverance through the Red Sea:

> The waters saw you, O God,
>   the waters saw you and writhed;
>   the very depths were convulsed. . . .
> You led your people like a flock,
>   by the hand of Moses and Aaron.

Not only does the structure of mounting intensity with dramatic reversal help create emotion, it can also, argues Robert Alter, shape worldview: "A particular poetics may encourage or reinforce a particular orientation toward reality. . . . What this means is that poetry of the Bible is concerned above all with dynamic process moving toward some culmination."[10] The Hebrews were exposed to poetry with this structure day after day, year after year, and through it their perceptions of God, self, events, and history were likely shaped. In the Hebrew mind, then, history is going somewhere, it has purpose, and although we are in distress, God has acted and will act again, so we can rest secure, for the long and winding road leads home.

The preceding discussion of structure in the psalms does not exhaust the subject. This brief overview, in fact, barely touches the hem of the garment, saying nothing about structural features like chiasmus, acrostic, and inclusio (a framing device).[11] Each of these devices produces its own effects and deserves consideration in studying individual texts. This chapter, though, has dealt with the most salient aspects of structure in Hebrew poetry—parallelism and intensification. Those should provide plenty of food for thought as we continue exegesis of psalms, asking not only what the text says but how it says it and with what effect.

Concrete Images

The third characteristic of the genre may be its chief literary feature: poets show rather than tell. Poetry makes the abstract concrete by embodying the universal in the particular. Like narrative, poetry incarnates its ideas so that knowledge is obtained vicariously through the author's experience. The subject matter of the psalms is human experience, not propositions.

Compare two genres (poetry and creed) that present similar ideas:

> The LORD is my shepherd, I shall not be in want.
>   He makes me lie down in green pastures,
>   he leads me beside quiet waters,
>   he restores my soul.
>
> (Ps. 23:1–3)

God the Creator of all things doth uphold, direct, dispose, and govern all creatures, actions, and things, from the greatest even to the least, by His most wise and holy providence.
—Westminster Confession of Faith

Poetry uses concrete nouns and verbs to create a picture of abstract ideas. The word *anger* does little to conjure up an image in our minds, but in the psalms *wrath* "kindles" and "burns." *Confusion* makes us "stagger"; *trouble* is an "arrow that flies by day"; *security* is a "shelter" from the sun or a "wing" to hide under; and *jubilation* causes "trees to clap their hands" and "seas to lift their voices." Rivers, fields, mountains, vineyards, gates, the Temple, and the heavens are the imaginative domains of the psalmists; donkeys, locusts, lions, and jackals walk its paths; brides, farmers, watchmen, and armies act on its stage. As Ryken observes, "Literature is concrete and experiential. It uses tangible images to convey the very quality of lived experience. It appeals to our imagination (image-making capacity)."[12]

Concretizing the abstract produces three rhetorical effects. First, it sparks the imagination. Like listening to an old-time radio play, poetry stages its scenes in the "theater of the mind." The curtain rises, though, only for those who yield to the literature. If the psalmist tries to carry us up the slopes of Zion or down to the sea, we have to go with him. We have to bring the right assumptions and skills to the text, and the chief skill is to read slowly. We must allow the images to form in our imaginations. Hear the roaring sea and the roaring lions. Feel the cold shadows and the hot sun. The psalms conjure images for those who yield.

The second effect of concretizing is to foster identification. Although David's headache is not my headache, when he describes his headache with concrete nouns and verbs, I identify. The psalmists knew that the way to communicate with a general audience is by being specific. We broaden a message by being narrow.

The third effect is to aid memory. "Your word is a lamp to my feet and a light for my path" (119:105) remains longer in the mind than "the Word of God provides direction in life and helps us make decisions."

When discussing poetry's concrete images, a special word is needed about metaphor and simile because nearly every psalm contains multiple implied comparisons (metaphor) or overt comparisons (simile):

> He is like a tree planted by streams of water. (Ps. 1:3)
> You will dash them to pieces like pottery. (Ps. 2:9)
> You are a shield around me. (Ps. 3:3)
> Let the light of your face shine upon us, O LORD. (Ps. 4:6)
> Their throat is an open grave. (Ps. 5:9)

Figurative communication resists instant assimilation. God is not really a rock! Like parallelism, metaphor and simile force the reader to ponder. As Ryken states, "Metaphor and simile place immense demands on a reader. They require far more activity than a direct propositional statement. Metaphor and simile first demand that we take the time to let the literal situation sink in. Then we must make a transfer of meaning(s) to the topic or experience the poem is talking about."[13] Robert Frost defined the poet's task as "saying one thing and meaning another."[14] Through metaphor, the communicator hopes to convey a rich concept, and yet he or she carries that concept through the back door of the receiver's mind. The term *metaphor* (*meta pherein*) means literally "to carry with." We carry meaning from one realm to another when we compare one object or person with another.

The rhetorical significance of indirect communication is subtle but profound. It prompts sender and receiver to collaborate, producing the meaning the author intends. Metaphor is a dance both parties must dance. When metaphor fails because the receiver doesn't understand the image or thinks the sender is speaking literally, then the dance becomes a wrestling match. But when metaphor works, it really works! Like an inside joke or irony, it's a language only insiders share.

In practice it looks like this: I want to inspire hope that God will deliver us from trouble. First, I need you to experience that trouble vicariously, how it makes you feel trapped and helpless, so I choose a compact and concrete image: "He will save you from the fowler's snare" (Ps. 91:3). My metaphor assumes three things: (1) you understand the image because you've seen poor birds tangled in a snare; (2) you'll decide that I'm not speaking literally; (3) you'll correctly decode my meaning by carrying it from the figure to the actual situation. If the metaphor works, if you "get it," the collaborative experience is a rich meeting of minds and hearts.

The book of Psalms is a storehouse of concrete images. Metaphor and simile fill much of that storehouse, but other forms of poetic language such as hyperbole, allusion, apostrophe, and personification also line the shelves.[15] Hebrew thought resists abstraction. It is concrete and experiential, prompting imagination, identification, meditation, and collaboration.

Intense Emotion

Already alluded to is the final literary feature of the psalms— intense, personal emotion. Psalms are, state Fee and Stuart, "intended to appeal to the emotions, to evoke feelings rather than propositional thinking, and to stimulate a response on the part of the individual that goes beyond a mere cognitive understanding of certain facts."[16] Ryken goes so far as to say that "the Psalms, being lyric poetry, exist primarily to give expression to the emotional side of religious experience."[17] The hues and tones of the psalms include terror, depression, loneliness, confidence, peace, amazement, humility, joy, and anger. This is the raw material of the psalms, which the poets mold and structure.

How can we preach these poems? How can we re-create some of the meditative, affective, imaginative, and collaborative effects the poets built into their hymns?

Try This

As stated in chapter 2, preachers who want to preach with variety need look no further than the text itself. Some of its strategies can be incorporated directly into our sermons, and some can be inferred.

The list below moves gradually toward innovative strategies that are not found directly in the text but that help us herald it faithfully. Remember that we are not "form fundamentalists." The goal is not to mimic the *exact form* of the text but to reproduce the *impact* of the text. If the text is meditative, we would do well to prompt meditation. That is the author's intent. If the text prompts emotion, we should too. If the text rebukes, we should rebuke. Here are nine ideas on how to preach psalms.

When Preparing, Meditate

As described above, poetry is a language of images and emotions that the reader must experience. This is how psalms work, and we must yield to their poetic nuances in our study. Henry Ward Beecher's words are especially applicable when we preach a psalm: "The first element on which your preaching will depend for power and success . . . is imagination, which I regard as the most important of all elements that go to make the preacher."[18] I recommend that you lock your door, take a walk, or take a drive to give yourself time and space to experience the poem. Meditation demands solitude. The only way I know to unpack a psalm's dense images and intense emotions is to slow down the normal mode of reading, linger over words, and imagine.

When I was a little boy, my dad regularly took my brother and me into the woods behind our house to sit on the "listening log." The log was a fallen tree, and we simply sat on it in silence trying to notice sounds. We were not allowed to move or make noise. We just had to listen. It was torture. Our sessions often ended with my dad exasperated by his sons who poked, giggled, and whined. Poking and giggling are natural to boys, of course, but I'm afraid the whining was the response of kids nurtured in a media-saturated culture. Silence is torture to a person brought up with constant visual and aural stimulation. Most Americans lack the ability to listen to silence and to imagine something not paraded before their eyes, but those skills are necessary to exegete the psalms. Is there any hope for channel surfers like you and me?[19]

To help spark imagination, Thomas Troeger recommends "logosomatic" study.[20] Get your body involved. If the text says we are like blind men, cover your eyes or take a trip to a cave. If the text says we are deaf, cover your ears. If we are captive, clench your hands and clamp your arms. If we stumble, stumble.

I also recommend listening to the text because poets write for the ear. Read the text aloud or listen to a professional recording. Robert Frost said, "The ear is the only true writer and the only true reader. I have known people who could read without hearing the sentence sounds and they were the fastest readers. Eye readers we call them. They can get the meaning by glances. But they are bad readers because they miss the best part of what a good writer puts into his work."[21] It is a happy circumstance that part of the aural quality of Hebrew poetry comes through even in translation because parallelism is one of the few poetic devices that transfers from one language to another. The psalmists wrote in balanced, pulsing, coordinate phrases, and we hear them that way even in English.

Use Concrete Language

The psalms use concrete language. There is no reason we shouldn't also, and perhaps every reason we should. We want the same rhetorical effects in our sermons that the psalms produce: imagination, identification, concretizing. Let us avoid Ralph Waldo Emerson's description of his own lectures: "fine things, pretty things, wise things, but no arrows, no axes, no nectar, no growling, no transpiercing, no loving, no enchantment."[22] The ancient rhetorician Quintilian spoke of "images by which the representation of absent objects are so distinctly represented to the mind, that we seem to see them before our eyes and have them before us. Whoever shall best conceive of such images will have the greatest power in moving the feelings."[23]

The key to communicating concretely is verbs and nouns. Rather than telling the story about "the man who went down the street," describe "the grandfather who shuffled" or "the CEO who strutted." Discipline yourself to use exact words not vague words. This does not mean, though, that you should use long words because they are often abstract. Just incorporate more of your reading vocabulary into your speaking vocabulary. It's not just a boat; it's a submarine, yacht, tugboat, or canoe. These words are not "highfalutin." They are simply concrete. Mark Twain once said that the difference between the right word and the almost right word is the difference between lightning and the lightning bug.

Try writing out a manuscript. This discipline helps slow the preparation process. It gives us time to choose vivid words. It also gives us a tangible document to edit. Caution: write a manuscript, but do not preach from it! Very few people can read conversationally. When we read, we sound like we're reading. Don't memorize the manuscript either. None of us has time for that. Just depend on the discipline of writing and editing to add some vividness to your speech. Some of the language from the manuscript will transfer to the sermon, and you'll have the best of both worlds—concrete language expressed conversationally.[24]

Spurgeon's language comes from a bygone era, but we can still learn from the master. Notice the sensory appeal:

> (*sound*) Our hearts . . . are beating funeral marches to the tomb.

> (*touch*) The heart is very slippery. Yes. The heart is a fish that troubles all gospel fishermen to hold . . . slimy as an eel, it slippeth between your fingers.

> (*taste*) Suppose you tell me that honey is bitter. I reply, "No, I am sure you cannot have tasted it; taste it and try." So it is with the Holy Ghost.

> (*smell*) The precious perfume of the gospel must be poured forth to sweeten the air.[25]

Let's talk the way the psalmists talk—with concrete verbs and nouns. Let's talk about sores, not Job's difficulties; Toyota pickups, not vehicles; and bloodshot eyes, not the signs of fatigue. Let's describe actions that wobble, heave, and growl. This is the way to prompt imagination and identification.

Use Metaphor

Another strategy of style that arises directly from the text is the use of metaphor. If you have a gift for artistic language, your gift can soar when preaching the psalms. Those who do not have that gift can at least avoid denuding the text's metaphors. Wiersbe parodies this approach in a preaching outline from Psalm 23. Here are portions of that outline:

    I.   A relationship that is precious ("the Lord is my shepherd").
   II. A resource that is plentiful ("I shall not want").
  III. A rest that is pleasant ("pastures . . . waters").
 VII. A repast that is peaceful ("a table before me").
  IX. A realization that is phenomenal ("follow me").
   X. A regularity that is positive ("all the days").[26]

Yawn! If we don't have the ability to spin metaphors as easily as a machine spins cotton candy, perhaps we can spin just one. A single metaphor can become a controlling image for an entire sermon, or even a series of sermons. I preached a five-part series on the problem of evil, for example, using the metaphor of a "long and winding road."[27] Each sermon used the metaphor of a journey with the last message describing heaven as "arriving home."

A controlling metaphor makes a great central idea used as a refrain:

It's Friday, but Sunday's coming.

—Tony Campolo

Payday someday.

—R. G. Lee

How is a king like a lion, a farmer like a cow, a dowager princess like her lapdog, a mafia chief like a snake?

—Haddon W. Robinson

Bear in mind when exegeting biblical metaphors that we may need to "translate" the images for modern audiences. Few of us know what a "lot" is, and even when we understand the gist of images such as sheep, arrows, oil lamps, and scrolls, we often need some explanation to appreciate the figurative language.

Create an "Emotional Outline"

This is David Larsen's phrase. He contrasts the emotional outline with the logical outline, arguing that a sermon needs "peaks and valleys. There need to be moments of effective intensity and then a backing off and moments of relief for the congregation. Working at half throttle all the time won't do, nor will going at full bore throughout delivery, like lightening which flashes all over but strikes nowhere."[28]

Using Psalm 77 again, notice how the emotional shape could be graphed like this:

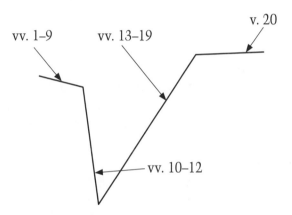

Fig. 3.1. The "Emotional Shape" of Psalm 77

The first nine verses angle sharply down, but then the psalm hinges in verses 10–12 and swings upward from that point onward as the author and readers (who are reading sensitively!) plow through the great deliverance at the Red Sea. Then the final verse "flattens out" with a summary as the Israelites continue their journey toward the Promised Land. The psalm leaves us higher than it started.

We can achieve a similar effect by carefully choosing and arranging materials not only for their ideational content (remember that we *are* teachers of the Word) but also for their emotional content. You may choose, for example, to use self-disclosure in this sermon about a time you felt "faint" (v. 3), "troubled" (v. 4), and "forgotten" (v. 9). As you well know, such self-disclosure is likely to crackle with emotional energy. The listeners will be riveted. Your story will help them experience the truth of the psalm on the downward slope, but you'll need to take special care to help them experience the upswing also. The psalm doesn't leave us in the depths. It rebounds with passion and leaves us in a higher state than we began. Perhaps you could describe the crossing of the Red Sea with vivid and dramatic language and then bring the text into the twenty-first century with testimonies of deliverance from folk who have seen God perform miracles (v. 14) and redeem his people (v. 15).

With this psalm, the preacher should probably not turn the experience into imperatives ("We should trust God just as the psalmist did"). Instead, the preacher should help worshipers remember how God delivered them. That will prompt trust.

Use Parallelism

If you want the congregation to slow down, meditate, ponder, and turn the prism this way and that, try doing what the Bible does: use parallelism. Here's a striking example of parallelism by Dr. S. M. Lockridge. This sermon was preached during Founder's Week at Moody Memorial Church in Chicago in 1981. Although Lockridge's text was the Lord's Prayer, not a psalm, he demonstrates what can be done with parallelism. By the way, no written transcript can do justice to this sermon, but maybe you can get a feel for it by reading:

> The Bible says that my King is a seven-way King:
>> He's the King of the Jews, that's a racial king.
>> He's the King of Israel; that's a national king.
>> He's the King of righteousness.
>> He's the King of the ages.
>> He's the King of heaven.
>> He's the King of glory.
>> He's the King of kings and He's the Lord of Lords.
> That's my King! Well, I wonder: do you know Him?
>
> My King is a sovereign King:
>> No means or measure can define His limitless love.
>> No far-seeing telescope can bring into visibility the coastline of His shore-less supply.
>> No barrier can hinder Him from pouring out His blessings.

He's enduringly strong.
He's entirely sincere.
He's eternally steadfast.
He's immortally graceful.
He's imperially powerful.
He's impartially merciful.
Do you know Him?

He's the greatest phenomenon that has ever crossed the
horizon of this world.
He's God's Son.
He's a sinner's savior.
He's the centerpiece of civilization.
He stands in the solitude of Himself.
He's august, and He's unique.
He's unparalleled, He's unprecedented.
He is the loftiest idea in literature.
He's the highest personality in philosophy.
He is the supreme problem in higher criticism.
He's the fundamental doctrine in true theology.
He is the . . . necessity of spiritual religion.
He's the miracle of the age.
He is the superlative of everything that you choose to call
Him.
He's the only one qualified to be an all-sufficient savior.
I wonder if you know Him today?

He supplies strength for the weak:
He's available for the tempted and the tried.
He sympathizes, and He saves.
He strengthens and sustains.
He guards, and He guides.
He heals the sick.
He cleansed the lepers.
He forgives sinners.
He discharges debtors.
He delivers the captive.

He defends the feeble.
He blesses the young.
He serves the unfortunate.
He regards the aged.
He rewards the diligent.
And He beautifies the meager.

I wonder if you know Him?
    He's the key to knowledge.
    He's the wellspring of wisdom.
    He's the doorway of deliverance.
    He's the pathway of peace.
    He's the roadway of righteousness.
    He's the highway of holiness.
    He's the gateway of glory.
Do you know Him?[29]

Here's another example, less inspired than Lockridge. It is from my own sermon on Psalm 77, in which I used concrete language and parallelism, trying to re-create the impact of the text:

If you think God has forgotten you, think again!

The disciples groaned as they pulled on the oars. The storm tossed them this way and that. They thought God had forgotten them, so Jesus said to the storm, "Hush."

   The disciples groaned when their friend Lazarus died. They waited in darkness while Jesus took his time getting there. They thought he had forgotten them, but then they had an attitude change when Jesus said, "Come forth."

      The disciples groaned when they saw Jesus on the cross. For three days they groaned as they huddled in silence because they thought God had forsaken Jesus and them. But then on Sunday morning, *Jesus rose*, and they remembered that fact all the days of their lives.

If you think God has forgotten you, think again.

Not only can we use parallelism for small units, but we can also use it to organize the entire sermon. State your point and develop it, then restate the point and develop it with more intensity, then restate it again. Sermons don't always have to march, they can also swirl in expanding arcs. If, however, you organize your message with synonymous parallelism, be careful that the arcs intensify just as the second part of a Hebrew line does. Sermons must not stall even when they state and restate themes.

In contrast to the swirling arcs of synonymous parallelism, antithetic parallelism lends itself to two-part structures. A text like Psalm 1, with its striking contrast between the godly and the wicked, could be organized with a strongly contrastive motif such as "This/Not this." The text is a dichotomy, and when the sermon is a dichotomy, it is expository in form as well as content.

Use Music

The psalmists used music; why shouldn't we? Try incorporating music into your sermon. This technique may jar the congregation, but before you skip to the next section of this chapter, remember that music is very powerful rhetorically and that the biblical poets intended their poems to be accompanied by music. And remember thesis 4: "There is no such thing as *the* sermon form." Maybe you could try one of these techniques:

- End the sermon with a hymn or praise song based on your psalm.
- Begin or end with special music that coordinates with the emotional and ideational content of the sermon.
- Insert a congregational song or special music in the middle of the sermon.
- Use musical background as the text is read.
- Insert your own singing into the sermon(!).

I've heard all of these done, and I've done all of them myself. My experience has been very positive . . . except when I sang. Like all homiletical/rhetorical practices, the use of music can be used to great advantage or disadvantage, but when done well it makes a powerful impact on the listeners.

Work in Concert with the Entire Service

This suggestion is closely related to the preceding one. Remember that the sermon is only *part* of the worship or evangelistic service. The liturgical tradition knows this and thoughtfully arranges the entire service as a unit. Those of us in the "free church" tradition should work with musicians and other leaders to create a holistic experience. Bill Hybels, pastor of Willow Creek Community Church, said in a lecture that the music, drama, Scripture reading, and prayer get him to the "five-yard line." All he has to do in the sermon is carry the ball over the goal line. Music, testimony, prayer, readings, communion, greetings, as well as the sermon, should be conceived as parts of a whole.

To re-create the impact of the text, try following your sermon with silence, a testimony, or a benediction. You may need to shorten your sermon to allow time for contemplation or discussion. Effective preachers think through such issues before they find themselves in front of their congregations.

Use Actual Images

Although the psalms communicate with words, not literal images, their language is so sensory, and our listeners are so attuned to visual communication, that the use of actual images may help us re-create the impact of the text.[30] One of the most stirring Scripture readings I have heard was of Psalm 8 ("the heavens declare the glory of God") accompanied by music and a slide show. Besides using pictures, preachers can use objects, as when Rob Bell, pastor of Mars Hill Bible Church, preached on Psalm 119 ("your word is a lamp to my feet") with an actual lamp onstage.

Remember that the Bible appeals to more senses than just sight. One of my students told me of a service in which her pastor set a bread machine in the back of the room. He programmed the machine to bake the bread during the service while he preached on the text, "One loaf . . . one body" (1 Cor. 10:17). The lovely smell of baking bread gradually pervaded the room, and after the sermon they used the fresh loaf for communion.

If your church discourages such communicative techniques for a Sunday sermon, perhaps you could use these ideas in other settings such as retreats, classes, or home groups.

Use an Expressive Voice and Body

Preachers convey meaning through two channels: sight and sound. What we look like and sound like are not incidental to preaching. They are inseparable from it.[31] In face-to-face communication, the nonverbal channel dominates the actual words. This is especially true when the nonverbal channel seems to conflict with the words. You have witnessed this clash when a greeter, scowling with a harsh voice, says, "Dear friends, it is good to see you. Welcome." When the two conflict, we believe the nonverbal; therefore, preachers who want to re-create the rhetorical impact of the text *must* embody it. God has ordained that his Word be incarnated in the voices, hands, and faces of preachers. How we look and sound is our medium, and if Marshall McLuhan overstated his argument that the medium is *the* message, we all agree that it is at least *a* message.

So if the text is joyful, we are to feel that happiness, then speak out of a full heart with a skillful voice and bearing. If the text is doleful, we need to enter vicariously the psalmist's experience and then communicate that experience naturally and sincerely. When we embody the text, the rhetorical impact is regenerated in the hearts and minds of the people. Some authors call this communication dynamic "empathy."[32] Listeners mirror what they see and hear from a speaker, as this description of Chrysostom's preaching illustrates:

> As he advanced from exposition to practical appeals, his delivery became gradually more rapid, his countenance more animated, his voice more vivid and intense. The people began to hold in their breath. . . . A creeping sensation like that produced by a series of electric waves passed over them. They felt as if drawn toward the pulpit by a sort of magnetic influence . . . some rose from their seats, others were overcome by a kind of faintness and the great mass could only hold their heads and give vent to their emotions in tears.[33]

Perhaps all of this advice on re-creating the impact of the psalms can be summarized in the old adage about writing: "If you're going to talk about a bear, it is of the utmost importance to bring in a bear." Bring in the bear with concrete language, metaphor, actual images, music, compelling delivery, and so forth. Turn the bear loose, and see what happens.

Chapter Checklist

- ❑ Meditate. Imagine.
- ❑ Get your body involved while studying.
- ❑ Read the text aloud.
- ❑ Listen to the text read aloud.
- ❑ Get alone.
- ❑ Find a listening log.
- ❑ Use concrete language—strong verbs and nouns.
- ❑ Write a manuscript.
- ❑ Write for the ear.
- ❑ Create some metaphors.
- ❑ Use a metaphor as a refrain.
- ❑ Translate metaphors as needed.
- ❑ Appeal to all the senses.
- ❑ Create an "emotional outline."
- ❑ Use self-disclosure.
- ❑ Don't (necessarily) turn poetry into propositions or imperatives.
- ❑ Use "microparallelism" (in a section).
- ❑ Use "macroparallelism" (for the structure of the whole sermon).
- ❑ Slow down and help people turn the "prism."
- ❑ Use a hymn or chorus.
- ❑ Use special music (before, after, or in the middle).
- ❑ Work in concert with the entire service.
- ❑ Use testimony.
- ❑ Use pictures.
- ❑ Use objects.
- ❑ Use other sensory experiences.
- ❑ Use variation in your voice.
- ❑ Use facial expressions, hand gestures, postures, and expressive movements.

- ❏ Practice.
- ❏ Think.
- ❏ Pray.
- ❏ Bring in a bear.

4

Narrative, Part 1

EVERYONE LOVES A STORY

Time didn't start this emphasis on stories about people; the
Bible did.

> —Henry Luce, founder of *Time* magazine,
> quoted in Wiersbe, *Preaching and Teaching*
> *with Imagination*

No story has power, nor will it last, unless we feel in ourselves
that it is true and true of us. . . . If the story is not about the
hearer, he won't listen. . . . A great and lasting story is about
everyone, or it will not last. The strange and foreign isn't
interesting, only the deeply personal and familiar.

> —John Steinbeck, *East of Eden*

Everyone loves a story. Witness the worldwide popularity of movies.
Witness the popularity of novels, magazines like *People,* and television dramas and sitcoms. Witness the chosen method of persuasion

most advertising companies use for TV commercials—brief stories. Witness the subject matter of most conversations—an account of what someone did and why they did it. Witness also the astounding consensus that has formed among scholars since the 1970s about the significance of narrative. Anthropologists, sociologists, rhetoricians, theologians, psychologists, philosophers, literary critics, and others all seem to be saying the same thing: "Narrative is present in every age, in every place, in every society; it begins with the very history of mankind and there nowhere is nor has been a people without narrative. . . . [N]arrative is international, transhistorical, transcultural: it is simply there, like life itself."[1]

Perhaps the pervasive presence of story can be explained because we live narratively as characters overcoming problems in a setting. An employee is stuck in traffic, late for work. She's a character overcoming a plot conflict in a setting. A father watches his son play tennis. The son is the protagonist in the court of decision against an evil antagonist. Daily experience is like a story. As philosopher Stephen Crites states, "The formal quality of experience through time is inherently narrative."[2]

This is true not only for the daily grind, but also for the metanarrative each worldview constructs: setting corresponds to the nature of the world (is the world a machine or a mirage?); character corresponds to the nature of humanity (are we accidents or demigods?); conflict corresponds to the problem of evil (does it arise because of the accidental collocation of atoms, or is it an illusion?); resolution corresponds to the remedy for evil (can we make this world a garden by pulling on our own bootstraps, or do we need enlightenment to discern the illusory nature of evil?).[3]

Because we communicate, live, and think narratively, we see story show up in unexpected places. One of those places is business, the bottom line world of making a buck. You wouldn't think that narrative had a seat in the boardroom, but in *In Search of Excellence*, Peters and Waterman tout its persuasive power: "We are more influenced by stories (vignettes that are whole and make sense in themselves) than by data."[4]

Another place where you might be surprised to see narrative is the sober world of tax law, but Attorney David Gustafson—who trains new attorneys in the tax division of the Justice Department, and who received a citation as "a teacher . . . of attorneys par excellence"—states, "When I lecture our new attorneys on preparing dispositive motions, I display an outline which ends with the admonition—in boldfaced and underlined—'Use your format to tell a story.' People understand and remember stories. Stories have beginnings and endings; they have plots and conflict and resolution; that's the way people like to (and habitually do) think about things."[5]

No wonder narrative is the largest genre of the Bible. By my estimate, it makes up more than 60 percent of Holy Scripture. Apparently, God values story as a form of communication. To borrow Cicero's three offices of the orator, it might be said that narrative teaches, delights, and moves.[6] But I'm getting ahead of myself. Before expounding the rhetoric of this genre, I need to define it.

What *Is* Biblical Narrative?

For the present purpose, biblical narrative can be defined as *a historically accurate, artistically sophisticated account of persons and actions in a setting designed to reveal God and edify the reader.*

The first phrase of this definition, "historically accurate," affirms the evangelical stance that Scripture speaks truthfully. It does so not only in what Francis Schaeffer calls the "upper story," the realm of faith and the unseen world, but also in the "lower story," the world of "brute facts."[7] Having affirmed the Bible's historicity, the province of this current chapter deals more with the second phrase of the definition: "artistically sophisticated." Although biblical narrators do not make up events and characters, they do select, arrange, and depict them with skill.

Narrators make these decisions in order to communicate doctrine and prompt response to that doctrine. As John states, if he tried to record everything Jesus said and did, the world could not hold the books, so he chose to describe some "signs" to prompt us to believe (John 21:25; 20:30–31). With the tools and skills of a biographer, storyteller, and poet, John argues his case that Jesus is Messiah. He selected, arranged, and depicted events and characters to move us to believe. Walter Kaiser makes the same point regarding the Old Testament: It is "critically important to recognize the larger context in which the narrative fits and to ask why the writer used the specific selection of events in the precise sequence in which he placed them. The twin clues to meaning now will be *arrangement* of episodes and *selection* of detail from a welter of possible speeches, persons, or episodes."[8]

For example, in the middle of the extended narrative of Saul (1 Sam. 9–31), chapter 14, the story of Jonathan and his armor bearer seems to gum up the plot. It feels like a clumsy digression, but closer study reveals how skillfully the narrator has placed the story. Jonathan serves as a foil to Saul, who by this point has showed that he cares more about himself than the honor of God. In contrast, Jonathan is jealous for the Lord's glory and risks his life to uphold it by attacking the Philistine garrison. The contrast is intensified in the second half of chapter 14 when Saul makes a rash vow and tries to have Jonathan put to death for eating a bit of honey. Saul is foolish, headstrong, self-centered, and a man-pleaser. Jonathan is wise, confident in the Lord, selfless, and a God-fearer. For this pair, "Like father, like son" does not hold true. We shake our heads in disapproval of Saul. We cringe at his rationalizations. We're not surprised when, in chapter 15, the Lord rejects Saul. The narrator's selection, placement, and shaping of the Jonathan incidents highlight the truth he wanted to communicate.

So biblical narrative is both historically accurate and artistically sophisticated. To use C. S. Lewis's terms, biblical narrative is both logos (something said) and *poiēma* ("something made").[9] Stephen Wright applies those terms to biblical literature that "points to realities" but is also an "object of contemplation which draws [us] into new experience. . . . *Poiēma* and *logos* have a symbiotic relationship. . . . Since logos comes to us in the framework of *poiēma*, literature is not reducible to the communication of facts; it invites us into experience."[10]

This current chapter, and this book, emphasize *poiēma*, but that emphasis may seem to devalue the Bible's historical and theological content, so let me cite Lewis again to summarize my stance: "The Bible is so remorselessly and continuously sacred that it does not invite, it excludes or repels, the merely aesthetic approach."[11]

The last phrase of my definition of biblical narrative asserts that it is "designed to reveal God and edify the reader." Those are the twin goals, and the New Testament uses Old Testament narratives for those goals:

Everything that was written in the past was written to teach us. (Rom. 15:4)

These things [stories from Exodus and Numbers] happened to them as examples and were written down as warnings for us. (1 Cor. 10:11)

All Scripture is God-breathed and is useful for teaching, rebuking, correcting and training in righteousness. (2 Tim. 3:16)

Another way to phrase the last part of my definition is to say that biblical narrative is theological and rhetorical. It was given to reveal the Lord God and to prompt a response to that revelation. As Eric Auerbach states, "The world of Scripture is not satisfied with claiming to be a historically true reality—it insists that it is the only real world. . . . The Scripture stories do not court our favor, they do not flatter us. . . . They seek to subject us, and if we refuse to be subjected, we are rebels."[12] Sailhamer, too, captures the theological and rhetorical nature of the Bible: "A text is . . . an embodiment of an author's intention, that is a strategy designed to carry out that intention."[13]

Sailhamer's assertion blends two aspects of "intention." The first is widely affirmed in evangelical circles, namely, that authors intend to communicate ideas, theological ideas in particular, but authors also intend those ideas to *influence* the readers. The second aspect of intention in Sailhamer's statement is that ideas are presented with a "designed strategy." Intentionality should be conceived of as both an idea and as a set of communication strategies for prompting a response.

Before turning to those strategies, this discussion of theology and intention raises a thorny hermeneutical and homiletical issue: preaching Christ from Old Testament narrative. This kind of preaching, sometimes called "historical-redemptive" or "Christ-centered," is often contrasted with preaching that uses the Old Testament stories to draw moral principles.[14] It seems to me that both approaches find warrant in the way the New Testament uses the Old. On the one hand, Jesus himself, "beginning with Moses and all the Prophets, . . . explained to them what was said in all the Scriptures concerning himself" (Luke 24:27). The Gospels, Acts, Paul's Epistles, and the General Epistles proclaim Christ from the only Scripture they had, the Hebrew Bible. On the other hand, the New Testament regularly uses Hebrew narratives to deduce and urge moral principles. First Corinthians 10, referred to above, uses the stories of the wilderness wanderings as "warnings." Hebrews 11 uses the old stories to exhort the readers to exercise faith. James inspires us to pray like Elijah because "the prayer of a righteous man is powerful and effective" (James 5:16). First John 3:12 clearly offers Cain as a negative moral example: "Do not be like Cain, who belonged to the evil one and murdered his brother." No wonder Goldingay concludes that "using biblical stories to provide examples of how believers should or should not behave is thus a quite biblical procedure."[15]

The tension between preaching Christ and preaching moral principles arises because biblical narratives are coruscating "speech acts" that perform many functions.[16] Fee and Stuart explain that Hebrew narratives communicate on three levels. The top level is the "macro-narrative" that portrays the creation and fall of humanity, the pervasive and universal effects of sin, and the need for redemption promised through Messiah.[17] The middle level centers on Israel—how God formed, blessed, watched, disciplined, and restored the chosen people. The bottom level centers on individuals, with hundreds of examples of virtue and vice. Using a different set of three perspectives, Goldingay says that Bible stories describe the commitments that the faith entails, the experiences that the faith may involve, and the events on which the faith is based.[18] These levels are all present in the story of Shadrach, Meshak, and Abednego, which, according to Old Testament scholar Richard Pratt, "served to guide readers into faithful living; it instilled a sense of pride in the courage of the young men; it inspired faith in the readers; and it offered doxology."[19]

I see both approaches—historical-redemptive interpretation and moral exhortation—as being legitimate when preaching from the stories of the Hebrew Bible. But preachers should remember that Fee and Stuart's lower level is always set within the context of the higher level(s). Moral principles must be urged, but as a result of God's powerful, faithful, and gracious provision. This is the way Isaiah 51 and Romans use the stories of Abraham.

It is hardly incidental that lifting up Christ and the glory of his Father is the best way to change behavior. Moralistic preaching without theological grounding feels like nagging with its never ending "do more, do better." It uses guilt to motivate behavior, a questionable pastoral practice that produces only temporary change; but a vision of God stirs holy affections, which is the seat of volition, and forms a profoundly Christian worldview.

Biblical narrative, then, is not only history told as story, it serves the intent of the author in revealing God and as it does so, it teaches, moves, and delights. How, though, does narrative do what it does?

How the Text Communicates, What the Text Does

The key features of narrative literature are plot, character, setting, and point of view. Each of these artistic components affects the reader.

Plot

Aristotle called plot the "soul" of story.[20] Of the four generic components mentioned above, it is first among equals because stories cannot exist without action. A tale could be told, at least theoretically, with no details of setting or character, but plot is the soul of the story. The action can be subtle and internal, but conflict drives the events.

Plot is the causally linked chain of events in a story that move from disequilibrium to resolution. "The king died, and then the queen died" is not a plot. It is a chronicle. "The king died and then the queen died of grief" is a plot because it describes events in causal relations. Plot is teleological in that the ending illuminates the beginning.

The biblical narrators were keen observers of causality: David avoids battle, then he looks on Bathsheba, then he commits adultery, then he murders. Peter trusts in his own strength, then he forsakes the Lord, then he repents, then he is restored as the leader of the early church. These "causally linked chains" deal with moral and spiritual choices even when the conflict involves physical battle as with David and Goliath. In the Bible the struggle of good versus evil, or God versus the Devil, permeates every story. As Ryken states, the external world "only provides the *occasion* for people to choose for or against God."[21]

Through plot, the authors *show* readers truth. They show us that God is sovereign (Job), that sinners who feel guilty try to hide their sin (Saul), and that God cares for the poor (Ruth). Occasionally narrators will intrude into their "showing" with "telling" (see Gen. 13:13; 29:18; 2 Sam. 6:8), but more typically they communicate ideas obliquely rather than stating them baldly as in genres like epistle and law. This "showing" provides readers with insight through vicarious experience. As narrative scholar Bar-Efrat states, "The plot serves to organize events in such a way as to arouse the reader's interest and emotional involvement, while at the same time imbuing the events with meaning."[22] I'll return to this idea below in discussing the rhetorical effects of plot.

Typical conflicts include the "quest," during which a hero strives to achieve a goal (Ruth); "death-rebirth," in which a hero endures death or danger and returns to life or security (Joseph); the "journey" (Moses and the Israelites); "crime and punishment" (Absalom); moving from "ignorance to insight" (Abraham).[23] Another way to conceive of plots is with the categories of drama: "comedy" and "tragedy." Comedy in the dramatic sense does not mean a story that produces waves of laughter, rather that the resolution of the conflict turns out positively for the protagonist. Tragedy, rare in biblical literature, means the opposite. The purest example is the story of Saul.

No matter how we categorize plots, they always develop a conflict, and the number of conflicts is surprisingly limited:

1. Person versus person (e.g., David vs. Goliath).
2. Person versus nature (e.g., the disciples on the Sea of Galilee).
3. Person versus self (e.g., Jesus wrestling in the Garden of Gethsemane).
4. Person versus supernatural being (e.g., Jacob wrestling with the angel).
5. Person versus collective (e.g., Jesus vs. the Pharisees).

Plots typically move through five stages:

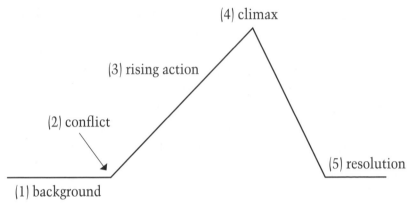

Fig. 4.1. The Five Stages of Plot

As an example, consider the story of Jesus and Zacchaeus from Luke 19:1–10.

- Background (usually brief, just enough to get the action started):

  Jesus entered Jericho and was passing through. A man was there by the name of Zacchaeus; he was a chief tax collector and was wealthy. He wanted to see who Jesus was. (vv. 1–3a)

  Note: Even this statement begins to create disequilibrium. A scoundrel wants to see Jesus! Why?

- Conflict (usually brief):

  He wanted to see who Jesus was, but being a short man he could not, because of the crowd. (v. 3)

- Rising Action (the longest portion of the story, it intensifies the conflict):

  Zacchaeus runs ahead, climbs a tree, is addressed by Jesus, takes Jesus home, bears the scorn of the people (see vv. 4–7).

- Climax (usually brief, the moment when the story turns toward resolution):

  Zacchaeus repents and receives Jesus' affirmation: "Today salvation has come to this house" (see vv. 8–9).

- Resolution (the outcome of the conflict and climax):

  Jesus affirms his mission: "The Son of Man came to seek and to save what was lost" (v. 10). God's self-revelation comes by means of a story depicting Jesus' kindness to an outcast scoundrel. The story functions as an argument, "proving" that Jesus truly does seek and save the lost.

As a preacher of narrative, you'll find it helpful in your exegesis to lay out the plot of your passage in these five sections. Merely laying it out does not, of course, make a sermon. Preachers must go further and determine the rhetorical significance of the plot's events. Plot functions rhetorically in three ways: it highlights ideas, induces suspense, and fulfills expectations.

The story of Jonathan and his armor bearer featured above demonstrates one way narrators highlight ideas, i.e., through contrast. If the book of 1 Samuel were a movie, the director would cut from Saul to Jonathan to juxtapose the contrast between father and son. When the spotlight suddenly swings onto a new scene, we naturally compare the new with the old and focus on the ideas the author intends.

Highlighting often occurs at the climax because that is the point of highest reader involvement. It is the summary of the action, indicating how the conflict is resolved. Thus, the story of Zacchaeus climaxes when the tax collector repents, and Jesus announces that salvation has come. Luke highlights the truth he wants us to embrace—that Jesus did indeed come to seek and save the lost.

The second rhetorical function, inducing suspense, is probably the most obvious role of plot. Whether it's the Red Sox in the bottom of the ninth, or Elijah battling the evil king and queen, we crave closure. We want to know who wins. We involuntarily ask, "How did this conflict start? What happened next . . . and next . . . and next? How did it turn out?" Preachers know, of course, the power of suspense.

They know that the moments of highest listener interest are likely to be their illustrations. Try saying, "That reminds me of the rainy summer of 1988 when I hiked the Appalachian trail," and watch the heads come up and the eyes focus.

The third rhetorical function, fulfilling expectations, in a sense safeguards the second. Some congregations already know the Bible stories you preach from, so suspense is reduced or eliminated. We already know who "wins," but plot still engages us with the third rhetorical function: setting up and fulfilling expectations. Even though we know, for example, that Dorothy and Toto arrive safely back home in Kansas, or that Luke Skywalker succeeds in blowing up the Death Star, we still enjoy watching classic films the second, third, fourth, or tenth time. Our enjoyment does not come from suspense. It comes because the plot establishes and fulfills expectations. Plots move from disequilibrium to resolution, and audiences find that movement as satisfying as the movement from an unresolved chord to a resolved one. Thus, congregations are still moved by the classic stories they've heard before: Elijah on Mt. Carmel, the Israelites crossing the Red Sea, the Prodigal Son, and so forth. Congregations do, indeed, say, "Tell me the old, old story."

In the words of Kenneth Burke, when a communicator points the "arrows of our desires" in a certain direction and then fulfills those desires, audiences find the experience satisfying.[24] Furthermore, when ideas imbue that affective experience, listeners naturally embrace the ideas. The rise and fall of the plotline, moving from background through conflict, rising action, and climax, opens the door for ideas to enter our hearts and minds. That entrance is likely to be through the back door, since narrators show rather than tell, but ideas do indeed enter.

Character

"Character" is the depiction of the persons in a story. It includes all of their physical, psychological, social, and spiritual attributes. The most important person in the story is the protagonist, a term that reminds us that plot and character cannot be separated: "protagonist" means literally the "primary struggler." The plot spins on the axis of the main character.

Narrative, like all art, universalizes particular experience. Characters carry a freight of meaning larger than themselves. By telling us the story of one man named Zacchaeus, who lived in Jericho, oversaw the collecting of taxes, and climbed a tree to see Jesus (hardly the experience of the people we preach to), we learn timeless truths about the kindness of God, the nature of repentance, and the complete pardon of forgiveness.

The art of characterization in ancient texts is much more succinct and reticent than the same art in modern texts. Thus, today's readers must use a slightly different set of conventions to read the old texts well. Here are seven of those conventions that convey character.

1. *Dialogue.* The primary way biblical narrators project character is by recording what the actors say. I estimate that nearly 50 percent of biblical narrative is dialogue, which means the quoted word carries the story's freight of meaning, yet the dialogue is compressed and crafted so that every word tells. Bar-Efrat explains, "Conversations in biblical narrative are never precise and naturalistic imitations of real-life conversations. They are highly concentrated and stylized, are devoid of idle chatter, and all the details they contain are carefully calculated to fulfill a clear function."[25] When Adam blames his wife and, by implication, God, the storyteller reveals the first man's psychological and spiritual state. The same is true of Saul's blaming the people, Aaron's blaming the people, and Jonah's blaming God. Dialogue reveals character, because words come from the heart.

2. *Action.* What actors do also conveys character. Pratt demonstrates this in the story of Ehud (Judg. 3:12–30).[26] Through action, the author shows this deliverer to be full of courage, canniness, and strength. We see that he possesses skill because he knows how to make his own double-edged sword. We see his physical strength in thrusting the sword all the way into Eglon's body. We know that he is trustworthy because the people place their tribute in his hands. We know he is brave because he faces Eglon alone, and he is crafty in his strategy and escape. Eglon, the antagonist, is heartless in that he oppresses the Israelites,

and he is a fool in that he leaves himself unguarded. Through careful selection of details, the author subtly depicts the physical, mental, and spiritual qualities of the players. Like their words, their actions also reveal the heart.

3. *Titles and names.* Ruth is a "Moabitess" and "daughter-in-law" (Ruth 1:22), Elisha is the "man of God" (2 Kings 5:8), Naaman is the "commander of the army of the king of Aram" (2 Kings 5:1), and Zacchaeus was the "chief tax collector" (Luke 19:2). These titles and names help us get to know the characters and help teach the truths the authors intend. Abram, "father," becomes Abraham, "Father of many nations." In his old age he bears "Laughter," who in turn bears a boy named "Deceiver," who is then renamed "Prince of God." The closer kinsman who accedes to Boaz is pélønî almønî, a vague phrase in Hebrew that leaves this shirker anonymous. He is simply "Mr. So-and-so." The apostles give to Joseph from Cyprus the nickname "Barnabas," the "Son of Encouragement" (Acts 4:36). If you appreciate Dickens, with his "Uriah Heep" and "Ebenezer Scrooge," you've got to appreciate the Bible's strategic use of names as a technique of characterization.

4. *Physical description.* Biblical narrators rarely describe the outer person, so that when they do, we need to sit up and take notice. When the storyteller includes the fact that Sarah was beautiful, or that Ehud was left-handed, or that Zacchaeus was short, we are supposed to recognize character that impacts plot. Berlin states, "The purpose of character description in the Bible is not to enable the reader to visualize the character, but to enable him to situate the character in terms of his place in society, his own particular situation, and his outstanding traits—in other words, to tell what kind of person he is."[27]

Absalom's handsome virility, for example, is suggested by describing his long hair weighing two hundred shekels (2 Sam. 14:26). In Hebrew culture, long hair was associated with strength. The description helps explain how he stole the people's hearts and foreshadows the irony of his being caught and killed by that hair. Perhaps the most fulsome physical description in the entire Bible is that of Goliath (1 Sam. 17:4–7). The author shows us that this warrior is a technological and biological terror, but even that description takes only four verses. Hebrew storytellers sketch with charcoal; they do not chisel marble.

5. *Authorial comment.* Another technique of characterization occurs when the author steps out from behind the curtain to insert his commentary into the flow of the plot. John, for example, explains Judas's complaint against the woman who anointed Jesus' feet with expensive perfume: "[Judas] did not say this because he cared about the poor but because he was a thief" (John 12:6). Authorial comments "are God's entrance as the ultimate storyteller into the story. Therefore, these comments become decisive in ultimately determining the meaning of the story."[28]

6. *Response from other characters.* How characters respond to each other provides a commentary on their natures. This commentary is entirely trustworthy when God or God's representative is the one responding. When Adam and Eve sinned, for example, God cursed them. That response is all the commentary we need to judge their actions as evil rebellion. Another example comes from the book of Acts. Because Sapphira lied, she was buried with her deceptive husband for she had, in Peter's words, "test[ed] the Spirit of the Lord" (Acts 5:9).

7. *Foils.* A foil is a deliberate contrast to the protagonist. When Orpah returns to Moab, we see Ruth's loyalty and courage in a stronger light. When Lot chooses the well-watered plains of Sodom, we admire Abraham's discernment. When the crowd grumbles that Jesus eats with Zacchaeus, the sinner, we esteem our Lord's courage and compassion; he was not deterred by the crowd's pressure. As discussed above, the depiction of Jonathan in 1 Samuel 14 serves as a foil to Saul, who is himself a foil to David, a man after God's own heart. In the same way, the insertion of Genesis 38, Judah and Tamar, seems to break the flow of the Joseph story, but Mathewson argues that the insertion not only heightens tension by suspending the plot but also positions Judah as a foil to Joseph.[29] Judah is sexually profligate; Joseph resists temptation. Judah is hypocritical; Joseph is true. Judah is foolish and blind; Joseph is discerning.

These seven techniques of characterization demonstrate that biblical narrators employ a subtle and artistic craft. But to what end? How does characterization advance the author's intention? The primary rhetorical function of character is identification. Ryken counsels readers to go through the story as a "traveling companion of the protagonist."[30] Storytellers induce empathy with heroes or antipathy with villains. As Pratt states, "Old Testament authors did not present characters simply to tell their readers about people in the past but to evoke responses. . . . Old Testament writers intended for many of their characters to elicit sympathetic responses of approval. Characters take on the qualities of heroes or models of appropriate attitudes and behavior that the audience was expected to appreciate and admire."[31]

When our minds are engaged in the flow of the plot and our feelings are bound to the characters, the values of the story begin to infiltrate our hearts. In contrast, defense mechanisms snap to attention when someone begins, "You are mistaken. Let me prove it to you." We know that they are arguing, trying to change us (and none of us likes that!), but when someone begins, "Once upon a time," we relax and yield to the form of the genre. The ideas expressed in that form enter the heart with little interrogation. Rhetorician William Kirkwood comments, "By ostensibly describing what and how, not why, . . . [narrative is] not readily susceptible to ordinary methods of analysis and refutation. Thus storytelling can briefly override auditors' immediate defenses and introduce views of life that would otherwise have been rejected before they could prompt self-examination in listeners."[32] This is what happened when Nathan confronted David with the story of the little lamb.

Setting

The third element of narrative is setting—the time and place where the characters act. As with characterization, the Bible is extremely selective with these descriptions. All we know about the setting of Ruth is that it takes place "in the days when the judges ruled" (1:1); it opens in Bethlehem, shifts to Moab, and then back to Bethlehem. Dearth of description can bore modern readers who are fascinated by the Louvre after hours (*The Da Vinci Code*, Dan Brown) or with the icy Himalayas (*Into Thin Air*, John Kraukauer), but boredom is mitigated when we learn to read with the right set of conventions.

Look again at Ruth. Perhaps this gem of a story shines more brightly as a foil to the dark days of the judges. Perhaps the move from Bethlehem to Moab implies disloyalty to the covenant and lack of faith. But look again. Is this all the setting the author supplies? No. We imaginatively arrive "as the barley harvest was beginning" (1:22). We enter "a field belonging to Boaz" (2:3), take a "short rest in the shelter" (2:7), are then transported to town (2:18), to the threshing floor (3:6), and the town gate (4:1). The clock spins as Ruth gleans "until evening" (2:17), and Boaz discovers Ruth "in the middle of the night" (3:8). The calendar rustles through the barley and wheat harvests (2:23). Setting in biblical narrative is subtle, but it is present for those with eyes to see. If the author tells us that the story takes place on a mountain, at a high place, in the desert, or in a garden, biblical preachers should take note.

Cultural and geographic study enhances our appreciation of setting. Using background tools, we discover what it was like to be in a boat on the Sea of Galilee, in the hold of the ship where Jonah slept, or fighting for life in a storm with Paul, bound for Rome. We discover how far Elijah ran, the size of the Holy of Holies, and the distance from Jericho to Jerusalem. We learn when barley harvest transpired, why the woman was drawing water at noon, and when the sixth hour occurred. We visualize the fiery furnace, the sycamore-fig tree, and the amphitheater in Ephesus.

Depiction of setting serves two rhetorical functions. The first is the ignition of imagination. Careful readers, those who are reading slowly and yielding to the intentions of the authors, feel the heat of the day, the cool of the cave, and the lurch of the waves. We see the Promised Land beckon, the desert shimmer, the walls loom, and the charcoal fire glow.

In the story of Zacchaeus, for example, Luke calls our attention to sparse details of setting, but each detail counts, helping us visualize the action and contributing to our understanding of the whole. A few minutes of background research will help you imagine Jericho—the city of dates, palms, and balsam; the city with Herod's gleaming winter palace; a crossroads city where a chief tax collector would indeed be "wealthy" (Luke 19:2). Notice also *when* the story occurs: Jesus is headed to Jerusalem for Passion Week. Knowing that the Lord Jesus had set his face like flint toward Jerusalem and the cross, each step taking him closer to the gallows, we see the kindness of our Savior in sharper focus. He wasn't thinking of himself, only his precious wandering sheep. He takes the initiative to seek and save one more outcast. Blessing waits for the one who slows down to soak in the setting.

Setting refers not only to extrabiblical details of time and place that spark imagination but also to intrabiblical allusions that prompt association. That is the second rhetorical function: association. Scholars such as Northrop Frye and John Sailhamer demonstrate convincingly that the Bible is *one* book.[33] Although written by scores of people over thousands of years, it is a self-reflecting constellation of meaning. States Frye, "The Bible as a whole . . . presents a gigantic cycle from creation to apocalypse."[34] Parts allude to other parts, and authors count on their readers to understand individual narratives in light of the metanarrative of redemptive history, Fee and Stuart's "top level."

Thus, the author of Ruth intends the reader to experience the sweet music of this story against the cacophonous jangle of the days of the judges. The author also intends the reader to gain understanding about the genealogy of David and the history of Israel.

Furthermore, the author expects the reader to possess prior understanding about the covenant of Deuteronomy, knowing that a faithful Jew would never remove himself and his family from the Land. Through intrabiblical allusion, the narrators communicate theology, but as we have seen, their craft is subtle. They embody their ideas in persons and places.

Biblical preachers can unleash the rhetoric of association in two ways. First, we can simply explain the allusions. We preachers are, in part, teachers, and we should not hesitate to unpack what God has packed in. Second, we should return again and again to the metanarrative. Over time, our congregations, by interpreting narratives on "level one," will begin to make associations themselves. They will see the Bible as a majestic story of creation, rebellion, and redemption. They will see themselves, as the authors intended, in the grand flow of God's story.

Point of View

The fourth and final generic feature of biblical narrative is point of view, the perspective or attitude from which a story is told. Point of view pervades the other three features, but for analysis it will be treated here as a separate category. This component is easiest to understand if we use the analogy of moviemaking, wherein point of view is literal. By means of the camera, directors control how we see the action, characters, and settings. The story can be told with sweeping panoramas, intimate close-ups, or a jerking you-are-there handheld camera. Directors also control point of view with editing techniques. Quick scenes pulse with energy by virtue of jump cuts, and slow scenes stroll with stateliness by virtue of slow dissolves. Most of us understand the grammar of movies because we have drunk from that well since kindergarten, but to understand the grammar of biblical narrative, most of us need to go to a different well. There, we imbibe and appreciate five techniques of perspective that biblical storytellers use to guide readers' responses to plot, character, and setting. You've met some of these techniques earlier in the chapter.

Degree of Omniscience

For the most part, biblical narrators, along with ancient storytellers in general, tend toward omniscience. In contrast to modern authors, who tend to limit their descriptions to what a single observer could detect, biblical authors speak authoritatively, sometimes revealing characters' thoughts and motivations, as when the author of Genesis tells us that Esau "held a grudge against Jacob because of the blessing his father had given him," and he also relates thoughts that Esau "said to himself" (27:41).

The Hebrew article *behold* (*wĕhinnēh*) sometimes indicates that the narrator is taking an omniscient point of view. It signals the reader that details are being seen through the eyes of the character.[35] The particle occurs three times in Genesis 28:12–13a to let the reader know what Jacob saw in his dream: "He had a dream, and *behold*, a ladder was set on the earth . . . ; and *behold*, the angels of God were ascending and descending on it. And *behold*, the LORD stood above it and said . . ." (NASB).

Another example of omniscience, or at least of the narrator taking an authoritative, teaching stance, occurs in the first line of Genesis 22: "Some time later God tested Abraham." This is the story of Abraham and Isaac, and the narrator doesn't want us to miss the point. By headlining the theme of the incident before we read it, we experience the following horrific episode (sacrifice your son!) with the expectation that God will not literally require human sacrifice. The author guides the reading process. Luke's quoting of Jesus at the end of the Zacchaeus story serves a similar headlining function, but this time the headline comes at the end: "The Son of Man came to seek and to save that which was lost." The author tells us what we have just experienced, like the moral of the story at the end of Aesop's Fables.

Amount of Detail

Like the movie director using close-up and panorama, storytellers also zoom in and out. Zooming out, of course, shows context and sweeping events: "He removed the high places and incense altars in every town in Judah, and the kingdom was at peace under him" (2 Chron. 14:5).

Zooming in creates intimacy and focus: "The other disciples followed in the boat, towing the net full of fish, for they were not far from shore, about a hundred yards. When they landed, they saw a fire of burning coals there with fish on it, and some bread" (John 21:8–9). This passage begins with midrange shots of the boat and the shore. Thus, we experience the story from a distance. Then the storyteller narrows our perspective, focusing on small details on shore—the charcoal fire with fish and bread. The author prompts us to see what the disciples saw so that we experience the events as one of the disciples, feeling like we've landed and are walking toward the fire.

This mention of the *charcoal fire* is itself significant. The Greek term is used only twice in the New Testament, here and in the story of Peter's denials in the courtyard (John 18:18). By using intrabiblical allusion, John carries the readers back to the scene of betrayal. Peter—and we—sees the fire, and Peter remembers his—as we remember our—denials. Peter's relationship with Jesus is fractured, and the time of confrontation has arrived. All of this and more is packed into a few verses that describe setting. All of this and more is accessible to us when we read according to the conventions the authors used.

Flow of Time

Similar to the control of the camera's distance is the control of time. The sacrifice of Isaac narrative in Genesis 22 illustrates this technique, highlighting and focusing our attention by skillfully managing the flow of narrative time. Three days of travel zip by like images flashing from a train window. Then the train slows as the narrator describes Abraham commanding the servants, climbing the hill, and building the altar. Then the train comes to a virtual stop as the narrator piles verb upon verb: he "bound his son," "laid him on the altar," "reached out his hand," and "took the knife." This slow motion technique creates suspense, prompting the reader to empathize with the severity of God's test.

Selection and Arrangement

As already seen, much of the artistry of biblical narrative lies in selection and arrangement. Pratt states, "Evangelicals often fail to consider the selectivity Old Testament writers exercised. 'They wrote about those events because that's what happened,' we say. This is certainly true, but Old Testament writers could have described the same events in countless ways without misconstruing the facts. What is reported, emphasized, de-emphasized, and omitted is largely a matter of choice."[36] The figure below illustrates the technique of selectivity:[37]

Luke's Story of Zaccheus (Luke 19:1–10)

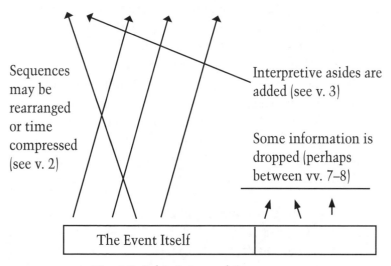

Sequences may be rearranged or time compressed (see v. 2)

Interpretive asides are added (see v. 3)

Some information is dropped (perhaps between vv. 7–8)

The Event Itself

Fig. 4.2. Selectivity and Arrangement as Techniques of Point of View

An intriguing use of selectivity occurs when the authors construct suspended plots, plots where some aspect of the conflict is left unresolved. In a suspended plot, the author deliberately withholds the climax of the story. Three major examples are the following biblical books:

1. *Jonah.* The book establishes a primary conflict between God and Jonah. God values the Ninevites and wants them to repent, but Jonah wants them to burn. By the end of the story, how is this conflict resolved? Does Jonah mend his attitude? Apparently not, but the reader doesn't know for sure. The story ends with a rhetorical question as God rebukes the selfish prophet: "Should I not be concerned about that great city?" This suspended plot produces an effect similar to Jesus' parables. The reader is drawn in and then left with choices. Will I side with Jonah or the Lord God? Do I feel compassion or contempt for pagans?

2. *Mark.* Assuming that the long ending of Mark is a scribal addition, this book ends at the tomb, not with Jesus' appearances after the resurrection. Here is the inspiring last line: "Trembling and bewildered, the women went out and fled from the tomb. They said nothing to anyone, because they were afraid." The effect of this anticlimax is similar to the one in Jonah. The writer tosses the ball back to the reader. What will we do with the fact that Jesus has risen—remain silent?

3. *Acts.* The ending is not as open-ended as Jonah or Mark, but it does lack complete closure. The curtain falls in Rome with Paul in his own rented house, boldly and without hindrance teaching and preaching about the Lord Jesus Christ. This conclusion creates a sense of forward momentum. The gospel has reached the capital. Nothing can stop it! Stay tuned for updates.

Besides these major examples, smaller pericopes may also use unresolved tension. See the story of Reuben's immorality in Genesis 35: "Reuben went in and slept with his father's concubine Bilhah, and Israel heard of it" (v. 22). See also the story of the floating axe head in 2 Kings 6:1–7.

Irony

When an author uses irony,[38] he counts on his readers to supply insider knowledge to detect incongruity as in Genesis 13:10, where Lot chooses the well-watered plains because they looked "like the garden of the LORD." What delicious irony—Sodom and Gomorrah compared to the Garden of Eden. Lot thought he was going to a place of prosperity, not destruction. We judge him because he lacked judgment, which led to God's judgment. Similarly, the reader knows that when Elimelech, Naomi's husband, removes himself from the Land, he cripples his opportunity to care for his family. Only an insider can sense the irony.

Verbal irony occurs when a character says one thing and means another, as when Michal mocks her husband, David: "How the king of Israel has distinguished himself today, disrobing in the sight of the slave girls" (2 Sam. 6:20). Dramatic irony occurs when the audience perceives what a character does not. The character says or does something without knowing the full implications, as when Sisera seeks refuge in the tent of Jael. He tells her, "If someone comes by and asks you, 'Is there anyone here?' [lit. 'any man'] say 'No'" (Judg. 4:20). He soon got the point. Situational irony occurs when experience turns out to be the opposite of what a character expected, as when Saul set out to find lost donkeys and returned with a kingdom (1 Sam. 9).

Point of view, then, provides two rhetorical effects. The first is, not surprisingly, that it controls the reader's point of view. The author, in order to teach us lessons and prompt attitudes, shapes how we respond to the characters and their actions. Readers who read imaginatively, yielding to the author's art, see the world as the author desires them to see it.

The second rhetorical effect, collaboration, travels with the first, and occurs especially with irony. As seen in chapter 3 when examining the collaboration produced by metaphor, readers of irony must supply what is missing. Booth notes, "In reading any metaphor or simile, as in reading irony, the reader must reconstruct meanings through inferences about surface statements that for some reason cannot be accepted at face value."[39] When speakers mean more than they say, or when they mean the opposite of what they say, they prompt us, in Booth's words, to dance an "intricate mental dance together."[40] The dance looks like this:

- The reader first senses incongruity, inferring that a statement cannot mean what it seems to mean, or means more than it seems to mean: "Lot thought the plains looked like the Garden of the Lord. How strange!"
- Then the reader invents a hypothesis about what it does mean: "Lot lacks discernment. His selfishness and spiritual blindness is leading him astray."
- Then the reader tests the hypothesis by what he or she knows about the speaker and the author's purpose: "Yes, that squares with the characterization of Lot I've come to expect. Furthermore, the purpose of this text is to contrast Abraham and Lot."
- Then the reader reconstructs the actual meaning: "Lot's selfishness and lack of discernment led him to choose the well-watered plains near Sodom and Gomorrah. His character contrasts with that of Abraham, whose restraint and wisdom derived from his relationship with Yahweh. Lot is a fool because he doesn't fear God." All of this happens in a flash of intuition. Irony is extremely economical since it takes ten times as many words to express the same meaning with literal talk.[41]

In his sermon "A Night In Persia," Don Sunukjian re-creates the irony of the book of Esther,[42] a book redolent with the sovereignty of God, yet a book in which God is never mentioned. Sunukjian conveys the irony by narrating the story through the eyes of an unbeliever. When striking "coincidences" occur, the pagan narrator muses, "Boy, those Jews are lucky!" But the listeners collaborate with Sunukjian to construct a different meaning: "That wasn't luck! That was the sovereign God at work." Such collaboration brings pleasure and binds speaker and listener in a kind of friendship.

As you can see, exegeting narrative calls for artistic sensitivity. Aren't you glad the Lord chose this fascinating genre as his primary way to communicate in the Scriptures? The next chapter asks how God's heralds can re-create some of the effects of the genre as we tell the old, old story.

5

Narrative, Part 2

EVERYONE LOVES A STORY

Men would rather listen to the biography of a miser than to a discourse upon the subject of avarice.

—John W. Etter

When we read only of doctrines, these may reach the understanding, but when we read or hear of examples, human affection doth as it were represent to us the case as our own.

—Thomas Hooker

This chapter discusses some suggestions for harnessing the enchanting form of story when preaching from narrative.

Choose a Passage with a Complete Plot

Standard homiletical doctrine tells us to preach thought units, but identifying those units in narrative can be tricky. When preaching from Psalms, the unit is usually obvious, an entire poem, but how should we preach units embedded within long stories such as Genesis or Mark? The answer is to identify and preach an entire plot: a clear conflict, rising action, and climax. Thus, a tidy story like Mary and Martha, only five verses long (Luke 10:38–42) forms a thought unit. Other clues to look for are changes in place (e.g., Gen. 18:33), persons (Gen. 19:1), or time (Gen. 22:1). These signal a transition from one scene to another.

Having used Luke 10:38–42 as an example, I should hasten to say that when preaching narrative, our texts are likely to be longer than this. Because narrative develops ideas by showing more than telling, our preaching texts are likely to be longer than when preaching from, say, an epistle. With short stories like Ruth and Jonah, you may want to preach the whole book in one sermon. In determining how to preach the big idea of a longer story, Don Sunukjian's sermon on the entire book of Esther is a model.[1]

Try Induction

Storyteller Flannery O'Connor says that stories speak "*with* character and action, not *about* character and action,"[2] so preachers who want to take their cue from the text may want to try induction. In an inductive arrangement the central truth of the sermon is stated only at the end after the preacher has "embodied [the idea] in a structure of events and persons, rather than in a structure of verbal generalizations."[3] For example, listen to radio storyteller Paul Harvey who always saves "now you know the rest of the story" for the conclusion.[4]

One way to preach inductively is by identifying the problem the passage addresses—what various homileticians call the "disease,"[5] "fallen condition focus,"[6] or "depravity factor,"[7]—and then determining how the theology of the passage provides the "remedy." At least half of the sermon should be devoted to analysis of the problem before getting to the solution. In this way, the sermon develops in a storylike way, introducing and intensifying a conflict before stating and expounding the solution. As Borden states, "Preaching this way enables you and your people to feel the story as drama. The sermon, which has its own plot, uses the pieces of the story that reflect the disequilibrium, reversal, and resolution they felt when they first read or heard the story."[8]

Gifted preachers can even imply, rather than expound, the big idea. Stories often carry their assertions and imperatives through the back door of the listener's mind. Why not try it yourself? Homiletician Sidney Greidanus states that preaching from narrative should be more by "suggestion than by assertion."[9] Robinson agrees: "Narratives are most effective when the audience hears the story and arrives at the speaker's ideas without the ideas being stated directly."[10] By prompting the listeners to infer your main idea, you may find your sermons to be more, not less, persuasive because physics and persuasion share a common axiom: "For every action there is an equal and opposite reaction." The "action" of argument causes people to push back. The "action" of story causes people to lean in.

Arrange Your Material Like a Plot

This suggestion is closely related to the one above about problem-solution arrangement. The goal is to arrange your material in a way that captures the rhetorical effects of the original plot. Alan Monroe and Eugene Lowry have developed methods of organization for speeches and sermons that move as a causally linked chain of events.

Monroe's "Motivated Sequence"

As a teacher of public speaking, Alan Monroe developed a way to organize sales presentations and other talks to achieve maximum persuasion.[11] In a sales talk, to get to the "close," Monroe said you must take your audience through a five-step process:

1. *Attention.* Focus attention on your product or idea.
2. *Need.* Surface a felt need for the same.
3. *Satisfaction.* Offer the product/idea as the solution to that need.
4. *Visualization.* After explaining your product/idea, heighten desire by projecting future consequences. Persuaders say, in essence, "If you adopt my proposition, your future will look like this. If you reject my proposition, it will look like this."

5. *Action.* This is the "close." Call for action. State clearly what you want the listener to do.

A sermon on Genesis 22 might look like this:

Attention	"God tests his friends." What is this we've read? He *tests* us?
Need	This makes us uncomfortable. Why does the Scripture teach that God tests us?
Satisfaction	Explain the definition and theology of "testing." State big idea: "God tests his friends for their own good and his own glory."
Visualization	Testing will come to you. "If you remember the story of Abraham, it will help you obey God and experience peace. If you forget this Scripture, you might flounder and wander from God."
Action	Thank God for his inscrutable ways. Thank him that he is trustworthy. Thank him that with every testing, we have the assurance that it is for our own good and his own glory.

Fig. 5.1. Monroe's Motivated Sequence Applied to Genesis 22

Lowry's "Homiletical Plot"

This method also arranges material in five steps designed to take the listeners through an experience in time.[12] Here are the steps with an example from Luke 19:1–10:

Upset the equilibrium.	Like Zacchaeus, sinners sin, and seekers seek.
Analyze the discrepancy.	Seekers seek Jesus because . . .
Disclose the key to resolution.	Seekers find Jesus because he is seeking them.
Experience the gospel.	The kindness of his grace leads to repentance.
Anticipate the consequences.	Forgiven sinners live lives of gratitude and holiness.

Fig. 5.2. Lowry's Homiletical Plot Applied to Luke 19

These methods may feel strange to someone who thinks all sermons have three points, but they have the advantage of being conversational and psychologically effective. Give them a try, especially when preaching from narrative.

Preach a Third-Person Narrative Sermon

Listeners love a good story, and God has inspired most of the Bible as story, so why not preach in story? This is the simplest way to incorporate nearly all of the rhetorical functions explored in the previous chapter: suspense, identification, imagination, collaboration, and so forth. Narrative sermons can be preached in either the third person ("David got up and walked to the roof of the palace") or first person ("My name is David. One day I got up and walked to the roof of my palace"). In this section I concentrate on the third-person sermon and in the next section on the first person.

The third-person sermon, rather than having points, shows ideas through events, characters, and settings. We would not, of course, simply repeat the story; instead we adapt and apply it to a particular congregation. To do so, give attention to the following three steps: (1) communicate the central idea, (2) shape the plot, (3) build identification with the main character.

Communicate the Central Idea

A narrative sermon, like every sermon, should aim to communicate a single dominant idea adapted to the listeners. Here are some techniques for communicating that idea while telling a story:

- *State the idea deductively in a traditional introduction.* Here's an example from my sermon on Acts 9, the conversion of Saul:

  When we think of Paul, we tend to think of him as . . . Paul: the apostle Paul, author of the New Testament, missionary, theologian, church planter, deeply devoted to God, and tender-hearted toward people. But he was "Paul" for only about half of his life. We don't think of him as "Saul," brilliant Pharisee, ruthless persecutor, enemy of Jesus, and hater of people. Today I want to tell you the story of Saul, Saul of Tarsus, and I want to show you how *the grace of God turns men around* [big idea]. Calvin said in his commentary on Acts 9 that the wolf became a sheep and then a shepherd. Here's how it happened . . .

- *State the idea bluntly in a traditional conclusion.* This can help some audiences feel that you have actually preached a sermon instead of merely telling a story, especially if you elaborate and apply the idea for a few minutes: "This story teaches us that . . ."
- *Weave the idea into the flow of the story.* Halfway through the sermon you could pause and reflect upon the characters and their actions, stating "Isn't God great? Look what he did for Saul. He turned him around and I mean 180 degrees around! That's what the grace of God does, you know. It turns us around."
- *Place the idea in the mouth of a character.* For example, "Ananias took Saul by the shoulders, looked him in the eye, and said, 'God has rescued you, brother Saul. He has stopped you

in your tracks and ransomed your soul. The grace of God has turned you around. Now serve him with a glad heart in newness of life.'"

- *Imply, but do not state, the idea.* This takes induction to a higher level, and it takes real skill, but when the audience infers your idea, they collaborate with you, and collaboration results in powerful communication. Prompt them by your storytelling techniques to think, "Wow, the grace of God turned him around."

Shape the Plot

However you choose to communicate the big idea, keep the plot moving forward steadily. Don't let it stall with unnecessary digressions for lengthy explanation or illustration. On the other hand, suspending the plot with *purposeful* support material can enhance the tension of the message.[13]

Barry Corey does this with his sermon on Nehemiah 5.[14] The first half of the sermon describes how the people lifted, hauled, and sweated for two months to build the half-erected wall. The twist is that they and their wives did this as volunteers, and they did it during a "depression." Food was scarce, usury was rampant, greedy merchants inflated the price of grain, people had to mortgage their fields, and some destitute families even had to sell their children into temporary slavery to pay off the greedy lenders. Corey states,

> So what does Nehemiah do about it? He sets a table for the hungry. . . . Here is Nehemiah the governor, and at his table, eating supper with him, are all kinds of folk. There are people from the city, commoners, and nobles. He even invited those from other nations to come to his table, to enjoy the finest of Mediterranean fare. . . . Nehemiah's banquet table was spread not for the few but for the many. . . . Was the wall done? No. Were times easy? No, people are struggling to make ends meet, they're tightening their belts. But in the midst of these difficult days with long hours of working, little discretionary money, families split up, there was a table set for them.
>
> There is a word that describes the way in which Nehemiah lived his life and the manner in which he opened his home

during difficult times. The word is *kindness*. And the question that this passage poses to us is this: Are you the kind kind?[15]

Corey then suspends the story of Nehemiah to tell another story from *Once Upon a Town*, by journalist Bob Greene, the tale of the North Platte Canteen, a train depot in 1941. During World War II, army trains stopped in North Platte for ten or fifteen minutes as they transported soldiers to the West Coast. The twelve thousand residents of North Platte wanted to express their thanks to the soldiers, so they started greeting them with baskets of food and treats. As Corey states, "Train after train, day after day, three to five thousand soldiers a day, six million over the course of the war, were welcomed by the North Platte Canteen. . . . The depot would be lined with tables and hosts, and the soldiers would climb out and to their delight find waiting for them birthday cakes and fresh bread, homemade sweets and coffee. They would ask 'how much?' and the ladies there would say, 'It's free.'"

After this charming story, the preacher returns to Nehemiah to finish the story and briefly exhort the listeners to show kindness, "kindness in the form of a meal."

Build Identification

In addition to retelling the events of the plot, the third-person narrative sermon creates identification with the main character. Listeners need to see themselves as Abraham tested, Zacchaeus seeking, or Ruth destitute. Without sympathetic connection, the sermon will lack credibility. It will seem merely like entertainment or a history lesson. In the sermon called "Mid-Life Crisis, Problem Ancient and Modern," notice how Haddon W. Robinson creates identification between his audience (pastors in midlife) and King David.[16] After describing David's success as a military and spiritual leader, Robinson states,

> But that doesn't mean that everything was right in David's life at forty-seven years of age. I'm sure he was bothered when he looked into the large bronze mirrors in the palace and he saw that decay was winning the battle over youth. There was the receding hairline, and the hair that was flecked with

gray. . . . And then there was that paunch. When David was a young man, leaping over walls to escape from Saul, he had been as lean and trim as a knife. Now he looked more like a fork. Even though his tailors could cut his garments so that no one noticed, David noticed, and it bothered him.

David also had trouble with his marriages. None of them turned out very well. Some of them could be shrugged off as marriages of convenience, but then there was Abigail. David could remember when he first met her. She made his blood run hot. She was a woman as brilliant as she was beautiful, a woman fashioned to be queen. As soon as he could, David made her his wife. That had been seventeen years ago. She hadn't done much for his blood pressure lately. In fact she had just settled down to become dear Abby.

That's the way it was in David's life. Everything seemed to have flattened out. That was true of his relationship to God. When he was a young man out there in the wilderness, there were times when psalms exploded from his soul, and he could hardly contain himself. There were other times when he cried out to God in his desperation. It seemed he could almost reach up and touch God. But there hadn't been many psalms in David's life lately. Of course, David could explain this. When you get along in years you get over the idealism of youth.

That's the way it was in David's life at forty-seven years of age. He was a king ruling in Jerusalem. He was successful. He was self-sufficient. He was complacent.[17]

I imagine that many of the pastors listening to this story about David felt that the preacher was telling their stories. They identified. If, in addition to creating identification, you're careful to include the central idea of the story and steadily advance the plot, your sermon will likely be highly effective.

Preach a First-Person Narrative Sermon

Most of the material above applies also to the first-person narrative sermon as well. As with the third-person message, the "dramatic monologue" needs a clear big idea, needs the plot to flow, and especially needs to create identification. In addition, the first-person sermon has its own set of considerations.[18]

One of those is costuming. I find that using a costume usually does not help the message and at times hinders it by implying that the sermon is "playacting." To be sure, the first-person sermon blurs the lines between acting and preaching, but never forget that you are a herald who, with freedom of form, is simply looking for the best way to re-create the rhetorical impact of the text and adapt to the constraints of each preaching venue. If you do use a costume, keep it simple and professional. No bathrobes, please.

When it comes to costuming, props, and blocking (stage movement), the key is to spark the listeners' imagination so that receivers participate vicariously in the message. To spark imagination, less is often more. Simple blocking and a simple prop are often enough to activate the mind's eye. Examine a sling stone or vial of ointment as you speak. Take up and set down a scepter at strategic moments. Or place three chairs on the platform to symbolize three stages of the narrator's life. Keep it simple.

Another special constraint of the first-person sermon is establishing who is speaking. This can be awkward because the people naturally expect you, not King Solomon, to address them, so you need to give the people sufficient clues to know how to process what they're hearing. To establish who is speaking, try using a traditional introduction to inform the audience of what you're doing. Don Sunukjian begins "A Night in Persia" this way:

> There's a book in the Bible where the name of God is never mentioned—the book of Esther. But even though God's name is mentioned nowhere in the book, you sense his presence everywhere, controlling what happens.
>
> It's like a dollhouse where the top has been removed and some big father can lean in, move the people around, rearrange the furniture, and do anything he wants. That huge father does not walk around in the dollhouse, yet he controls everything that happens. That's how it is in the book of Esther. You don't see or hear God there, but you sense his presence dominating everything.

I would like to tell the story of Esther through the eyes of one of the minor characters in the story. The man is on the palace staff, an attendant to the king. He's on the inside. He knows everything that's going on. How would this man, who never hears the name of God and yet sees everything that happens, view it? What sense would he make out of it all? [Pause]

My name is Harbona.[19]

If you plunge directly into the story without a traditional introduction, let the audience know that someone else is speaking:

"I suppose I should introduce myself to you. My name is David."[20]

"My name is Hosea. My profession is prophet of the Lord Jehovah."[21]

"I still don't know my way around the palace. You ought to see all the rooms. And it's kind of hard to get around (*motioning toward his mangled feet*). . . . My name is Mephibosheth."[22] [Note: When I saw Sunukjian preach this sermon in 1999, he entered the stage with crutches; thus, even before the verbal communication began, he established character nonverbally.]

Also let the audience know if you are addressing them directly or if they are overhearing the monologue, as in this example, in which the staging shows Mary writing a letter:

"Dear Elizabeth,
   It's a boy! . . . After my visit to you . . . I went back to Nazareth."[23]

Just as the introduction of the first-person sermon needs special attention, so does the conclusion. Coordinate well how you will transition into the next part of the service. I find it best for the preacher to simply exit at the conclusion of the message and have someone else pray or continue the service. If you continue the service as yourself, having dropped the character, the juxtaposition may jar the listeners and cause them to analyze the performance rather than contemplate how God has spoken.

Another constraint of the dramatic monologue relates to gender. Should men represent women, and vice versa? No. It's best to stick to your own gender. Physical appearance is a constant reminder that we are either men or women, and audience members can't get past the evidence of their senses. Most audience members, in fact, find it nearly impossible to set aside their perceptions of the preacher's gender. Members will usually grant that, for the duration of the sermon, I (a male) am taking the role of a male character, but they balk when called upon to imagine me as a female character.

Concerning language and delivery, discussed in more detail below, remember that you are creating a character. While it is not necessary to act, it is crucial to suggest the character and motivation of the speaker. Is he bitter, homespun, calm, intelligent, or guilt ridden? Show the audience. Is she simple, determined, or full of doubt? Help the listeners infer those qualities by your word choice and nonverbal delivery.

Use Vivid Language

This suggestion is standard homiletical doctrine, but it deserves special notice when preaching from narrative because the stories of the Bible tend to show more than they tell. So do not merely state, "Moses was angry"; also describe his narrowed eyes and clenched jaw. Prompt the listeners to infer Moses' anger. Don't tell us, "It was hot in the desert." Describe heat waves, dust devils, the tawny hue of rocks and dirt, and squinting against the painfully bright sun. Vivid language appeals to the senses and re-creates experience so that we learn vicariously. Jay Adams comments, "It is true that *we learn best what we see, touch, or hear* and that, in discursive language, a story comes closest to the very experience of an event."[24]

The Bible, with its roots in orality, also uses a lean style, and when preaching we should too. Notice how communication is enhanced when words are eliminated:

Zacchaeus stared at the tree ~~for a really long time~~. Should he? What would people think? And besides that, could he? He hadn't climbed a tree since he was a ~~little~~ boy. Looking ~~slowly~~ up and down the trunk for ~~some possible~~ handholds ~~which would make the job a lot easier~~, he ~~finally~~ made up his mind. Up he went ~~quickly~~. He wasn't used to this boyish exertion! But by pushing and pulling ~~really hard~~, he soon ~~found himself~~ perched in the ~~many~~ branches ~~like a bird~~. And here came Jesus!

When using vivid language to spark imagination, a question arises: "How much is too much?" After all, the text does not say that Zacchaeus stared at the tree. He might have sprung up without a thought. My response to this legitimate question is twofold. First, do good exegesis. I've found that careful study supplies all the food for imagination preachers need. Use your atlases, handbooks, commentaries, and encyclopedias to lead out all that the storyteller intended. Luke knew about chief tax collectors, the likelihood of a man climbing a tree, and the characteristics of the sycamore-fig tree, and he presumably intended for the reader to mentally supply that same knowledge, but since we are separated by hundreds of years and thousands of miles, we must hit the books.[25] When we do so, we position ourselves to discover all that the author has put in without going beyond what he has put in. Good exegesis aids imagination.

Second, when in doubt about the exact details (such as Zacchaeus's hesitation), we can qualify our statements with phrases like, "I imagine he hesitated because men of stature in that culture did not climb trees." Brief qualifications or disclaimers do not hinder the rhetorical impact of imagination even as they preserve us from "flights of fancy."

For Effective Delivery, Reexperience the Text

As with vivid language, the importance of delivery is a homiletical commonplace. We all know that the nonverbal must reinforce the verbal in every sermon, but in narrative preaching, delivery assumes even greater importance. This is because of the communication law of empathy, that dynamic whereby audiences unconsciously imitate the emotional state of the speaker, which is projected through signals from the voice and body. Storytelling, even more than lecturing, demands effective delivery, because the affective and imaginative elements are on center stage.

The key to prompting empathy in listeners is to imaginatively reexperience the text in both your study and the pulpit, and then to express those feelings with conviction. If you do, the audience will come along for the ride as in William Ward Ayer's description of Billy Sunday: "When he preached on Elijah, he did it so vividly that I thought I was looking at Elijah. When he preached on Naaman going down into the dirty Jordan, I suffered all the agony that Naaman suffered. For nearly an hour Naaman lived in Billy Sunday."[26]

Read aloud the passage above about Zacchaeus. Empathize with the wee little man. Contemplate with him, "Should I climb the tree or not?" Let your eyes, gestures, pauses, and facial expressions convey Zacchaeus's thought process as he hesitates. If you empathize, the people will too. And you won't need the extraneous words that are crossed out.

Use Wisdom

Having recommended narrative, image, and induction, I must now offer a word concerning balance. Use wisdom when deciding to preach narrative sermons.[27] I urge caution for three reasons. The first is pastoral. Narrative form will strike some listeners as mere entertainment. I believe they're wrong, but the way to convince them is not through force-feeding. Use pastoral wisdom as you minister to your particular group. As stated above, the use of a traditional introduction and/or conclusion often helps listeners feel comfortable with your sermon even when the majority of it is narrative. The mixture of traditional sermonic form with narrative form may work well for you. Caution is needed especially with the first-person sermon. Sometimes this form prompts listeners to concentrate on the preacher's skills, and as Lowry states, "Whenever listeners move back to watch, they do not lean forward to hear."[28] You might try introducing the dramatic monologue at Christmas or Easter. These holidays tend to permit creativity and artistry.

A second reason for wisdom is exegetical. Expository preachers who take seriously the text's form will not cavalierly jettison that form in their sermons. There may be good reasons for adopting the first-person perspective, such as when the text displays unusual psychological insight, as in the stories of Saul and David, or when the text itself is in the first person, as in Nehemiah and parts of Daniel and Acts. But most biblical narrative is third person, and that format should be our standard procedure.

A third reason is epistemological. Narrative may be the most common genre in the Bible, but it is not the only genre. Other modes of discourse are also crucial in forming a Christian worldview—soaring poetry, witty sayings, subversive parables, straightforward discourse, and so forth. Even homiletician Fred Craddock, the godfather of induction and narrative preaching, after studying the indirect methods of Kierkegaard, concluded, "Whether we learn it from Jesus or from Kierkegaard, the wise course to follow is to keep both direct and indirect . . . present in the content and style of our communicating."[29] No one can live successfully only through indirection. Sometimes we must shout, "Fire!" Sometimes we must say to the kids, "Don't play in the street." Sometimes prophets must follow their stories with indictments: "Thou art the man."

While it may be true that the human mind translates abstract statements into concrete scenes, the opposite also seems to take place. Narrative prompts the mind to ask what the story means. Propositions and narratives belong together. Philosopher Stephen Crites has explored the relationship between the two: "The mind and imagination are capable of recollecting the narrative materials of experience into essentially non-narrative forms. Indeed there seems to be a powerful inner drive of thought and imagination to overcome the relentless temporality of experience. One needs more clarity than stories can give us."[30] Knowing the necessity of both image and idea, we are not surprised that the Bible uses both and that our Lord used both in his preaching. We should do the same.

In light of these cautions, use narrative preaching wisely. Ask the Holy Spirit for wisdom as you strive to be a biblical preacher and discerning pastor. Keep in mind that an effective style is appropriate not only to the material but also to the listeners and to your personality.

Use Testimony

Biblical preaching coupled with personal testimony is a dynamic combination, and it works well no matter what genre you preach from, but I mention it in this chapter because it is most congenial to narrative. When the text recounts a personal story, augmenting your teaching with a personal story seems fitting. Testimony is more than a story of salvation, although it should certainly include such accounts. Testimony is the experience of a disciple who is trying to walk faithfully.

The use of testimony produces the effects we want—especially identification and suspense—when preaching narrative. Testimony also makes the abstract concrete. Those of us who have been in the faith for a long time tend to forget how vague our church services can be. Listen to our songs through the ears of a seeker, and listen to your sermons too. "We are filled with unspeakable joy" is a precious truth that longtime disciples subconsciously translate into their own experience, but for seekers, the phrase may sound like hyperbole. Concrete incidents should demonstrate that the Lord has indeed "done great things." Testimony carries truth down the ladder of abstraction, depositing it at the feet of every listener.

When the preacher uses testimony in his or her own sermon, we call it "self-disclosure," and I heartily recommend it as a way to incarnate the truth of the text.[31] True, self-disclosure can be done poorly, derailing the message by self-promotion or self-flagellation, but judicious self-disclosure builds trust, and influence occurs only between people who trust each other. A July 1999 New York Times/CBS poll evaluating trust levels revealed that 63 percent of people interviewed believe that in dealing with "most people" you "can't be too careful." Thirty-seven percent believed that "most people would try to take advantage of you if they got a chance." The same survey, however, also reported that of the people they "know personally," they expect that 85 percent of them would "try to be fair."[32] The moral of that story is that we should help people get to know us in and out of the pulpit. It builds trust. Furthermore, self-disclosure holds our feet to the fire, helping us live the life we exhort others to live.

Much, much more could be said about preaching narrative, but the ideas in these two chapters should keep us busy for a while. Here's a checklist to help you be a biblical preacher in form as well as content.

Chapter Checklist

☐   Use your imagination in exegesis. Slow down.
☐   Remember that biblical narrative communicates theology. We should too.
☐   Preach Christ, but don't be afraid to preach moral principles (if you ground them in theology).
☐   Remember the three levels.
☐   Exegete plot—the five stages.
☐   Exegete character—the seven techniques.
☐   Exegete setting—time and place.
☐   Exegete point of view—notice details.
☐   Don't let irony pass over your head.
☐   Preach from a unit of Scripture, an entire plot.
☐   Try preaching a whole book.
☐   Try induction.
☐   Try Monroe's Motivated Sequence.
☐   Try Lowry's Homiletical Plot.
☐   Try a third-person sermon. It's flexible!
☐   Try a first-person sermon.
☐   But use wisdom.
☐   Show, don't just tell.
☐   Use a lean style.
☐   Reexperience the story in your study and in the pulpit.
☐   Use testimony.
☐   Use self-disclosure.

6

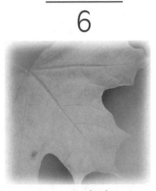

Parables

HIDDEN LAND MINES

He did not say anything to them without using a parable.
—Matthew 13:34–35

Parables are tiny lumps of coal squeezed into diamonds, condensed metaphors that catch the rays of something ultimate and glint at it in our lives.
—Walter Wink, quoted in Larsen,
Telling the Old, Old Story

Parables are imaginary gardens with real toads in them.
—Snodgrass, *Dictionary of Jesus and the Gospels*

The problem with too many teachings is that when they're over, they're over.
—Rob Bell, "Subversive Preaching,"
lecture given June 3, 2004

It is not down in any map; true places never are.
—Herman Melville, *Moby-Dick*

When we come to the parables, we come to the heart of Jesus' ministry. In fact, we come to the heart of Jesus himself—his values and mission. He depicts himself as the Good Shepherd, the Good Woman, and the Patient Father (Luke 15). He describes his mission as establishing God's kingdom, which is leaven, a mustard seed, and a fishnet (Matt. 13). He tells us to participate in the kingdom by watching, investing, and inviting (Matt. 25:22). Even theologically liberal exegetes, often skeptical about the authenticity of the Gospels, affirm that in the parables we hear the *ipsissima vox* (the very voice) of Jesus.

Jesus spoke fifty to seventy parables, depending how you define the term, so that approximately 43 percent of his words in Matthew, 16 percent of his words in Mark, and 52 percent of his words in Luke are parables.[1] The word *parabolē* occurs fifty times in the New Testament. All but two of these occurrences appear in Matthew, Mark, and Luke. (The other two are Heb. 9:9 and 11:19.)

Parables seem to have been rare in the Near East around the time of Christ.[2] The Hebrew Bible contains only a few, with Nathan's story in 2 Samuel 12 as the best parallel to Jesus' stories,[3] but parables dominated the Lord's teaching. If, then, you want to expound the Savior's heart, you've got to preach the parables, but the task can be daunting because a tsunami of scholarship, perhaps the most extensive in the vast ocean of New Testament studies, has confused and frightened many preachers.

You may feel it is best to leave the parables in the hands of scholars or poets, but the critical attention lavished on parables attests to their hidden depths. We are fascinated by them. They are deep wells, and we haven't come to the bottom yet. The goal of this chapter is to help you understand the power of the genre and preach it with power.

What *Is* a Parable?

The term *parabolē* means literally to "throw alongside," and that's what parables do. They make comparisons. They align one thing next to another to clarify the second. They portray scenes from everyday life—kneading, sowing, fishing, traveling—which morph into spiritual lessons. *Parabolē* is closely linked to the Hebrew term *māšāl* ("to be like"), which, as you'll see in the next chapter, is the characteristic term for proverb. But Old Testament *māšālîm* and New Testament *parabolai* are broad categories that do not have exact parallels in English literature. They include riddles, allegories, and sayings.

Here's a simple classification of parables, from shortest to longest:

- Figure of speech: "A city on a hill cannot be hidden" (Matt. 5:14b).
- Similitude: "The kingdom of God . . . is like yeast" (Luke 13:20–21).
- Parable proper: The parable of the Tenants (Matt. 21:33–44).

This current chapter centers on the "parable proper," a *parabolē* with at least minimal narrative elements of plot, character, and setting. David Buttrick estimates that thirty-three parables fall into this category, fifty if you count duplicates,[4] but while this chapter focuses on the parable proper, it will help you preach the shorter forms as well.

The old saw says that a parable is "an earthly story with heavenly meaning." The cyclone of scholarship has merely unfolded and unfurled that definition. A parable is a "*picture* that becomes a *mirror* and then a *window*."[5] As we gaze at the scene in the parable, we see ourselves; then we see truth.

C. H. Dodd's classic definition has stood the test of time: "At its simplest the parable is a metaphor or simile drawn from nature or common life, arresting the hearer by its vividness or strangeness, and leaving the mind in sufficient doubt about its precise application to tease it into active thought."[6] With admirable succinctness, Dodd's definition not only summarizes the content of the parables—analogies "drawn from common life"—it also hints at their rhetorical power—they "arrest the hearer" and "tease the mind into active thought." Ryken's definition echoes these themes: "Realistic stories, simple in construction and didactic . . . in purpose, that convey religious truth and in which the details often have a significance beyond their literal narrative meaning."[7]

How the Text Communicates, What the Text Does

It goes without saying that Jesus spoke his parables for edification, not entertainment, although they certainly are entertaining. His interpretation of two of his parables in Matthew 13 demonstrates that he was *preaching* by means of these stories. Furthermore, his didactic purpose is apparent when we remember that Jesus told many parables to answer questions. The Son of God came preaching and teaching, and he used parables to communicate his message.

Jesus also used parables for a purpose we ourselves are unlikely to use: to conceal. Mark 4:11–12, following the parable of the Four Soils, clearly states its purpose: "But to those on the outside everything is said in parables so that, 'they may be ever seeing but never perceiving'" (quoting Isa. 6:9–10). This statement is so disturbing and seems so out of character with Jesus' mission to save the lost that we may be tempted to explain it away. Yet there it stands, and the meaning is as it appears.

One reason Jesus' told parables, or at least the parable of the Soils, is to conceal. An exploration of context helps us understand why. First, the context indicates that Jesus is speaking to the faithful. Jesus often explained his parables to the disciples (Mark 4:34), and in this instance, they needed to know why some people (some of the "soils") rejected the Word of God. Jesus says plainly that those people are "on the outside" (Mark 4:11). They have not accepted Jesus' offer to become his disciples and become "insiders."

The context indicates, too, that, in contrast to the disciples, "those on the outside" refers to the "teachers of the law" (3:22)—those who rejected Jesus, attributing his works to the Devil. To these scoffers, the parable was simply a confusing story, nor did they make the effort to ponder it and query Jesus as the disciples did. The obscure parable thus confirmed the rejecters in their blindness.

Isaiah's preaching served that purpose also. When the Israelites rejected Isaiah's preaching, they showed where their loyalty lay, thus warranting God's judgment. Matthew also emphasizes this causality when he recounts the same parable (13:13–15). He says that Jesus taught in parables *because* the outsiders were blind; he spoke to them in obscure analogies because they would not receive his teaching.

When we combine Matthew's handling of the parable with Mark's, we see the full picture: when hard-hearted scoffers reject God, he rejects them and hardens them in their unbelief (cf. Rom. 1:21–28).

As I stated, though, when we preach from parables, we will not often adopt the purpose of concealment. We don't know who are the insiders and outsiders, so we won't intentionally veil the truth. As pastors and teachers, we follow Jesus' other goals in using the beguiling form of parable, goals that aid teaching such as holding attention, causing people to ponder, and helping doctrine lodge in memory. We leave the concealing function to the inscrutable wisdom of God, knowing that he has communicated plainly to the scoffers (but was rejected), and will communicate plainly again in the day of judgment (Mark 4:21–23).

The communication dynamics that parables engender are so complex that they can seem inscrutable, but we can get a handle on them by exploring three qualities: their realism—what some scholars call "verisimilitude"; their folktale qualities—they are simple narratives; their nature as analogies—they compare one thing to another. These three qualities are the means that convey Jesus' didactic purpose.

Realism

Jesus' parables amble through everyday life in the ancient Near East. We meet homemakers, widows, virgins, servants, tenants, fathers, and sons. We see them light lamps, sow seed, invest money, and invite to weddings. The stories are realistic. Although the stories often exaggerate, as will be discussed below (mustard plants don't *really* grow as large as trees), there are no talking animals, dragons, or haunted forests. Parables are not fairy tales. They are concrete stories that use the secular world to communicate spiritual truths. (For fascinating insight into the parables' realism, see the works of Kenneth Bailey, who lived in the Middle East for many years.)[8]

Because the parables plant their feet in the soil of the ancient Near East, it goes without saying that preachers must plow that soil. We must exegete Jesus' stories to hear them the way his original hearers did. Modern Western interpretation tends to read, for example, the parable of the Good Shepherd (Luke 15) through an individualistic worldview. We value each person as a unique individual, so we focus on the shepherd's affection for the lost sheep. While this is a valid insight, plowing the soil of Middle Eastern culture reveals another insight foreign to modern Westerners. The shepherd throws a party not only to rejoice in the rescue of the poor sheep, but to celebrate his own integrity.

The literary context and the cultural context suggest this interpretation. Notice the literary context—the verses immediately before the parable: "Now the tax collectors and 'sinners' were all gathering around to hear him. But the Pharisees and the teachers of the law muttered, 'This man welcomes sinners and eats with them'" (Luke 15:1–2). Luke clearly indicates that Jesus' didactic purpose in telling the parable was to defend himself and his "inclusive policy" of eating with sinners. He implies that his calling, his responsibility, is to shepherd the people of Israel. If a sheep strays, he seeks and saves it, although this costs him dearly. The shepherd says in essence, "I labored to carry this animal [weighing between fifty and seventy pounds]. I walked far in the wilderness. I have fulfilled my calling! Celebrate this testimony to my strength, courage, and character! I haven't lost a single sheep!" You and I have been socialized to view such boasting as the puffing of a blowhard. Not so in the cultural context of Jesus' day, when people took innocent joy in being responsible adults who exemplify their values.[9]

What is the sermonic payoff of such plowing? Theology. Behind this drama, the incarnation hides in the wings as God comes to earth to regather his flock. The atonement casts its shadow across this "simple" story—regathering demands self-sacrifice. The magnificent but paradoxical glory of God, that glory displayed in humility, flashes around the corner of this realistic narrative. The Pharisees may criticize Jesus for consorting with sinners, but the Pharisees are dead wrong. He calls them to recognize his compassionate courage and celebrate with him. The kingdom is arriving! The shepherd is regathering his flock!

Another example, also from Luke 15, shows how concrete details function in parables.[10] We have the rare picture of a *woman* entrusted with the household "cash box." Jesus, in a move even more startling than comparing himself to a lowly shepherd, compared himself to this woman. Why? To teach the same theology in light of the Pharisees' criticism. Just as the shepherd took responsibility to seek and save the lost, so does this woman. In fact, she takes full responsibility. The coin is not a perambulating sheep with a mind of its own. It is inanimate. She calls it "the coin which I lost." In first-century Palestine, homes were dark, the windows little more than slits high in the walls. The floors often had large cracks because they were paved with irregular stones, and into one of those cracks it seems the small silver coin fell.[11] So she lights a lamp and sweeps the floor, devoting herself to the task, and she celebrates when the task is done well.

Parables teach theology; they also prompt us to respond to that theology. They do so through three rhetorical implications that are embedded in the realism of parables. The first is identification. By depicting himself as a woman and a lowly shepherd, for example, Jesus blasted the conventions of his day; his apprentices include women, not just men, and the lowly, not just the mighty. He identifies with them. In Jesus' kingdom, women count! He deliberately but indirectly honors them by representing himself as a responsible, diligent household manager.

The second rhetorical implication is imagination. Parables express truth concretely, not abstractly, and the realism sparks our imaginations. Vivid and concrete stories transport us to the rugged wilderness and a dark home. The original hearers would have visualized the landscape and felt the cool floor. That's the way stories function, prompting vicarious experience.

The third rhetorical implication is implied in this chapter's title: parables are "hidden land mines." They are explosive but concealed. They take the mind off the thing they would put the mind on. On the literal level they depict secular, mundane life. Only one takes place in "church" (the Pharisee and Tax Collector, which takes place in the Temple, Luke 18:9–14), and only two mention the name of God (the Rich Fool, Luke 12:16–21, and the Persistent Widow, Luke 18:2–8), although many parables include God's name in the explanations that follow the parables (e.g., Luke 16:13, "You cannot serve God and Money"). Realism prompts listeners to drop their defenses as when I engage you with this story: "I was reading the newspaper this morning and saw a story about some high-powered Wall Street executive who embezzled from his company. You know what that scoundrel did? He went to his boss, gave him a sob story, and . . ." Your imagination is prodded, your feelings are aroused, and you listen with shields lowered but, before you know it, you discover that you're standing on a land mine. You might be the scoundrel! Ask the Pharisees and the teacher who wanted to justify himself . . . or King David . . . and they'll tell you about land mines.

Folk Stories

Just as the mundane realism of parables functions to teach theology and prompt response, the second characteristic—narrative form—does the same. Parables are a subgenre of the larger genre of narrative. Thus, most of the material from chapter 4, "Narrative, Part 1," applies here also. Parables have plot, character, setting, and point of view. Their rhetorical functions are similar to the ones engendered by historical narrative, just as the experience of attending a play—which is one type of narrative—is similar to the experience of reading a novel, another type of narrative.

Parables are a *type* of narrative, however, not pure narrative. As seen in chapter 4, pure biblical narrative is extremely laconic compared to modern narrative, but parables are even more laconic. This is true not only of biblical parables but of parables worldwide. Hasidic tales, Sufi stories, and Zen anecdotes, as well as New Testament parables, average only one hundred fifty to two hundred fifty words.[12] Parables are sketched with pencil, not painted in oil. They are best thought of as *folk stories*, reflecting their genesis in oral communication.

Two qualities of folk stories—simple plots and simple characters— enhance Jesus' didactic purposes. The plots are somewhat formulaic, often constructed in three scenes, as with the Prodigal Son and the Good Samaritan. Three-scene plots are common in oral communication such as in joke-telling ("There was a priest, a rabbi, and a minister . . ."). The conflicts that drive the plots are simple: seeds struggle for survival, persistent widows pester judges, and stewards mishandle money. Only in the Prodigal Son, by far the longest parable, is there anything resembling a subplot. The plots are often built on archetypes, and as Amos Wilder observes, "Human nature has always responded to stories about quests and adventures, ups and downs, rags to riches, lost and found, reversals and surprises; . . . masters and servants, the wise and the foolish, rewards and penalties, success and failure."[13]

Besides the simplicity of the plots, consider the simplicity of the characters. They are "types": faithful and slothful stewards, wise and foolish builders, children playing in the marketplace. Only one of the characters, Lazarus, has a name. As the *Dictionary of Biblical Imagery* states, "Never has such immortality been thrust upon anonymity,"[14] yet these simple folk populate the parables. Herman Horne calculates that persons, not objects, constitute the majority of the subjects in Jesus' parables:[15]

Inanimate objects	26%
Plants	11.5%
Animals	7%
People	55.5%

The simple plots and characters enhance Jesus' didactic purpose in four ways. First, stories disarm resistance. Narrative form prompts listeners to listen, not resist. In order to follow a story to its end, we as listeners have to yield to the form of causally related events and characters: "person x went to town, and then person y did so and so, and that action caused person x to . . ." If the narrator argues that person x did not go to town, we won't "get" the story. Only at the end, when we realize that the story is also an analogy, do we see that person x is really us and that we must mend our ways. Rhetorician William Kirkwood contrasts how listeners respond to narrative parables and to abstract arguments (which he calls "theories"):

Whereas narratives portray sequences of unique events, theories . . . describe generalizable connections between non-unique events. While one can readily question the validity of each successive, general claim in the development of an argument or explanation and thus defend against its eventual conclusion, it is more difficult to dispute the highly particular events set forth in a parable. Paradoxically, if a teaching story makes no pretense at being factual (as many do not), it is still more difficult to deny; one can hardly "refute" an admittedly invented, non-necessary sequence of unique events.[16]

While the conclusions Jesus intended could not be avoided, the development of the ideas leading to those conclusions invited reception. The parable form is thus a means of persuasion.

As folktales, parables also polarize responses, like when we see the good guys wearing white hats and the bad guys wearing black. Parables prompt us to take sides. They leave no options. This is not to imply that the parables are simplistic, just simple. Even when the bad guys are clearly marked as bad guys—anyone with eyes can see their black hats—we may be shocked to see who is under the hat. Priests, Levites, Pharisees, and rich men wear black hats in Jesus' world, and Samaritans and tax collectors wear white! The parables push us to take sides, sometimes against our inclination.

A third rhetorical function these simple folk stories engender is memory. Like proverbs, the parables were transmitted from person to person through oral communication. To be permanent they had to be simple, brief, with the form of the utterance aiding transmission. Thus the parable form allows no digressions, abstractions, or lengthy explanations. The previous comparison of parables to jokes applies here also. We can remember jokes, even though we don't write them down, because of their brevity and simple form—stock characters, a single conflict, a formulaic rise in action, and a sudden turn or punch line.

Fourth, the simple plots focus attention on Jesus' most important teaching, which often materializes at the climax with the last event or speech in the plot. This focusing technique is called "end stress": the last group invited is the one that enjoys the banquet, the last soil is most fertile, and the last steward is judged most harshly. By the end of the parable, Jesus passes moral judgment, although he may not have pronounced that judgment. Instead, he prompts the listeners to judge themselves. He leaves them to ponder the implications of the truth stressed at the end, having aroused their feelings and focused their attention. Part of the end stress of the Prodigal Son, for example, is joy. Jesus didn't shout to the Pharisees, "You should feel joy, not bitterness, when sinners repent," but he did cause their consciences to whisper that truth. They understood his point, and he left them with a choice about how to respond.

Although these folk stories are simple and realistic, they sometimes possess unrealistic or paradoxical elements such as the preposterous size of the mustard plant and the outlandish pay scale of the workers. The surrealism, what Dodd calls "strangeness," prompts us to look behind the details. It warns the reader, "Beware! Do not take this at face value." The surrealism is another quality of the genre that prods listeners to think. The quality of "strangeness" leads us to the final generic characteristic.

Analogy

As the term *parabolē* suggests, parables are analogies. Wilder explains, "There is the picture side of the parable and there is the meaning or application."[17]

The long, scholarly, sometimes heated debate on how to interpret these beguiling stories may be the most complex in the vast field of New Testament studies, but the term *analogy* simply and accurately captures the range of meaning of *parabolē*. In the Septuagint (LXX), *parabolē* is used of an *event* that has become emblematic (see 1 Sam. 10:12), just as we might say that such-and-such a failure was the leader's "Waterloo." In the LXX the term also describes *persons* who've become emblematic (see Jer. 24:9; Job 17:6). We do the same when we say he is a "Quisling" or "Machiavelli." The term is also attached to an *allegorical story* (see Ezek. 7:1–10). In all of these cases, *parabolē* is a figure of speech that compares one thing to another.

Individual parables can be located on a sliding scale between simple simile ("the kingdom of heaven is like . . .") and intentional allegory (the four soils stand for the heart conditions of four hearers). That sliding scale has baffled scholars because we have no parallel literary form. Thomas Long summarizes the long history of parable interpretation under three terms: *code, vessel,* and *metaphor* (which he calls *object of art*).[18]

The first hermeneutical approach, code, is the earliest and most enduring. For nearly two thousand years interpreters saw parables not just as analogies but as allegories with intricate equivalencies hiding under the surface. Parables are a code that must be cracked. This hermeneutical stance grew out of a sacramental worldview. Ancient believers saw the invisible world in the visible, so their default beliefs prompted them to look for "spiritual truth" beneath the folk stories.

This instinct is not entirely misplaced because parables *do* compare things of this world to the kingdom of God. Jesus' own practice gives warrant to allegorical interpretation because he used deliberate allegories at least twice: Matthew 13:1-9, the parable of the Seed, with the allegorical explanation in verses 36-43; Mark 12:1-11 where he compares God to the vineyard owner, the Pharisees to the wicked tenants, and himself to the owner's son whom they killed.

Some parables, then, are allegories, but we must not assume that *all* are. *Parabolē* means more than "allegory," so we must not allegor-*ize*, assuming that every parable is a code to be cracked. We must not impose meaning the author never intended. Augustine did so with his well-known handling of the Good Samaritan. Even though Jesus told the story to answer the question, "Who is my neighbor?" Augustine turned the parable into an allegory of the fall and redemption of humanity:

- The "certain man" going from Jerusalem to Jericho = Adam
- The thieves = the Devil and his demons
- They stripped him = took his immortality
- They beat him = tempted him to sin
- The priest and the Levite = the ministry of the Old Testament, which does nothing for Adam
- The good Samaritan = Christ
- He binds his wounds with oil and wine = he restrains sin with hope and an exhortation to work with a fervent spirit
- The inn = the church
- The innkeeper = the apostle Paul[19]

The guidelines below will help prevent such excess, but when allegorical interpretation *is* warranted, what rhetorical effects attend it? Confirmation—it confirms what readers already know.[20] No new information is imparted, but old truths materialize in the consciousness of the ones who crack the code. Allegory also unifies the hearers since they are insiders. They experience cohesiveness, bonding, and solidarity as does a group of friends with their inside jokes and distinctive vocabulary. Hearers say, "I get it."

The next development in the history of interpretation viewed parables as vessels. The person most responsible for this theory was the German scholar Adolph Jülicher, whose massive work, *The Parables of Jesus* (1899), taught that parables make one point and one point only. That point is accessible, not hidden, because Jesus did not intend to obscure his ideas. A parable is a vessel that contains a theological concept. Parables are like sermon illustrations. Simile replaced allegory as the dominant interpretative framework. In other words, every parable could be paraphrased to say, "This truth is like . . ." While Jülicher undoubtedly overstated the case, his theory was a needed corrective to the excesses of allegorization. Some parables are indeed vessels.

The rhetorical effects of simile are pedagogical. These parables teach and illustrate. Perhaps this is why Aristotle recommends the use of parables as examples that clarify and prove propositions.[21] They move from one "field of experience" to another, as when a teacher tries to explain the color scarlet to a man born blind: "It is *like* the sound of a trumpet blast." Parables move from the known (everyday life in the ancient Near East) to the unknown (the kingdom of God).

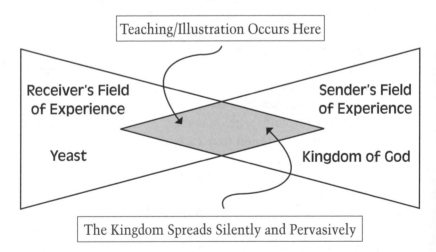

Fig. 6.1. Parables and Fields of Experience

Vessel parables respond to questions that the hearers ask such as, "Lord, are only a few people going to be saved?" (Luke 13:23—the parable of the Narrow Door). The answer? Comparatively few. Many will stand outside knocking. When a hearer understands the comparison, he or she learns something new. The hearer says, "I see!"

Our Lord also used vessel parables to redirect the hearers. In the same parable (Luke 13:22–30), Jesus personalized the theological question, exhorting the hearers to "make every effort to enter through the narrow door." He says, in essence, "Make sure that *you* get on the narrow road, and worry less about who's in and who's out."

The current emphasis in the hermeneutics of parables is that they are metaphors. Like the previous schools of interpretation, there is much to commend this one. The rhetoric of metaphor was covered in chapter 3 on "Psalms." You will remember that metaphor sparks intuitive perception as we see similarity in dissimilar things. Metaphor thus demands imagination and collaboration. A metaphorical parable provokes listeners to seek meaning, whereas that meaning might be rejected if expressed in propositional terms. When metaphor "works," the reader says, "Oh my!" Metaphor is a deeper experience than either allegory or simile. Buttrick compares the effects of simile and metaphor.[22]

Simile	Metaphor
Their cotton candy looks like a puffy pink umbrella.	They held high their cotton-candy umbrella to ward away a world of tears.
Translation: With its cardboard cone and billowing top, the sweet treat looks like an umbrella.	*Translation:* Is one possible? The meaning of the metaphor is not easily reduced to a proposition.
Rhetorical effect: The comparison is obvious and pleasing. It helps us understand what the cotton candy looks like.	*Rhetorical effect:* This language prompts more thought than the simile: How is cotton candy an "umbrella"? Is it a shield? What is the relationship between candy and sorrow? The ideational content and the rhetorical effect are intertwined as the metaphor prompts the listener to collaborate, imagine, and ponder.

Fig. 6.2. A Comparison of Simile and Metaphor

So how should we interpret parables? How can we decide if a parable should be read as code, vessel, or metaphor? Most parables contain elements of all three. The key to interpreting parables is the same as interpreting any biblical literature for preaching—we should be guided by authorial intent. Evangelical hermeneutics is based on the conviction that God has spoken through his Word (2 Tim. 3:16), graciously making himself known through the Bible. Thus, an interpreter's goal should be to exegete, or lead out, the meaning that God intended. We are not free to eisegete, or read in, our own meaning.

Evangelical hermeneutics also affirms that humans wrote the Bible. The personal styles and experiences of authors like Luke, David, and Matthew are evident in their books. How, though, are we to understand this dual authorship? Second Peter 1:21 provides an answer through a word picture: Like wind in the sails of a ship, the Holy Spirit "carried along" the authors of the Bible, ensuring that their words were also his words. While we do not completely understand the mystery of God's sovereign oversight being executed through human agency, this seems to be the position Jesus affirmed (see Matt. 22:43) and that the Scripture itself assumes (see 2 Peter 3:15–16, where Paul's writings are called "Scripture"; Heb. 3:7–11, where Ps. 95 is attributed to the Holy Spirit; and Heb. 1:8–9, which attributes Ps. 110 to God). Thus, when we interpret a parable or any other portion of Scripture, our goal should be to discover what our heavenly Father intended to communicate through the human authors.

But how do you find authorial intent?

1. Carefully note the literary context and form.
    *   Sometimes the story's *lead-in* clarifies its meaning, as with the Good Samaritan. A religious man asked, "Who is my neighbor," so Jesus' intention was to define the term and prompt the man to act like a neighbor. The lead-in establishes a set of expectations in the listener/reader so that we expect the parable to illustrate a concept. At the end of the parable, we say, "I see!" and as soon as we say that, we realize that we're standing on a land mine. Our next comment is, "Oh my! Am I a compassionate neighbor?" With uncanny economy Jesus teaches and challenges. This parable

is part vessel and part metaphor, but it is not an allegory. The lead-in has nothing to do with the fall and redemption of humanity.

- Sometimes the *placement* of the parable in the Gospel suggests meaning. For example, Jesus tells the parable of the Unmerciful Servant (Matt. 18:23–35) following Peter's question, "How many times shall I forgive?" This parable answers that question. Like the parable of the Good Samaritan, it functions as a vessel and metaphor.
- Sometimes parables use the obvious *language of comparison:* "the kingdom of heaven is like . . ." We know we're in the arena of simile with a vessel parable.
- Sometimes Jesus *summarizes* the parable's truth in a maxim. These parables make one point such as, "Watch therefore, for you know neither the day nor the hour." Jülicher would be proud! Jesus closes the parable of the Pharisee and Tax Collector (Luke 18:10–14) with the proposition, "Everyone who exalts himself will be humbled, and he who humbles himself will be exalted." Take note that this same parable starts with a lead-in, "To some who were confident of their own righteousness and looked down on everybody else, Jesus told this parable. . . ." Both Luke and Jesus are determined that we get the point!
- Remember the rule of *end stress.* The spotlight of authorial intention often falls here. Only at the end of the Good Samaritan do we learn what it means to be a good neighbor.

2. Carefully note the cultural context. A parable can mean only what it once meant. As argued above, parables are analogies that compare one thing with another—the everyday world with the spiritual world. Thus to understand the spiritual world, we must first understand the everyday world of the ancient Middle East—vineyards and fields, builders and shepherds. While a modern reader can often get the general idea of the parable without knowing details of ancient civilization, cultural study adds color to the black-and-white picture. (See the works of Kenneth Bailey to understand the culture of the Near East.)

3. Related to the point above, interpret as the original audience would have. Picking on poor old Augustine again, the parable of the Good Samaritan cannot yield his fantastic equations, because when Jesus told the parable, the apostle Paul was still the Pharisee Saul! The original audience would not have arrived at Augustine's interpretation. In contrast, the original audience of Mark 12:1–11 *would* have inferred Jesus' allusions to Isaiah with the vineyard, hedge, pit, and tower. This parable functions as an allegory, and the hearers got the point. They responded by looking for ways to arrest Jesus!

4. Carefully note the rhetorical effect. Does it confirm something already known? Does it teach something new? Does it prompt thought and imagination? We know what Jesus intended to do by experiencing what he does do. For instance, the plot of the Laborers in the Vineyard (Matt. 20:1–16) prompts us to ponder the economy of the kingdom. What drives that economy—"fairness" or grace?

Jesus used parables, then, to communicate theological concepts. Parables do so through realism to which the listener can identify and easily call up in imagination. Their simplicity makes parables comprehensible to everyone and sparks an emotional response. Parables are analogies, using something that is familiar to the listener and comparing it with something the narrator wants the listener to understand. Jesus spoke *in* parables, but we speak *on* parables.[23] Here are some ways to do so.

Try This

Remember that the goal is to reproduce the rhetorical dynamics of the genre. How we communicate, not just what we communicate, is crucial—not incidental—to our preaching, just as it was crucial to the preaching of Jesus, Nathan, and other users of parables.

I believe that we have considerable freedom when preaching parables, for this genre uses numerous devices and produces numerous effects. Some parables are simple; some are complex. Some confirm what we know; some startle us. Some make us feel like insiders; others alienate us. Nearly all of them challenge us. It follows, then, that this genre cannot be reduced to a simple set of rules. Thus, select and tailor the suggestions below for each text and each preaching context. Put on the homiletical shoe only if it fits the textual and contextual foot.

Interpret the Parables on Two Levels—the Literal and the Didactic

Since parables are analogies, responsible interpreters seek the point(s) of comparison to understand Jesus' didactic intention. Again, study the cultural context to understand the literal level. To arrive at authorial intent, we must walk the dusty roads of Israel. Careful exegesis of the culture permeating the Prodigal Son parable, for example, helps us understand God's copious grace:

- Men of dignity and age did not *run*!
- The best robe was probably a ceremonial robe of high distinction.
- The ring was probably a signet ring, a symbol of authority.
- Shoes were a luxury, not worn by slaves.
- Killing and eating a fatted calf was uncommon in a land where meat rarely was eaten.

The story overflows with abundance.

In the early 1900s William Barton delighted readers with parables published weekly in *The Christian Century* and other religious periodicals. Notice how the impact of the didactic level would be lessened if you did not understand the details of the literal level:

> Now I entered the Kitchen, and would have passed through. But Keturah [Barton's wife] was there; so I waited: and she cast Divers Things into a Great Bowl, and did stir them with a Great Spoon.
>
> And I asked her, saying, What hast thou in the Bowl? And she said, Sugar and Spice, and all that's nice. . . .
>
> And she took the Dough out of the Bowl, . . . and she rolled it with a Rolling-Pin; and she cut it into round cakes. And in the midst of every several cake there was an Hole. And a great Caldron hung above the Fire, and there was Fat therein that boiled furiously.

And Keturah took the round Cakes of Dough, and cast them into the Caldron; and she poked them with a Fork, and she turned them, and when they came forth, behold, I knew then what they were. And the smell of them was inviting, and the appearance of them was exceeding good. And Keturah gave me one of the Doughnuts, and Believe Me, they were Some Doughnuts.

And I said, To what purpose is the Hole? If the Doughnut be so good with a part Punched Out, how much better had it been if the Hole also had been Doughnut!

And Keturah answered and said, Thou speakest as a Fool, who is never content with the Goodness that is, but always complaineth against God for the lack of the Goodness which he thinketh is not. If there were no Hole in the Doughnut, then . . . though the Cake were Fried till the Edges thereof were burnt, . . . yet would there be uncooked Dough in the middle. Yea, thou shouldest then break thy teeth on the outer rim of every Several Doughnut, and the middle part thereof would be Raw Dough.

And I meditated much on what Keturah had told me. And I considered the Empty Spaces in Human life; and the Desolation of its Vacancies. . . . And I pondered in my soul whether God doth know that save for these, our lives would be [brittle or unformed]. . . .

[We must not be] like unto one who rejecteth a Doughnut because he Knoweth not the Mystery of the Hole.[24]

Translate

Since many parables speak with the accent of ancient Israel, we will often need to "translate" them for modern listeners. The parables are rooted in the soil of Palestine, so we must "transplant" them to our culture. Ideally, we shouldn't have to interpret a parable. Listeners should simply get it like a joke, but "in a fallen world, separated by miles and centuries from Jesus' original milieu, we may not always 'get it,' so we need to be prepared *both* to explain *and* to contemporize the parables."[25]

For example, the original hearers must have been shocked to hear Jesus make a tax collector the exemplar with the Pharisee as the foil

(Luke 18:10–14). Tax collectors were traitors! Modern audiences need to feel the shock. Perhaps we could translate with a story of how the Dutch treated collaborators after World War II. They hated and persecuted the collaborators who had sided with the Nazis to ravish their land. They saw the collaborators as traitors, just as the Jews saw the tax collectors who collaborated with the Romans as traitors.

We'll probably need to translate the story of the Prodigal Son, too.[26] Jesus' listeners would have expected the father to take offense when his son left. To help our listeners respond to the story in the same way, perhaps we could show the scene from *Fiddler on the Roof* when Tevye pronounces his daughter "dead" for marrying a Gentile.

David Wells retells the Persistent Widow with a contemporary "translation":

> You will be appalled by the story I am about to relate to you. Appalled, that is, if you have any kind of social conscience.
>
> A poor black, living on Chicago's South Side, sought to have her apartment properly heated during the frigid winter months. Despite city law on the matter, her unscrupulous landlord refused. The woman was a widow, desperately poor, and ignorant of the legal system; but she took the case to court on her own behalf. . . . It was her ill fortune, however, to appear repeatedly before the same judge who, as it turned out, was an atheist and a bigot. The only principle by which he abode was, as he put it, that "blacks should be kept in their place." The possibilities of a favorable ruling to the widow were, therefore, bleak. They became even bleaker as she realized she lacked . . . a satisfactory bribe. Nevertheless, she persisted.
>
> At first, the judge did not so much as even look up from reading the novel on his lap before dismissing her. But then he began to notice her. Just another black, he thought, stupid enough to think she could get justice. Then her persistence made him self-conscious. This turned to guilt and anger. Finally, raging and embarrassed, he granted her petition and enforced the law. Here was a massive victory over "the system"—at least as it functioned in his corrupted courtroom.[27]

Don't Be Afraid to Make a Point

True, Jülicher overstated his case, but he had a case. Jesus told parables to communicate truth. They are fiction enlisted to battle false ideas. "In a sense, the parable has the character of an argument; it invites the hearers to choose [an] alternative view of reality."[28] Adapting to the needs of the listeners, Jesus often spelled out the point of the argument. We can too. I stress this in case you've been unduly influenced by the current trend in interpretation, namely that parables are works of art that cannot and should not be reduced to propositions. As with Jülicher's assertion, this too is an overstatement, yet, as I'll affirm below, the case is not grossly overstated. Here, I'm simply presenting a reminder that Jesus used this genre to communicate ideas. Parables may be more than ideas, but they are not less. Don't be afraid to explain, summarize, and make points.[29] You could, for example, state the main idea of your sermon in the conclusion just as Jesus did in the conclusion of the Unmerciful Servant: "This is how my heavenly Father will treat each of you unless you forgive your brother from your heart" (Matt. 18:35).

Don't Be Afraid **Not** to Make a Point

Dodd says that a parable leaves "the mind in sufficient doubt about its precise application to tease it into active thought."[30] This is not to say that your preaching should be aimless and that you should be cloudy about what you're trying to communicate. It is to say that parables often achieve their effects inductively and subtly. Sometimes Jesus left his stories open-ended, and if we would preach like Jesus, at times we'll do the same. But "most preachers have a hard time leaving things unsaid."[31] I certainly put myself into that category.

My point about not making a point is especially pointed when we preach to postmodern listeners since they value mystery, imagination, narrative, and silence. They recoil from pat answers and formulas that package the truth with brown paper, strapping tape, and ribbon. As actor Sean Penn stated, "When everything gets answered, it's fake. The mystery is the truth."[32] As early as the mid-70s, theologian Sallie TeSelle argued this point:

> For many of us the language of the Christian tradition is no longer authoritative; . . . Much of it has become tired clichés,

one-dimensional, univocal language. When this happens, it means that theological reflection is faced with an enormous task—the task of embodying it anew. This will not happen, I believe, through systematic theology, for systematic theology is second-level language, language which orders, arranges, explicates, makes precise the first-order revelatory, metaphorical language. [Renovation will take place through] poems, stories, even lives—which will image [truth] to us, in our total existential unity.[33]

Open-ended preaching demands faith—faith in the sovereign Spirit to apply the truth, and faith in the capability of the listeners to ponder the truth.

Tolstoy knew the power of leaving things unsaid, even when he wanted to communicate something vital. In "How Much Land Does a Man Need?" Tolstoy tells the story of a peasant named Pahom who covets land.[34] Pahom mused, "'If only I had plenty of land, I shouldn't fear the Devil himself.'" But "the Devil had been sitting behind the stove, and had heard all that was said." The Tempter took up the challenge and gave Pahom land, making the onetime peasant a wealthy landlord. Pahom broke tenants, gobbling their land when they couldn't make their payments. His farms and pastures spread wide, and he relocated again and again, always searching for greener grass.

Finally he ventured to the outskirts of the kingdom where the people were "as simple as sheep" and the land could "be got for almost nothing." Pahom gave the people trinkets for their land, and they reciprocated those "generous" gifts by allowing him to take as much land as he was able to walk upon in one day. The only condition was that he had to return to the starting spot by sundown.

At dawn Pahom climbed a hill to survey the vista. His "eyes glistened: it was all virgin soil, as flat as the palm of your hand, as black as the seed of a poppy, and in the hollows different kinds of grasses grew breast high." He chose his route, and began walking. Using a spade, Pahom occasionally dug turf to mark the boundaries of his new realm. He walked all morning, eating bread and drinking water on the march. He walked all afternoon, growing weary and discarding all encumbrances.

As the sun began to set, he realized he had walked too far and had to hurry to the hill where he started. "It was very hard walking, but he went quicker and quicker. He pressed on, but was still far from the place. He began running," and fear made him breathless. "His breast was working like a blacksmith's bellows, his heart was beating like a hammer, and his legs were giving way." In despair Pahom saw the sun dip below the horizon just as he reached the foot of the hill. Then he heard the tribesmen shout to him from the top of the hill because the sun had not yet set up there. In a final burst of determination, Pahom crested the hill, claimed his prize, and fell forward. The chief exclaimed, "Ahh, that's a fine fellow! He has gained much land!" But Pahom was dead, blood flowing from his mouth. "His servant picked up the spade and dug a grave long enough for Pahom to lie in, and buried him in it. Six feet from his head to his heels was all he needed."

Another modern parable that leaves the didactic point unstated is Pam Faro's tale of "Two Brothers," a beautiful story that exemplifies self-sacrificial love. Told with restraint, the concrete language, simple plot, and patterned refrains draw us in and open our hearts. Space doesn't allow me to transcribe the whole story, but I hope the adapted summary of the story presented below illustrates the rich dynamics that occur when a parable makes its point without "preaching."[35]

Two brothers farmed a single plot of land. One of them had a large family, and the other had none, and each of them said, "It's not fair." The one with the large family felt rich in the blessings of this world, for his family helped him with the farm, surrounded him with love, and would support him in his old age. He felt "it was not fair" that his brother had none of these blessings, for that poor soul had to work alone and could not produce as much grain. So at night the brother with the large family secretly carried a heavy sack of grain across the fields and deposited it in the adjoining barn.

The brother with no family also felt, "It is not fair," for he had much land and grain to himself while his brother had many mouths to feed, so he too secretly deposited a large bag in his brother's barn. In the morning each was confounded when he counted the number of bags in his barn. None was missing!

That night they repeated their loving stratagems, only to be perplexed again the next morning. The ruse became a pattern, as night after night each tried to comfort and care for the other. Then one night, laboring under their heavy sacks, the brothers met in the middle of the field. They "saw the answer to their puzzle, set their sacks down, stepped toward each other, and embraced. It is said that God in heaven looked down upon those two men and said, 'This will forever be a holy place, for here I have witnessed great love.'"

Prompt Meditation with Imagination

As I've discussed in nearly every chapter of this book, biblical preachers should seek to reproduce the *effect* of the text, not just its ideas. If the text prompts meditation by using imagination, biblical preachers should try to do the same. Assuming that we can't improve Jesus' methods of preaching and teaching, we too will prompt our listeners to ponder. David Larsen calls this pondering "inner ignition," which he illustrates with Henri Nouwen's personal story of viewing Rembrandt's painting, "The Return of the Prodigal Son." Nouwen first saw the painting as a poster, and he was so enthralled that he journeyed to St. Petersburg to see the original. He visited the painting again and again "with no small difficulty," meditating ever more deeply. From that meditation came his profound book on the subject of fathers, sons, and brothers.[36]

If the Parable Gives You a Shock, Pass It On

Don't disarm Jesus' land mines. Pass on the blessing. Here is a parable from a Max Lucado sermon that joshes along until it administers a mild shock at the end.

> A strange thing happened to me and my family not long ago. We were on a trip in an airplane. My oldest daughter pointed out that there was a fly in the plane. Do you know what that fly was doing? That fly was flying. I don't know what you do when you see a fly flying in [a plane], but I'll stop and talk to the fly. I said, "Come here, buddy. Why are you flying?" And he buzzed over to me and said, "I gotta fly. It's up to me to keep this thing airborne." I said, "You're kidding!" He said, "If I stop we could crash. It's entirely up to me to keep this thing in the air." And he buzzed off.

But when he came back a few minutes later, he was tired. And I said, "What's wrong?" He said, "It's hard keeping this thing up." And I said, "Listen to me, my friend. Look to the right, look to the left. You are kept airborne by virtue of a power that is not yours. You can sit down and rest and relax. You can enjoy the journey." He didn't believe me. He told me to get lost. He told me to buzz off.

Sometimes we feel like that fly, don't we? I fear there is something within us that thinks, "I've got to stay very busy, for if I don't stay busy, something is going to drop. My salvation is going to be in jeopardy." And what I said to that fly, I . . . say to you: It's not up to you. It's really not. It's not up to you.[37]

One of Jesus' favorite places to plant land mines was in the garden of materialism. As Blomberg observes, "It is impossible to expound any significant cross section of Jesus' teaching in parables without having to come to grips repeatedly with money matters—Christian stewardship, to be more precise."[38] If preaching is "truth through personality," we need to do some frank soul searching before we can faithfully recommunicate Jesus' sobering teaching that "no servant can serve two masters" (Luke 16:13, following the parable of the Shrewd Manager).

Other areas strewn with land mines are God's fearsome justice—the day of judgment is coming; God's magnificent grace—he forgives freely and loves lavishly; God's rigorous demands—he expects his followers to follow. When speaking of parables, through all and in all is the theme of the kingdom, the "already but not yet" reign of God. Ultimately, "all the parables of Jesus are kingdom parables," the rule of God in our hearts and in our society.[39]

Tell Narratives "Narratively"

If the Lord wisely chose to shock, confirm, perplex, and enlighten the crowds with *stories*, we do well to follow in his steps. One way to preach parables narratively is by creating a modern equivalent as Wells does with the Persistent Widow.

Another way is to compose an original parable, as Lucado does. Adopting a less fantastic stance, Sid Buzzell preaches a sermon called,

"The Story of Anna McLeash."[40] Although this sermon expounds a proverb, "Guard your heart," it shows what can be done to create a realistic fictional narrative. What follows is a summary of the sermon's controlling story.

Anna was a millionaire who lived on a vast estate in Bryn Mawr, Pennsylvania. After carefully checking references, she hired a Bible college student named Sonny to care for the grounds of the estate. With justifiable suspicion, she wisely guarded her wealth. But then she fell in love with a fellow named Tony, who turned out to be a crook. Claiming to be acting as her agent, he invested Anna's wealth, bilking the heiress of all her money. She did not guard her heart, and she was burned. In the end, the *Philadelphia Inquirer* reports that "Anna McLeash, daughter of the wealthy and deceased Seamus McLeash, was found dead in the 1700 block of Arch Street, a homeless indigent."

A third way to preach narratively is by following the parable verse-by-verse in a running commentary. If we can avoid turning our exegeses into cadavers, this method can reproduce many of the rhetorical effects the original audience experienced. The key is to react to the story as it unfolds, prompting the congregation to react as well. Much of that reaction will be communicated nonverbally with our tone of voice and facial expressions, but we'll also use explanation, analogy, and other support material. When preaching the parable of the Lost Coin, we could say, "Jesus then compares himself to a woman. A woman? Yes, you heard me: a woman! Or *did* you hear me? Maybe those words simply glided over your ears, but they certainly would *not* have glided over the ears of the Pharisees. Those words would have clanged in their ears. A woman? How degrading! Put yourself in their shoes. How would you like your mighty Messiah to picture himself as an illegal alien who picks fruit, a telemarketer who can hardly mumble his script, a cocktail waitress chewing gum and shimmying from table to table, or as an aged, muttering greeter at Wal-Mart? Some Messiah."

With the parable of the Barren Fig Tree (Luke 13:6–9), your sermon could develop as you react:[41]

- "The tree is dead"—*acknowledge* the fact.
- "Cut it down"—*agree* with the logic.

- The gardener requests, "One more year"—*absurd!*
- Application: God gives time for repentance—*wonder* at this absurd, merciful patience.

Use the suggestions in the preceding sections to help you preach with joyful and creative conviction. In doing so, you can help your congregation understand what parables are and how they communicate. Parables do, indeed, contain land mines; they are also a gold mine!

Chapter Checklist

☐ Do your homework—cultural context is crucial.
☐ Do your homework—literary context is crucial.
☐ Look for lead-in statements, summary statements, and end stress.
☐ Don't allegorize.
☐ Expect analogy.
☐ "Translate" or explain as necessary.
☐ Create your own parable.
☐ Be concrete and realistic.
☐ Add a twist or some "strangeness."
☐ Make your point obvious.
☐ Don't make your point obvious.
☐ Preach about the kingdom.
☐ Prompt imagination.
☐ Prompt identification.
☐ Prompt meditation.
☐ Keep the plot simple.
☐ Keep the characters simple. Dress them in white and black hats.
☐ If you preach verse-by-verse, react along the way.
☐ Confirm what we already believe.
☐ Teach something new.
☐ Shake up values and expectations.
☐ When preaching to postmoderns, avoid packages with ribbon.
☐ Read Tolstoy.

7

Proverbs

SHORT SENTENCES LONG REMEMBERED

A maxim is a conclusion upon observation of matters of fact.

—Samuel Coleridge, quoted in Ryken,
How to Read the Bible as Literature

The proverb shares with other literary forms the desire to overcome by means of arresting strangeness the cliché effect of ordinary discourse.

—Leland Ryken, *How to Read the Bible as Literature*

One cannot dictate an aphorism into a typewriter. It would take too long.

—Karl Kraus, quoted in Williams,
Those Who Ponder Proverbs

People need the kind of portable and memorable wisdom of the nuts-and-bolts variety that a proverb is designed to provide. The question is not will people live by proverbs, but what kind of proverbs will they cherish.

—Thomas Long, *Preaching and the
Literary Forms of the Bible*

Proverbs are a universal literary form. Like stories and poems, they are common in nearly every culture and era. Consider these:

- Chinese: Talk does not cook rice.
- Sumerian: A donkey eats its own bedding.
- Spanish: He who knows little soon repeats it.
- French: All are not hunters who blow the horn.
- English: Call a man a thief and he will steal.
- Nigerian: A single partridge flying through the bush leaves no path.
- Modern American: Different strokes for different folks.

The largest repository of biblical proverbs is, of course, the book of Proverbs, but this literary form, the shortest of all genres, is scattered throughout the Bible. First Samuel 10:12, for instance, says, "It became a saying [proverb]: 'Is Saul also among the prophets?'" And in Hosea 8:7 is found, "They sow the wind and reap the whirlwind." Crossan estimates that there are one hundred thirty aphorisms in the Gospels alone.[1]

Proverbs abound in modern Western culture just as they did in the ancient world. We see them on T-shirts, coffee mugs, posters, and calendars. Parents quote them to children, teachers quote them to students, friends quote them to friends, and the media quotes them to everyone. Advertising is the primary creator and transmitter of proverbs today, telling us to "be all that you can be," expecting "no pain, no gain," with the result that "you deserve a break today"!

Proverbs embody and transmit the *zeitgeist*—the spirit of the age. As such, proverbs are windows into culture. Folklorists, anthropologists, rhetoricians, and literary scholars see them as the building blocks of worldviews. What the alphabet is to reading and notes are to music, proverbs are to cultural ethics. But the ubiquitous presence of proverbs does not mean they are easy to define.

What *Is* a Proverb?

A single, clear definition of *proverb* has not arisen out of literary or biblical scholarship. Paroemiologist (an expert on proverbs) Andrew Guershoon's statement from 1941 holds true today: "[We] are not yet at one as to the definition of the term 'proverb.' It seems as though there will always be differences of opinion on this subject. . . . [But] every specialist and most laymen know what a proverb is."[2]

Novelists and poets may best capture the essence of the proverb:

A short sentence founded upon long experience, containing a truth.[3]

—Cervantes

A winged word, outliving the fleeting moment.[4]

—anonymous

The wisdom of many, the wit of one.[5]

—Lord John Russell

The most common Hebrew term for *proverb* is *māšāl*, but English doesn't have an equivalent term. The range of meaning for *māšāl* includes "proverb," "riddle," and "similitude." The Septuagint uses the term *parabolē* to render *māšāl* because, like parables, proverbs are rooted in daily life and have meaning beyond literal denotation. The verbal stem of *māšāl* means "to be like."[6] Crenshaw describes *māšāl* simply as a "similitude" or "powerful word," offering the general term "saying" as the best equivalent.[7]

For the present, we can sidestep most of the scholarly conundrum. Our purpose is to understand the general formal and rhetorical features of the genre—how this genre communicates and what it does—so that we can reproduce some of those features in our sermons. The material in this chapter applies mainly to the short maxims in chapters 10–29 of Proverbs, but it also informs understanding of the longer wisdom poems of chapters 1–9 and 30–31.

How the Text Communicates, What the Text Does

Three questions reveal the key literary and rhetorical features of proverbs: who speaks (and listens to) a proverb, what do proverbs say, and how do they say it?

The Words of the Wise: Who Speaks (and Listens to) a Proverb?

Proverbs are found on the lips of authorities. The teacher guides the student, "Haste makes waste!" The parent warns the child, "He who walks with wise men will be wise, but a companion of fools suffers harm." The master guides the disciple, "We reap what we sow." And the sage corrects the naïve, as when Gandalf reorients the hobbits' impression of Strider: "All that is gold does not glitter, not all who wander are lost."[8]

Each of the first seven chapters of Proverbs begins by addressing "my son" as the father urges his child, "accept my words" (2:1), "do not forget my teaching" (3:1), "pay attention" (4:1), and "listen well to my words of insight" (5:1). The book of Proverbs clearly is a repository of advice from an authority to a subordinate.

Even in peer relationships, the one who speaks a proverb signals a desire to act as an authority. A child, for example, may justify rough play in soccer by telling another child that "all is fair in love and war." The child wants to be seen as referee, or at least as justified in using brute force. Paroemiologist Neal Norrick states, "In citing a proverb, the speaker signals . . . that he wants to or at least is willing to assume the role of teacher/advisor for his hearers. One would hardly expect a child to utter proverbs to his parents or teachers."[9] The use of the proverb allows the speaker to borrow authority from traditional wisdom.

That phrase *traditional wisdom* is crucial in understanding the rhetorical force of proverbs because these anonymous sayings circulate as the distillation of cultural values. No one knows who first spoke a proverb, but its anonymity may actually add to its authority. Says Norrick, "Hearers tend to react to proverbial utterances as they would to directives from authoritative sources. The weight of traditional or majority opinion inculcates proverbial utterances with authority."[10] Aristotle lists proverbs with the type of proof called "ancient witnesses" and received opinions.[11] Proverbs are "common sense," thus speakers easily incorporate them like "commonplaces" into myriad discussions. "Commonplaces" were stock arguments from classical rhetoric, which could be plugged into nearly any argument.[12]

Proverb users take the mantle of authority, but this does not imply that listeners are automatons who respond like Pavlov's dogs. On the contrary, proverbs prompt listeners to collaborate with the speaker to discern the intended meaning. That's because proverbial meaning can be determined only from the context of its utterance. This rhetorical phenomenon occurs because proverbs are pithy and often use poetic language. More about these features below, but here my point is that proverbs are so short that they cannot present a nuanced argument, and their language may be so figurative that meaning is not readily apparent.

The proverb "Silence is golden" could, for example, be used in the following situations: A mother could order her child to be quiet; a girl could console her shy date when awkward pauses enter their conversation; a hiker could exude contentment over the stillness of a forest.[13] Each speaker expects the "interpreter" to rely upon context for correct interpretation.

When Jesus speaks proverbs in the Gospels, we have sufficient context to understand the potentially ambiguous sayings, but the book of Proverbs supplies less context. While chapters 1–9 are unified poems, most of the other chapters are simply a catalog of maxims. Yet even within this catalog, the compiler has given us some context by grouping sayings dealing with topics like the drunkard (23:29–35), the king (25:2–7), and the sluggard (26:13–16). Some scholars, such as Garrett, believe that context also exists on a more subtle level than obvious cohesion by theme,[14] while other scholars such as Ryken believe that beyond the wisdom poems and obvious groupings, "the structure is miscellaneous and the unity nonexistent."[15] Both of these positions suggest that context is crucial for interpretation. The first stance suggests that the compiler of Proverbs recognized the difficulty of "proverbial hermeneutics" and tried to give us some context. The second implies that Proverbs is a collection of free-floating maxims that speakers apply to apt situations as in the "Silence is golden" example above.

The necessity of context for interpreting proverbs produces two communication dynamics. The first dynamic is collaboration. This is one of the recurring themes in this current book: literature, being indirect rather than propositional, demands collaboration between speaker and receiver. Metaphor, irony, allegory, and figurative language in general call for speaker and receiver to work together. Proverbs, being somewhat ambiguous, also demand collaboration.

Here's how collaboration takes place. First the speaker sees something about his or her situation that calls for comment. Then the speaker chooses a proverb to capture and comment on that situation. Finally the speaker communicates the proverb, encoding meaning that he or she expects the listener to grasp. The listener must decode the speaker's intention, working through the process in reverse order. An example from Shakespeare illustrates the dynamic of encoding and decoding. In *Richard III*, one murderer says to another, "I'll go hide the body in some hole . . . [and then] I will away, for this will out, and then I must not stay" (1.4.280–84). The line "for this will out" is an allusion to the proverb "Murder will out." As Norrick argues, Shakespeare counted on his Elizabethan audience to recognize the proverb and agree with the notion that justice will catch up with murderers.[16] Thus, Shakespeare encoded a complex set of values and motives in a four-word allusion to a proverb, and he prompted the audience to figure out for themselves why the murderers flee. It "made sense" to them as they supplied recognition, premises, and conclusions to Shakespeare's subtle argument. Of course, the collaborative encoding and decoding took place in a flash, in a much shorter span of time than it takes to read a labored exegesis like this. With a pithy proverb Shakespeare enrolled the listeners as coplaywrights.

You may be thinking that this is risky business, and you're right. That's the second dynamic of using proverbs. When communication is more than "information dump," when it is transactional not linear, when it depends on insight from the listener, then it is risky. Thomas Long notes that "this is the irony of the proverbial form: it speaks wisdom, but it also *requires* wisdom to be rightly heard and employed."[17]

The risk is similar to what occurs when a speaker uses irony. The point lies in authorial intention, not always in literal language, and the audience must reconstruct the author's meaning. On a stormy day I may say to you, "Nice day." My intention is to communicate the opposite of the literal words, and I depend on you to figure that out. As we all know, sometimes it works, and sometimes it doesn't, but when it *does* work, the dynamic unites sender and receiver as they collaborate to construct meaning.

The pithy and figurative sayings in Proverbs seem folksy on the surface, but the more you get to know them, the more you see the complex dynamics that occur when sages speak. What, though, do the sages speak about? The following section describes the content of Proverbs.

Apples of Gold in Settings of Silver: What Do Proverbs Say?

The purpose of the book of Proverbs is to give "prudence to the simple, knowledge and discretion to the young" (1:4). Dundes calls proverbs "charters for belief and models for action."[18] Biblical proverbs give prudence by transferring *ḥokmāh* ("wisdom/skill") from parents to children: money can't buy happiness (Eccl. 5:10); pride comes before the fall (Prov. 16:18); he who guards his lips guards his life (13:3); don't invest in get rich quick schemes (v. 11); honor the king (19:12); lazy men go hungry (v. 15); never stop learning (v. 27).

These biblical proverbs may sound like the oratory of inspirational speakers. Indeed, self-help books show fondness for proverbs.[19] The quality that makes biblical proverbs different from humanistic proverbs is not so much their content as their theological underpinning, namely the fear of the Lord, which is the beginning or "chief part" of *ḥokmāh* (1:7). Reverencing and trembling before God mitigates the potential hubris of Proverbs. These snappy sayings sound like self-help humanism only if we see the world as existing independently from the King, but "for Israel the experiences of the world were always divine experiences, and experiences of God were always experiences of the world. The world is never experienced as purely secular, as apart from the Lord who controls it and who is revealed in it."[20]

Proverbs transfer *ḥokmāh* by making observations on repeated phenomena. These observations are made in present tense, indicative mood, implying that "this is the way things are." The intention behind the book of Proverbs is, of course, admonitory, but it makes its admonitions by calling us to observe that the contentious wife is irksome, the hotheaded man makes enemies, and the gossip loses friends. These sayings admonish us to take action, but the admonition does not burst through the front door in a huff. It comes through the back door and invites us to concur before we act. Thus, proverbs often communicate indirectly.

Because proverbs summarize phenomena and yet are quite short, they must distill insight. Ryken calls them "moments of epiphany."[21] For example, how many cases and studies have you seen of money not bringing happiness? All of those cases are distilled in Ecclesiastes 5:10: "Whoever loves money never has money enough." As Ricoeur states, "Without being a 'narrative,' a proverb implies a 'story.'"[22]

Before uttering Proverbs 18:21, "The tongue has the power of life and death, and those who love it will eat its fruit," the sage has seen the parent criticize the child and then alienate that child. The sage has watched the coach belittle the softball team and then seen the players adopt a don't-care attitude and lose the rest of their games. The sage has heard the boss yell at the employees and then noted the increase in the number of sick days taken. Those who sow deadly words *will* eat the fruit.

Since proverbs distill general categories of human experience, we must remember that they are not promises. The biblical sage has observed that the fear of the Lord adds years to life (9:11), but presumably the same sage would agree that holy men and women have, indeed, been martyred. Ryken explains, "Those who utter proverbs do not worry about possible exceptions (neither do lyric poets); they trust people to use their common sense in recognizing that a proverb need not cover every possible situation."[23]

The clearest demonstration that proverbs are general principles that must be applied with skill is Proverbs 26:4–5:

> Do not answer a fool according to his folly,
>   or you will be like him yourself.
> Answer a fool according to his folly,
>   or he will be wise in his own eyes.

Verse 4 is often true and we should take heed, but verse 5 is true, too. There is a time to remain silent, and there is a time to engage fools. *Ḥokmāh* tells us which is which. As Long observes, "A proverb is larger than one case, but not large enough to embrace all cases. . . . As wisdom, they transcend a single situation, but they do not have indiscriminate force to be applied anywhere and at all times."[24]

Proverbs, then, give wisdom to the simple, but in striving to preach genre-sensitive sermons, the third question is particularly interesting because much of the rhetorical force of a genre or sermon lies in its form.

Pleasant Words Are a Honeycomb: How Do Proverbs Talk?

The most obvious stylistic feature of proverbs is that they are short. An entire literary unit can be as few as six words in Hebrew and not many more in English. Smith explains, "To epigrammize an experience is to strip it down, to cut away irrelevance, to eliminate local, specific, and descriptive detail, to reduce it to and fix it in its most permanent and stable aspect, to sew it up for eternity."[25]

Brevity makes proverbs memorable. Nonliterate cultures often embody, preserve, and transmit their laws and customs in proverbs, because they are easy to remember, and, as argued above, even literate cultures circulate proverbs as repositories of collective wisdom. Proverbial style makes it easy to "bind [these sayings] around your neck, [and] write them on the tablet of your heart" (3:3). According to Alter, "The didactic poet does not want to set up eddies and undercurrents in the unruffled flow of his language, because the wisdom itself derives from a sense of balanced order, confident distinction, assured consequences for specific acts and moral stances."[26]

Even though proverbs can be quite short, we must not forget that they are poems. They utilize all the devices of lyric poetry, such as figurative language, hyperbole, and chiasmus. All forms of parallelism saturate Proverbs, and the parallel lines intensify just as they do in the Psalms. Proverbs 14:11, for example, says that the "house of the wicked will be destroyed, but the tent of the upright will flourish." The terms *house* and *tent* are not mere synonyms. The sage intensifies the images, saying that a mere tent, flapping and temporary, is more secure than a house, founded and firm, if righteousness is found within the tent. Without repeating the material from chapter 3, I call attention to a few of the more striking features of proverbial style.

Like all literature, proverbs comment on the universal by way of
the particular. A part stands for the whole. This is called synecdoche.
The *tongue* stands for the awesome power of language, a *faithful
witness* stands for the body who speaks truth,[27] and the *tent* in the
example above stands for the family unit. Sometimes this figurative
language needs "translation" from one culture to another, as when
Ecclesiastes 9:4 speaks of the living dog and dead lion. In ancient
Israel dogs were despised and lions revered. Exegetical digging yields
homiletical treasure.

As brief poems, the aural qualities of proverbs are prominent.
Rhythm and rhyme, alliteration and assonance help proverbs lodge
in memory and exhibit their roots in oral communication.[28] "Birds
of a feather flock together" stays with us better than "Persons whose
characters bear striking resemblance tend to associate with one
another."

Many of these aural qualities are mitigated when translated, so if
you have the ability to read Proverbs aloud in Hebrew, I suggest you do.
The compact nature of Hebrew, particularly evident in proverbial style,
gives these gems a brilliance that is lost when words swell in translation. Here is a literal translation of Proverbs 16:18, "Before breaking,
pride. Before stumbling, haughtiness." Sometimes a commentary or
felicitous translation will maintain Hebrew's aural qualities, as with
Williams's rendering of Proverbs 12:11,

> The tiller of soil has his fill of bread:
>   but the pursuer of vanities has an empty head.[29]

As stated above, biblical proverbs display every form of parallelism
and even add a few twists. "Better . . . than" statements are common
in chapters 10–22 ("Better to live in a desert than with a quarrelsome
and ill-tempered wife," 21:19); rhetorical questions make us think
("Who has gone up to heaven and come down? . . . tell me if you
know!" Prov. 30:4); merism—naming the outer poles and including
all between—functions as synecdoche ("The tongue has the power of
life and death," 18:21); numerical sequence such as Proverbs 30:15–31
helps us memorize *māšālîm*.

Proverbial style not only enhances memory, it also adds its own
kind of authority. As argued in the introduction of this book, form

functions rhetorically to prompt listeners to yield to the content. Kirshenblatt-Gimblett explains:

> Proverbs sound authoritative. The truths they proclaim feel absolute. . . . The proverb's form reinforces this effect by sounding so "right." Neat symmetries and witty convergences of sound and meaning, tight formulations of logical relations, highly patterned repetitions, structural balance, and familiar metaphors encapsulate general principles and contribute to the feeling that anything that sounds so right must be true.[30]

Before moving to the next major section of this current chapter, which talks about how to preach proverbs, two other stylistic features deserve attention. The first is Proverbs' fondness for humor. Just for fun, look at a translation like Today's English Version or The Message. Those versions help capture the impish spirit of stones tied in slings (26:8), thornbushes in a drunkard's hand (v. 9), dogs returning to their vomit (v. 11), lions roaming the street (v. 13), sluggards too lazy to withdraw their hands from the dish (vv. 14–15), and a man grabbing a dog by the ears (v. 17).

Like all humorists, the sage of Proverbs makes us grin by unexpected or incongruous juxtaposition. Proverbs 27:20, for example, sets a dark tone by beginning with "Death and Destruction," which are "never satisfied," but in a flash the proverb transports us to the mall! The shoppers' *eyes* [italics added] are never satisfied. They are as relentless as the grave." Similarly, the parallelism of 11:10 sets us up to expect rejoicing with prosperity and wailing with perishing, but instead we hear "shouts of joy" when somebody perishes. That's what happens when the "wicked" perish. Yippee!

A final stylistic feature is the prominence of the female roles—both literally and figuratively—in Proverbs. Female roles are present literally when depicted or described as mothers, wives, and harlots, and they are present figuratively when the noblewoman personifies the role of wisdom as in chapter 8. McKenzie argues that the unusual presence of the female in wisdom literature fits the genre well. Speaking generally, not descriptively of every case, women and proverbs both focus on the mundane specifics of daily experience. As the province of women usually encompasses things like child care, household management, and interpersonal communication, so are proverbs planted on terra firma, dealing with things like relationships, business, and lifestyle. Proverbs are *ḥokmāh*—practical wisdom for living in the fear of God.

Women—speaking generally again, not descriptively of every case—and proverbs both tend to communicate indirectly. Women view communication as a shared experience, dialogue not monologue, striving to make decisions or give directions through collaboration.[31] Proverbs, too, as demonstrated in the previous section of this chapter, also foster collaboration through indirect communication. The sender of a proverb uses laconic and figurative language, which the receiver must decode, using clues from context. McKenzie further spells out the connection between women and proverbs: "Though often excluded from formal, public arenas, . . . women occupy a role as informal historians and social critics and arbiters of morality. Given the place of women in the traditional social order, it makes sense that wisdom, a highly pragmatic religious tradition, would be imaged in female form."[32]

Proverbs, then, contain literary and rhetorical features. These cagey sayings communicate with folksy simplicity *and* unexpected complexity. How, though, can we preach them?

Try This

Preachers have many options for recommunicating proverbs since these sound bites of *ḥokmāh* connect with "secondary orality"—cultures in which people *can* read, but tend to think as oral learners do, with stories and proverbs. Most people learn and verbalize their faith this way. The suggestions below help preachers move toward what Tisdale calls "preaching as local theology and folk art."[33]

These suggestions are arranged roughly in chronological sequence moving from exegesis to delivery.

Preach Observations, Not Promises

As you study your text, remember that proverbs are general observations. That is the nature of the genre. To be sure, they are *inspired* general observations, but they are not promises. God has arranged the world so that cause-effect and action-consequence are normal patterns, but as we all know, those patterns have plenty of exceptions. Proverbs summarize the normal patterns, and the books of Ecclesiastes and Job handle the exceptions. They describe how the righteous think and behave when bad things happen to good people. The seventh suggestion below expands this point, but here let it suffice that as you study do not make a categorical (or genre) error. Do not force these round pegs of observation into the square holes of promise, and remember that the Bible itself presents two strands of wisdom, what some scholars call the conservative and radical strands. The conservative strain operates within the framework of an orderly world: obedience brings blessing, disobedience results in failure and punishment, the world functions regularly under God's sovereign rule. Most of the proverbs are conservative, whereas Job and Ecclesiastes are radical. They explore life when it seems out of control, when it seems that God is not playing by his own rules.

Perhaps you could preach two series to honor that balance. The first could be called "You Reap What You Sow," and the second "What to Do When You Plant a Carrot but Get an Onion." The same strategy could be used in a single message, as described below in the eighth suggestion.

If we can't give our listeners an ironclad promise (such as skillful parenting *guarantees* that our children will walk with God, Prov. 22:6), what *can* we give them? We can give the truth that God has given: parents have enormous impact on children; God has arranged the world so that children naturally want to please their parents; parents are obligated to train their kids to fear the Lord; when parents do so with *ḥokmāh*, kids respond. But since there are no perfect parents or perfect kids, we may need to talk about onions, too.

Do Not Preach Selfish Behavior, Humanism, or Materialism

I've heard many sermons that walked a fine line (and sometimes went over the line) when offering all that God offers—"the fear of the LORD brings wealth and honor and life" (Prov. 22:4)—but they leave out the fear of the Lord. Proverbs are not prescriptions for the American dream. They are prescriptions for how to live skillfully in a world created by the sovereign, generous, and fearsome Master. The first step in living skillfully is to revere God. To use proverbs to enthrone self is to make another categorical error, or as Long states, "To listen to a proverb without at the same time hearing its covenantal background is to pry a gem from its setting."[34]

"Health and wealth" sermons are common in the prosperity gospel movement, and a subtle form also shows up in the seeker-targeted movement. As part of that latter movement, I walked the line myself for many years. Ask God to give you wisdom to handle biblical proverbs the way the compiler handled them—as motivation and instruction to walk the straight path, not as a way to baptize carnal desire.

Preach Thought Units

This is standard procedure when preaching any genre, but I call attention to it here because determining thought units in Proverbs can be tricky. While the long poems of chapters 1–9 and 30–31 are self-evident units, the catalog of individual proverbs needs careful study. As Garrett demonstrates in his commentary, short proverbs are often grouped with other short proverbs of similar theme, but sometimes the connection is subtle.[35] You may not see immediately what proverb x has to do with proverb y, but look again. Expect unity. A good commentary will help.[36]

Although units often encompass more than one verse, a topical approach is also possible as a genre-sensitive way to preach from the catalog. The book of Proverbs tosses out observations on themes like old age, gossip, laziness, alcohol, and humility. You can gather all the proverbs on that theme and preach a message or series on the topic. In a sense, your "text" is the entire book from which you glean a number of short pericopes.

Use Your Imagination

As poetry, this genre communicates with images, so in our study we should imagine those images. This is what the original authors intended, that we understand their ideas and respond to their values by engaging our imaginations. Try to see, hear, and feel the firebrands, pigs, jewels, trees, crowns, rods, scales, and fountains. Ryken suggests that "one of the most helpful aids to a literary approach to . . .

Proverbs and Ecclesiastes is to work at finding visual commentary on each proverb."[37]

As you use your imagination in exegesis, remember that many images need "translation." We no longer live on our roofs (Prov. 25:24). Even in their own day, those images were synecdochical, or representative, of classes. So the mocker shooting "firebrands and deadly arrows" (26:18) may in our day toss dynamite and shoot a shotgun, or drop napalm and discharge a cannon.

Show as Well as Tell

Proverbs admonish, but they often do so by simply observing phenomena. For example, "Stone is heavy and sand a burden, but provocation by a fool is heavier than both" (Prov. 27:3). The clear intention of the proverb is exhortation: "Don't be a fool! Don't burden people with silly aggravation," but the exhortation is made in the indicative mood. In other cases, proverbs mix the imperative and the indicative moods as in Proverbs 27:1: "Do not boast about tomorrow, for you do not know what a day may bring forth." The intent is always to produce volitional change, but observation is the horse that pulls the cart.

Preachers who want to reproduce the rhetorical impact of the indicative, even while clearly intending the imperative, should make observations by using statistics, examples, current events, and stories. Remember that a story, or a group of stories, lies behind each proverb. *Show* the congregation the result of cheerful words. *Show* them what is happening in society because of alcohol abuse. Encourage and warn by describing the way things are.

Turn on the Spotlight

As an extension of this suggestion, McKenzie tells us to turn on the spotlight, not the floodlight.[38] This means to rove mentally through society searching for particular situations that should be illumined by a particular proverb. To use a different figure, "like the binoculars one finds at scenic overlooks, the proverb beckons us to pull over just for a moment and look through it out over the landscape of our journey, looking for situations to which it can bring ethical clarity."[39] Proverbs describe and provide *ḥokmāh* for apt situations, not all situations. The sage knows the difference, but the fool doesn't. That's why a proverb in the mouth of a fool is as useless as a lame man's legs (Prov. 26:7).

In terms of our preaching, this means that apt "narratives, vignettes, story-like threads that the proverb tugs from the fabric of everyday life would be told, each thread punctuated by the proverb itself, quoted as an interpretive refrain."[40] For example, when preaching from Proverbs 18:20–21 ("Death and life are in the power of the tongue,"NASB), I found apt examples of the power of language wielded in advertising campaigns and the abortion debate, and I told the following story from Amy Tan's *The Joy Luck Club.*[41]

A little girl with an extraordinary gift for chess could see "the secrets" of the chessboard. At age nine she was a national champion with unlimited potential. Her only liability was her mother, who sometimes envied her daughter's gift and manipulated her. The mother goaded and humiliated the daughter, and eventually the little girl dared to speak back. The mother responded with ice-cold silence (which was, itself, a form of communication). The girl stopped playing chess to try to manipulate the manipulator, but eventually the strategy of silence crushed her spirit and she announced, "I'm ready to play chess again." But her mother shouted, "No! It is not so easy anymore." The little girl tried to play again, but what the mother had said became a curse. She no longer could see the secrets of the board. She recounted, "I could only see my mistakes, my weaknesses." By age fourteen she had stopped playing, saying, "I had lost the gift and turned into someone quite ordinary."

Let the roving spotlight swing across society to find situations illumined by the proverb.

Make Your Central Idea "Proverbial"

For more than two thousand years, since Plato and Aristotle, teachers of oratory have stressed the differences between oral and written communication, and they have instructed us how to speak for the ear. In particular, theorists have emphasized with uncanny unanimity the value of communicating one unified idea.[42] Just as the fear of the Lord is the beginning of wisdom, so is the central idea the beginning of public speaking. That central idea will lodge in memory if you word it like a proverb, with brevity, balance, image, and sound values. By doing this, we preach not only as the sages spoke, but also as the listeners listen because in the age of secondary orality, the distilled, memorable phrase is as common as cornflakes. Advertisers coin jingles to lodge in memory, and politicians summarize their messages in sound bites to make the evening news. We live in the age of the one-liner. Here's an e-mail I received, containing a list of tongue-in-cheek headlines that report the end of the world:

> *USA Today:* "We're Dead."
> *Wall Street Journal:* "Dow Jones Plummets as
>   World Ends."
> *Sports Illustrated:* "Game Over."
> *Readers Digest:* "'Bye."
> *Rolling Stone:* "Grateful Dead Reunion Tour."

One way to make our central ideas proverbial is by using the proverb itself. I did this in the sermon cited above, "Death and life are in the power of the tongue" (18:21 NASB). That powerful statement was the single idea I stated and restated over the course of my thirty-minute sermon. The book of Proverbs is full of concise, striking, memorable statements, just the kind you want for your big idea.

You can also coin your own proverb. This is a chance for you word-smiths to exercise your gift. When preaching on how to overcome bitterness, John Piper argued that people who hold grudges try to take judgment into their own hands, not trusting God to dispense justice. The argument was dense, so Piper gave the people a nugget to take home: "If you hold a grudge, you slight the Judge."[43] When I preached on old age from Proverbs 16:31, here's the nugget I used: "A head of gray is a crown of glory, at the end of a righteous story." In Hebrew, the phrase in the proverb "crown of splendor" rhymes, so I simply borrowed the proverb's own style.

Sometimes an "interpretive refrain" can become a motto for an entire ministry or church. Timothy Keller, pastor of Redeemer Presbyterian Church (New York City), often summarizes the gospel with this memorable statement: "He lived the life I should have lived and died the death I should have died." In a church where I was teaching pastor, we so emphasized "speaking the truth in love" that an informal motto evolved in the church: "The truth is our friend." Rather than seeing the truth as our enemy, feeling that it will bring pain and conflict, we renewed our minds with God's Word. The truth sets us free, and the maxim helped us practice the truth day in and day out.

Another way to preach proverbs "proverbially" is by rephrasing a modern proverb. We can "learn a lesson from the parodist who boldly goes where he is not supposed to go."[44] Instead of "Seeing is believing," we can proclaim "Believing is seeing." Or try this one: "Life is short, pray hard."[45]

Dueling Proverbs

Compare and contrast modern proverbs with biblical ones. McKenzie calls this "dueling proverbs."[46] This technique focuses two spotlights on the same situation, evaluating culture's repository of wisdom against God's. Sometimes our culture speaks truth, and sometimes it is found wanting.

For example, "Money makes the world go round" could be paired with Proverbs 11:28, "Whoever trusts in his riches will fall, but the righteous will thrive like a green leaf." American proverbs that embody values such as progress ("Records are made to be broken"), money as the measure of value ("Time is money," "You get what you pay for"), and what McKenzie calls "visual empiricism" ("A picture is worth a thousand words," "What you see is what you get") need theological and homiletical scrutiny.[47] We must help our people take every thought captive to the obedience of Christ. When preachers know the Bible's proverbs and are mindful of the proverbs circulating in culture, they are "equipped to offer the dehumanized consumers in the pews an alternative identity, worldview, and way of life."[48]

Dueling proverbs can even be used with a set of biblical proverbs in the same way that Proverbs 26:4 and 5 does. Show, for example, how it is sometimes wise to hold your tongue (10:19), but other situations call for speech (27:5–6). If you do this, be careful not to imply that the Bible contradicts itself. Instead, use the sermon to demonstrate that proverbs are generalizations that call for discernment in application.

Dueling proverbs can also help us teach that there are conservative and radical strands of wisdom. This technique can help us preach, for example, a full theology of suffering or success. Borrowing an English proverb, I preached a sermon called "Barking Dogs Never Bite (except now and then . . .)."

Borrow the Proverb's Movement

To organize your message in a way that responds to how God communicated, not just what he communicated, try to reproduce the proverb's flow of thought and feeling. Antithetical parallelism is found on every page of the book of Proverbs (e.g., "The lips of the righteous know what is fitting, but the mouth of the wicked only what is perverse," Prov. 10:32), as is synthetic (e.g., "He who puts up security for another will surely suffer," 11:15) and synonymous (e.g., "When a wicked man dies, his hope perishes; all he expected from his power comes to nothing," Prov. 11:7). For more advice on organizing according to parallelism, review the fifth suggestion in the chapter on preaching psalms (pp. 54–57). You can also organize with other proverbial forms such as acrostic (e.g., Prov. 31:10–31).

Adopt the Teacher's Stance

Authorities speak proverbs to students or children. How can preachers reproduce that pedagogical tone and attitude? Not by being authoritarian—since proverbs aren't (they make *observations*)—but by encouraging listeners to ponder and draw conclusions for themselves. As George MacDonald said, "The best thing you can do for your fellow man, next to rousing his conscience, is—not to give him things to think about, but to wake things up that are in him; that is, to make him think things for himself."[49]

Rhetorical theorists use the term *enthymeme* to describe the strategy MacDonald suggests. Aristotle first described the enthymeme as a "rhetorical syllogism."[50] As you know, a syllogism is a closely reasoned argument that has three parts:

1. *Major Premise:* All men are mortal.
2. *Minor Premise:* Socrates is a man.
3. *Conclusion:* Therefore, Socrates is mortal.

In contrast to the syllogism, the enthymeme does not state one or two of those parts. The parts are still crucial to the argument, but if the audience already believes them, they can be left unstated. Since, for example, you already believe that everyone is mortal, I could simply argue, "Socrates is just a man. He's mortal!" and you would concur. I could, in fact, jump straight to the conclusion, "Socrates is mortal," since you believe the major and minor premises before I even open my mouth. Skillful rhetoricians analyze the audience to determine their existing beliefs and values, and then they use those presuppositions in their own persuasion. According to Lloyd Bitzer, this is the essential feature of the enthymeme—*"the audience itself helps construct the proofs by which it is persuaded."*[51] Skillful speakers "awaken things already present" to move them toward things absent.

Teachers know how to do this. They *engage* the students in order to surface latent knowledge, beliefs, and values. Here are some "pedagogical/enthymemic" techniques I've used when preaching a series from Proverbs:

- *Quiz.* I asked the congregation multiple choice questions, such as "What does the word 'fear' mean in the phrase 'the fear of the Lord'?":

  A. Reverence/respect.
  B. Concern/anxiety.
  C. Dread/terror.
  D. All of the above.
  E. None of the above.
  (By the way, which would *you* choose?)

- *Participation.* In a message directed to young people from Proverbs 4:20–27, I gave them a space to draw as we looked at the passage. The passage describes the ears, eyes, lips, heart, and feet of one who pursues wisdom, and the young people drew these body parts on a stick figure.

- *Discussion.* I quoted a line from a hymn, which one church had rewritten—"'Twas guilt that taught my heart to fear and pride my fears relieved"—and then asked the congregation what presuppositions about fear lie behind that hymn. That is, why did the church rewrite the original line, "'Twas grace that taught my heart to fear and grace my fears relieved"? Since the congregation was large, the "discussion" was hypothetical, taking place in their minds, but it nevertheless took place.[52]

Feature Women

Even though women make up more than 60 percent of evangelical congregations, preachers (mostly men) usually do not address their needs and questions. We may lob Proverbs 31 to the congregation on Mother's Day, but we need to do more. Proverbs can help. It gives us the opportunity to correct this imbalance. Praise the role women play in God's kingdom, address them directly, and choose illustrations that connect with them.[53] For example, consciously employ illustrations that show women acting courageously. Speak of Elisabeth Elliot's return to the Auca tribe in South America. She went back to complete the work their team had started—bringing the gospel to a people group who had never heard. She did so in spite of mortal danger and in spite of the heartbreaking memory that the Aucas had killed her husband.

Use Some Humor

Many proverbs use exaggeration and quirky juxtapositions. That's how God has communicated to us. Try it yourself as you recommunicate the Word. When preaching from the proverb about grabbing a dog by the ears (26:17), you could tell the humorous story of the first puppy you got as a child and how your "training" backfired. If you don't have a gift for humor, though, you might want to stick with the suggestions above.

Use Homespun Language

Proverbs are poetry, but they are not the "high poetry" of Psalms. If your personality or background is down-to-earth and homespun, you should feel at home with proverbs. They're full of common sense and wry observation. Don't say, "Dear ones, we have gathered today to make supplication before the Father of lights, the only Wise God, the Potentate of time." Say, "Well, folks, I'm glad you're here. Tonight we're going to pray. The Lord is here, and he's the only one who can answer our prayers, so we're going to pray. Life is short; pray hard." Language is not simply a conveyor belt that carries thought. It also shapes thought and feeling. To capture the tone of Proverbs, "talk natural."

Chapter Checklist

- ❑ Don't preach promises; remember the onions.
- ❑ Do preach wisdom.
- ❑ Don't preach self-help, humanistic, anthropocentric health and wealthism.
- ❑ Do preach *ḥokmāh*—skill for living in the fear of God.
- ❑ When discerning a thought unit, look for unity with the surrounding verses.
- ❑ Don't be afraid to preach topics.
- ❑ Exegete with imagination.
- ❑ Expect synecdoche.
- ❑ Translate images.
- ❑ Use examples and current events as a spotlight.
- ❑ Use statistics too.
- ❑ Especially use stories. Proverbs imply stories.
- ❑ Craft your central idea. Make it proverbial.
- ❑ Use sound values like rhythm and rhyme to make your idea memorable.
- ❑ Use the central idea as a refrain.
- ❑ Make a biblical proverb duel with a worldly proverb. Pistols at ten paces.
- ❑ Make biblical proverbs duel each other, but don't let either one take out the other.
- ❑ Use antithetic, synthetic, or synonymous parallelism for your outline.
- ❑ Use anything else the proverb gives you, such as acrostic.
- ❑ Be an authority, but don't be authoritarian.
- ❑ Use dialogue, discussion, quizzes, participation, and other pedagogical methods to make students think thoughts for themselves.
- ❑ Address women.
- ❑ Make 'em laugh.

8

Epistles

ONE SIDE OF A CONVERSATION

Instead of impersonal phrases, rich in etiquette and convention, Paul threw himself into his letters with emotions bared. The letters arose in response to reports from specific contexts, and Paul treated each situation as unique and important; he was not so much forging religious dogma as conveying his understanding of how Christianity might be structured in the concrete situational contexts of the particular addressees.

—William Doty, *Letters in Primitive Christianity*

If the form of the sermon influences faith, Paul's preaching is a reminder of the importance of direct speech and argumentative discourse in the formation of Christian consciousness.

—James Thompson, *Preaching Like Paul*

Our point is that the personal dramatic character of the Gospel itself involves confrontation, . . . the living encounter of heart

and heart, voice and voice, and that this has inevitably regis-
tered itself in the ongoing story of Christ and in the style of
the New Testament. . . . [I]t is as though God says to men one
by one: "Look me in the eye."
                               —Amos Wilder, *Early Christian Rhetoric*

Epistle is the dominant literary form of the New Testament, com-
prising approximately twenty-one of its twenty-seven books.[1] This
highly flexible genre was so useful that it continued as the primary
form of written communication in the early church with the apostolic
fathers using it extensively. Later, the generic pattern continued in
papal encyclicals and letters.[2]

Of all the genres covered in this book, the epistle is most like the
sermon. Both are created to address specific circumstances; both
argue ideas and employ "support material," such as illustrations and
quotations; both are markedly aural. No wonder preachers often feel
at home in the epistles. Poetry, narrative, parable, and proverb tend to
hide their rhetoric, using induction and imagination for persuasion,
but epistle flies its rhetorical flag for all to see.

The goal of this current chapter, like the other chapters, is to
increase understanding of the rhetorical functions of the genre and
suggest ways to incorporate those functions into sermons. Preachers
pay attention to rhetoric because, as Wayne Booth states, "Rhetorical
study is the study of *use*, of purpose pursued, targets hit or missed,
practices illuminated for the sake not of pure knowledge but of further
(and improved) practice. . . . We want to know *why* one story or technique works better than another, because . . . our practice as tellers
and listeners can always be improved."[3]

What *Is* an Epistle?

An epistle is a letter designed for wide circulation that addresses
current issues and revives personal relationship. At the turn of the
century, Adolf Deissmann sharply contrasted "epistle" and "letter."[4]
Epistles were formal, literary, long, and intended for the public. Letters were informal, dashed off, short—no longer than one sheet of
papyrus—and intended for a private party. Deissmann placed Paul's

writings in the "letter" category, but in reality they belong on a continuum, Romans being close to the "epistle" end of the continuum and Philemon close to the "letter" end. For our purposes, the terms are used interchangeably, but I believe that most of the New Testament texts are closer to Deissmann's "epistle." They were designed for groups of people (churches), not individuals, and they are much longer than the personal letters of that day.

Letter writing was quite common in the classical world. Handbooks and rhetorical schools taught epistolary style.[5] Thousands of papyri (short letters) have survived, as have the formal epistles of public figures such as Isocrates, Cicero, and Seneca. Today we have no modern equivalent to the epistle (that is, the formal, public letter), but perhaps our "letter to the editor" comes close. Conversely, we still have letters today. The explosive growth of telecommunication may be tolling the demise of the private letter, but it isn't dead yet.

Epistles substitute for the personal presence of the author, that presence being summarized by Koskenniemi as *philophronēsis* ("friendly relationship"), the extending of oneself that occurs when we talk; *parousia* ("presence"), the reviving of relationship between separated friends; and *homilia* ("dialogue"), the continuance of a conversation.[6] Regardless of content and style, the simple act of writing is rhetorical. It is a speech act, a reaching out to another person. The telephone company AT&T tells us to "reach out and touch someone," and they're right about the touching. By means of a phone call, we obliterate space to extend our "presence." Letter writers do the same. Through epistles, the apostles reached out to touch the fledgling church.

Yet their reaching out and touching was not literal. The epistles substituted for personal presence, but it was presence-in-absence, the result of physical and temporal distance. Under Augustus, the Roman emperors established their own postal services with vehicles, horses, and inns, all largely restricted for imperial use, but an official letter from Rome to Caesarea still took fifty-four days.[7] For private letters, no postal system existed, and with the dangers and inconveniences of travel in the first century, New Testament letters, dependent on personal carriers and weather, undoubtedly took longer to arrive. In addition to physical and temporal distance, mediation also added to the epistles' quality of presence-in-absence. Paul, James, John, Jude, and the other epistolographers sent their messages via envoys. Someone such as Timothy or Silas read the author's words to the churches.

As a result, this presence-in-absence quality gave the author and the receivers time to think. It reduced the "risks" rhetorician Carrol Arnold describes when communication is face-to-face—risks accompanying nervousness, loss of attention, or breakdown of speaker-audience relationship.[8] Compare receiving these words through an intermediary, to hearing them from the speaker who is looking you in the eye: "I am astonished that you are so quickly deserting the one who called you by the grace of Christ" (Gal. 1:6), and "Now listen, you rich people, weep and wail because of the misery that is coming upon you" (James 5:1). Presence-in-absence mitigates the sharp edge of rebuke so that a cut has time to heal before the recipient responds to the communication.

Amos Wilder argues that the apostles gravitated to this genre because it mirrors the theological center of the New Testament—the incarnation. That is, because Jesus is the Word made flesh, and Christianity is a personal encounter with that Word, the New Testament authors chose written forms of communication that approximate face-to-face encounters.[9] The epistle is perfectly suited for that enterprise. No wonder the genre has something of a favored status in the New Testament. Furthermore, this genre is highly congenial to preaching, so we turn to our subject with expectation and delight.

How the Text Communicates, What the Text Does

We still write letters, so we probably have an intuitive sense of what makes this genre work, but a few surprises may surface as I delineate three literary/rhetorical features. The first feature deals with content, and the next two deal with form.

Content: "Occasions" Met with Theology

Perhaps more than any other literature of the Bible, epistles address specific situations or "occasions." Reading them is like listening to one side of a telephone conversation.[10] Like speeches and sermons (or phone calls), epistles are direct address, using first- and second-person pronouns. We overhear Paul instruct young Timothy how to oversee the church in Ephesus. We overhear John speaking to the "chosen lady and her children" who were troubled by deceivers (2 John 1, 7). Even a text like James, a catholic or general epistle, addresses the circumstances of the "twelve tribes scattered among the nations" (James 1:1). Epistles arise from and address specific exigencies. Thus, a hermeneutical commonplace states that exegetes need to understand, as much as possible, the background, author, and recipients of the letter.

We should think of Paul and the other letter writers as practical, not systematic, theologians. Their theology is, in the words of Fee and Stuart, "task theology"[11]—theology at the service of particular needs. Paul uses the word "justification," for example, fifteen times in Romans and eight times in Galatians, but only two times in the rest of his letters. In Rome and Galatia the church planter battled the false belief that we can earn salvation, so he defended justification by faith, but apparently that particular false belief did not trouble other churches. James battled the opposite problem, what we today call "easy believism."

Remembering that the epistles address specific occasions will preserve us from theological myopia, that is, building a system on a portion of the epistles' rich doctrine or even on a single metaphor. Some audiences need to hear that salvation cannot be earned. Others need to hear that faith without works is useless. These messages do not contradict each other; they focus the light of revelation on different circumstances. The behaviors and thought patterns of the recipients determine which portion of the spectrum the authors applied.

While stressing the fact that epistles are pastoral theology, let's not downplay the fact that they are theology. Taken together, they create a profound worldview—a way of understanding self, family, society, evil, temptation, salvation, authority, morality, and the future. That theological worldview provides answers to even the most mundane questions. Should a woman wear her hair loose while praying (1 Cor. 11)? The answer can be found in the headship of the husband, Christ, and God. Should a believer take a fellow believer to court (1 Cor. 6)? The answer is implied by our view of the eschaton when the saints will judge the world.

This theological worldview provides the rationale for behavior by grounding the imperative in the indicative. That is, the epistles

command, rebuke, and exhort, but they do so on the basis of the character and work of God. Because God loves us (indicative), we should
love each other (imperative) (1 John). Because Jesus will come again,
we should not grieve like those who have no hope (1 Thess. 4). Because
Jesus became poor for us, we should give generously (2 Cor. 8). In the
epistles, action is motivated by the facts of theology.

This ordering of the indicative and imperative is, in the opinion of
Allen Verhey, a profound reflection of the essence of the Christian life:
"The indicative mood has an important priority and finality, . . . but
the imperative is by no means merely an addendum to the indicative
or even exactly an inference drawn from the indicative. Participation
in Christ's cross and resurrection (the important priority of the indicative) and anticipation of the new age of God's unchallenged sovereignty
(the important finality of the indicative) are *constituted* here and now
by obedience to God's will (the imperative)."[12]

One function of this use of theology is what the rhetoricians call
"transcendence," a type of argument based on first principles and
core values rather than pragmatism.[13] For instance, Peter might have
urged his readers to rejoice in trials because of the health benefits
that attend a positive mental attitude—and there are indeed such
benefits—but instead he links trials to something deeper: "Rejoice
that you participate in the sufferings of Christ" (1 Peter 4:13). Most
people argue on the basis of self-interest or utility, but the typical
pattern of argumentation in the epistles is based on the character of
God and union with Christ.

Even in cases of the epistles' arguing pragmatically, they set
pragmatism within transcendence. Notice the pragmatism in these
commands: "He who loves his wife loves himself" (Eph. 5:28); "Do
you want to be free from fear of the one in authority? Then do what
is right and he will commend you" (Rom. 13:3). But before Paul gives
the pragmatic argument to love our wives, he first grounds it in the
ontology of Christ and the church. That is, because marriage is an
earthly picture of a spiritual mystery, we ought to love our wives.
The command from Romans is also set within a transcendent understanding of reality: "Everyone must submit himself to the governing authorities, for there is no authority except that which God
has established" (Rom. 13:1). Love and fear of God is to motivate us.

The New Testament writers lift our eyes to view circumstances and relationships in light of the will of God, eternity, and the profound but often unseen essence of reality.

By addressing mundane occasions from a profoundly theological world, the epistles model what we should do in our preaching. The way to build Christian communities is by patiently teaching about God's provision and character, and then by drawing implications for behavior from those facts.[14] I'll return to this idea in the final section of this chapter.

Form: Adapting Generic Conventions

Just as letters today have a defined form, so did ancient letters. The following form, remarkably calcified, was used in the Mediterranean world for eight hundred years:[15]

- Prescript (with name of sender to name of receiver)
- Greetings (often with a wish for good health)
- Body (with many stereotypical formulae)
- Conclusion (often with greetings to others and a final salutation or prayer)[16]

The New Testament writers, Paul in particular, maintained these conventions but modified them by "the demands of his unique ministry, by his theological commitments, and by his personal creativity."[17] A major modification Paul made was to greatly expand the length of letters. The average length of a letter of Cicero was 295 words; Seneca, 955; but Paul's epistles averaged 2,500 words![18] No epistles in the ancient world come close to this. As you'll see below, such documents could not be dashed off. Here are some other ways Paul adapted the letter form:

- In the prescript, he often included his title, such as "apostle" (1 Corinthians; 2 Corinthians; Ephesians) or "servant of Jesus Christ" (Philippians), and this sets the tone for the letter. To the maverick Galatians, for example, Paul begins with the abrupt "Paul, an apostle—sent not from men nor by man, but by Jesus Christ and God the Father" (Gal. 1:1). A modern equivalent would be, "Randy, what were you thinking?"[19] In the prescript, Paul also regularly included his co-workers such as "Paul, Silas, and Timothy to . . ." (1 Thess. 1:1). The apostle worked with a team and did not hog the stage.

- Paul modified the Hellenistic *charein* ("greetings") to the theologically loaded *charis kai eirene* ("grace and peace" to you). He also regularly added a prayer of thanksgiving for the recipients, not merely a wish for their good health (e.g., Colossians; 1 Thessalonians; 2 Thessalonians; 2 Timothy; Philemon). These blessings often foreshadow the content of the body (e.g., 1 Cor. 1:4–7).
- Paul expanded the conclusion with components like warnings (Rom. 16:17–20), benedictions (1 Cor. 16:23–24; 2 Thess. 2:16–17), and final charges (1 Tim. 6:20–21).

Rhetorically, these modifications can be understood as cultural adaptation. As every missionary knows, effective communicators adapt. Paul and the other New Testament letter writers borrowed the form of their day, but they also adapted and enriched it for ministry. They illustrate Donald Bryant's definition of rhetoric: "Adjusting ideas to people and people to ideas."[20] They adjusted their ideas not by compromising convictions but by flexing form. Genre became a help, not a straitjacket, for the gospel.

Form: The Suppleness of Discourse

Epistle is "discourse," a mode of communication that is like speech. As such, it is extremely supple, incorporating other genres within its framework and combining appeals from logos, pathos, and ethos. Epistles are like speech in four ways: they employ various small forms, argue with linear logic, cite or allude often, and are composed for the ear.

Employing Small Forms

Just as narratives like 1 Samuel or Luke incorporate proverbs and poems within the flow of their stories, epistles also incorporate other forms within the larger generic structure, but epistles do this with much greater frequency than any other genre.[21] Some of these subgenres are proverbs (1 Cor. 15:33; Gal. 5:9), creeds/hymns (Gal. 5:14;

1 Tim. 3:16; Phil. 2:6–11; Col. 1:15–20), lists (Rom. 1:29–31; Gal. 5:22–23), rhetorical questions (James has the highest proportion, but Rom. 8:31–35 has the highest concentration—seven in a row), apostrophes (1 Cor. 15:55), doxologies (Rom. 11:33–36), and apocalyptic visions (2 Thess. 2). As discourse, the genre of epistle, like the genre of sermon, is, as stated, supple.

Discourse employs features of language commonly associated with poetry, metaphor in particular. Many metaphors in the epistles derive from the Greco-Roman world of athletics ("All the runners run, but only one gets the prize," 1 Cor. 9:24), warfare ("If the trumpet does not sound a clear call, who will get ready for battle?" 1 Cor. 14:8), law courts ("We must all appear before the judgment seat of Christ," 2 Cor. 5:10), and farming ("You are God's field," 1 Cor. 3:9). The most extended metaphor in the New Testament epistles is Ephesians 6:10–17, the armor of God. Many other metaphors derive from the history and customs of Israel with its sacrificial system, law, and exodus. Greidanus agrees, saying that "the Epistles contain many more metaphors than one generally perceives—metaphors such as redemption, adoption, liberty, the new creation, peace, expiation, and justification."[22]

This quality of suppleness maintains attention. The listener never knows what's coming next. It might be a hypothetical dialogue, a current proverb, or, most likely, a quotation from the Old Testament. You can read barely five verses of discourse without a shift of perspective. The weaving of other sources into the flow of the epistle's argument, what today we call the use of quotations, is so prominent it deserves the separate attention given below.

Citing or Alluding Often

An astonishing portion of New Testament epistles is "quoted" material. The word *quoted* is place inside quotation marks because the ancient world had different standards of citation than we have today. They depended on memory and did not often "check references." This is because exact references were difficult to locate. Few manuscripts existed, and most of those were scrolls, laborious to unroll and reroll. Furthermore, manuscripts contained no visual indicators such as page or verse numbers signaling which portion was being quoted.

Entire sections ran together without breaks even between words. Additionally, ancient standards of citation differ from ours because intellectual property was not considered private property. In the oral world it was a communal possession. It had no existence apart from a speaker speaking it to listeners, who later kept it alive by speaking it again. In contrast, knowledge in the typographic world is the product of a writer who has frozen it on the page. Knowledge is equated with those frozen symbols on the page and the author who scratched the symbols.[23]

Thus, when New Testament letter writers cite others, their "quotations" range from exact reproduction (our modern concept of quoting), to paraphrase, to echoes of the original words. James provides a striking example. He rarely quotes verbatim, but in dozens of places he alludes to the Old Testament and to Jesus' words, especially the Sermon on the Mount, so that "Jesus' pervasive influence underlies the whole of James's teaching."[24]

Most citation is taken from the Old Testament, usually the Septuagint, but citation also comes from hymns, creeds, sayings of Jesus, and even pagan poets (Titus 1:13). As much as half of an epistle can be quoted, what scholars call "preformed material." Ellis estimates the following percentages:[25]

Romans	27%
1 Corinthians	17%
2 Corinthians	11%
Galatians	32%
Ephesians	54%
Philippians	7%
Colossians	42%
1 Thessalonians	37%
2 Thessalonians	24%
1 Timothy	43%
2 Timothy	16%
Titus	46%
Philemon	0%

Fig. 8.1. Percent of "Preformed Material" in Paul's Epistles

This heavy freight of citation creates a dual rhetorical function. Most obviously, the author borrows the ethos of the original source to bolster his own message. When James alludes to the Sermon on the Mount, he aligns himself with his Master, showing that he did not invent his message, but is simply applying it to the recipients' circumstances. More subtly, when an author uses allusion rather than verbatim quotation, he engages the listeners to participate in their own persuasion. Allusions are brief and sometimes veiled so that authors count on their listeners to get the point. And in that we see yet another instance of collaboration, the same dynamic I discussed in previous chapters.

To support the claim that "faith without works is dead"(NASB), James alludes to the stories of Abraham and Rahab (James 2:20–26). He expects his audience to recognize the allusions, supply the information he breezes over, and assent to his idea. I can imagine his readers saying, "Yes, that's right. When Abraham sacrificed Isaac, God said to him 'Now I know you fear God. . . . I will surely bless you . . . because you have obeyed me' (Gen. 22:12, 17–18). If Abraham had merely mouthed the right words, he would not have received God's blessing. Real trust cannot be divorced from action. Yes, James, you are right! Faith without works is useless." Allusion draws us in, engages our minds, and prompts us to participate in our own persuasion.

Arguing with Linear Logic

A third feature of discourse is its linear flow of logic. This is not to imply that epistles march like syllogisms (although sometimes they do), rather that their flow is topical and logical, in contrast to the flow of events in narrative or the flow of images and feelings in lyric poetry. "This means that the flow of the argument of the Epistles is established by a series of interrelated assertions in which the various statements are related to one another *logically*."[26] To interpret epistles well, look for ideas—how they are argued, illustrated, and applied—not individual words or even phrases. Modern translations break the text into paragraphs, and these can often be helpful in discerning blocks of ideational content.

Epistles are not, of course, simply sterile beakers of ideas. They are also means of extending one's personality, and they can overflow with emotion. They are rhetorical texts par excellence that provide myriad opportunities for full employment of logos, pathos, and ethos.

Writing for the Ear

The fourth feature of epistolary discourse is that it was meant to be heard. Although epistles are written, they were transmitted orally by a reader, clearly indicated by internal evidence: "I charge you . . . to have this letter read to all the brothers" (1 Thess. 5:27); "After this has been read to you, see that it is also read in the church of the Laodiceans" (Col. 4:16); "Blessed is the one who reads [aloud] the words of this prophecy, and blessed are those who hear it and take to heart what is written in it" (Rev. 1:3). Even the letter to Philemon, the most personal in the New Testament, is addressed to Philemon "and to the church that meets in your home" (v. 2).

External evidence also compels the conclusion that the epistles were received aurally. In the ancient world silent reading was virtually unknown.[27] Even solitary readers, like the Ethiopian eunuch (Acts 8), read aloud. The Greek term *epistolē* originally referred to an oral communication sent by a messenger. Eventually the term came to mean a written communication sent by a messenger, but the text was still delivered orally by the envoy who would then expound or clarify it. This was true in the secular realm, and Paul followed the practice.[28]

Knowing that most of their recipients would hear, not see, their letters, the authors used aural devices to signal emphasis and transitions of thought. Written communication, of course, uses spatial devices like the ones used on this page: headings, paragraph indentations, fonts, and punctuation. In orality, emphasis is achieved by repetition and parallelism.[29] See 2 Corinthians 4:8–12 and 6:4–10, two of the most passionate passages in the New Testament. Aural style contributes to their energy.

Another aural device the epistles use is chiasmus (see 1 John 1:6–7; Rom. 10:9–10). Modern readers often overlook chiasmus, but in the ancient world it was a major stylistic device, so that Richards asserts, "Ancients noticed and enjoyed chiasm much as we notice and enjoy rhyming sentences today. For us, rhyming makes something easier to remember and often gives us an appreciation that the writer thought carefully when constructing his material. . . . Readers in Paul's day viewed chiasm the same way."[30]

Not only were the epistles received aurally, they were also composed through speech. Authors dictated to scribes because writing on papyrus was irksome and demanded skill. In the ancient world the ability to read did not guarantee the ability to write, just as today the ability to read does not guarantee the ability to type. Or, to use another analogy, today literacy does not guarantee the ability to write calligraphy.[31] In the first century, the secretary had to mix ink, make pens, glue sheets of papyrus into scrolls, and write legibly on rough papyrus. Even in the late 1800s, operetta composers Gilbert and Sullivan noted how businessmen appreciated the skill of a junior clerk who could write in a "good round hand" (from *The Pirates of Penzance*).

Paul probably worked with a team (Timothy, Silas, etc.) on early drafts of his epistles before a secretary eventually prepared the final text.[32] Peter also acknowledges "the help of Silas" (1 Peter 5:12). As Richards argues, this dialogic, communal approach to composition means that the letters originated as oral texts.[33] Preliminary ideas and early drafts generated in discussion were captured on reusable wax tablets and went through multiple revisions before final dictation to the secretary. Epistles were not simply dashed off. The whole process was laborious and expensive, especially when you consider the extraordinary length of most of the New Testament epistles. Richards estimates the following:[34]

Epistle	Number of hours to make a final copy	Cost in dollars (from the year 2004)
Romans	11.5	$2,275
1 Corinthians	10.7	$2,108
Galatians	3.6	$722
1 Thessalonians	2.4	$484
1 Timothy	2.8	$554

Fig. 8.2. Time and Money Invested to Produce a NT Epistle

The simple but often overlooked fact that epistles were composed orally and received aurally leads to three rhetorical effects. The first is vigor. Like one side of a phone call, the epistles use first- and second-person pronouns, rhetorical questions, exclamations, and other devices typical of face-to-face communication. Sometimes epistles even provide both sides of the phone call by creating hypothetical dialogue ("But someone will say, 'You have faith; I have deeds,'" James 2:18). This style is as close to conversation as written language can come, and the result is vitality. To be sure, the spontaneous, dialogic quality brings with it grammatical oddities and suspensions of the flow of thought,[35] but energy pulses in the letters because we feel that something was at stake—the health of a newborn baby, that is, the first-century church. These letters are not philosophical treatises; they are one-half of a real conversation between real people with real problems.

Orality in the epistles also enhances ethos, that mode of proof, in contrast to logos and pathos, that arises from the speaker's relationship with the listeners. Let me explain: In the ancient world words were thought of as phonemes (sound), not graphemes (marks on paper). The only way words were communicated was by the human voice so that words could not be divorced from the speaker of the words. As you read the words on this page (black graphemes), your relationship with me is distant and cool. The result is that you evaluate the ideas I'm presenting divorced from my personality. You hold my ideas at arm's length, turning them this way and that, treating words as conveyors of disembodied ideational content. But in the oral world, words were encounters with persons. In a sense largely foreign to us, the original recipients of biblical epistles felt the presence or voice of the author, even when the message was delivered by an envoy. Thus, epistolary rhetoric gives full scope for the use of ethos as an available means of persuasion.

John emphasizes, for example, his role as "the elder" to warn his "children" of antichrists (1 John 2:18) and deceivers (2 John 7). In these letters, he certainly uses logic, but he also persuades the readers on the basis of his status and relationship with them. He loves them and wants only their good; he is wise and sees things they do not; he is responsible for them as their shepherd. Who would not submit to such a man? Even after two thousand years, John's ethos comes through the written word; how much more would it have come through the oral word as the recipients sat in John's "presence."

The final implication of epistles as oral rhetoric is that they speak concretely, not abstractly. The oral mind is conditioned to conceive of ideas as embodied and tied to experience, not detached or speculative. "As African pastor John Oginga put it, 'There is no idea without a head.' To oral communicators like him, . . . no idea exists in a free-floating abstract state. Every idea is attached to the person who uttered it and the context in which is was uttered."[36]

Thus, in the epistles, values and virtues are embodied. As Davis states, "One acts a certain way not because it is 'right' but in order to follow the example of a hero."[37] We are not surprised to hear Paul urge generosity by praising the Macedonians (2 Cor. 8:1–7), or to hear him use Timothy and Epaphroditus to illustrate the kind of men we should honor (Phil. 2:19–30). He even uses himself as a role model (Phil. 3:17), not necessarily a mark of conceit in an oral culture.[38] Furthermore, just as virtue was embodied, so was vice. It could be seen in persons like Hymenaeus and Philetus (2 Tim. 2:17) and "the heathen, who do not know God" (1 Thess. 4:5).

Even when the epistolographers do not use literal examples, they are likely to use figurative ones, the metaphors I described earlier. Timothy is to be a soldier, athlete, and farmer (2 Tim. 2:1–7). The tongue is a bit in the horse's mouth, a rudder, and a fire. Animals, birds, reptiles, and creatures of the sea have been tamed, but not the tongue. It is full of poison (James 3:3–8).

Epistles, then, offer several literary and rhetorical characteristics. They are one side of a conversation, addressing occasions with profound theology and a variety of forms. The challenge is to preach epistles faithfully in accord with their form.

Try This

Because of the affinity between the epistle and the sermon, most preachers feel at home in this genre. That's good. Traditional homiletics—with its emphasis on the importance of the central idea, logical flow with strong transitions, and illustrations—fits the genre like a die and casting. But we can do more. Because we are expository preachers, we can stretch a bit to preach epistles in other ways that are faithful to form as well as content. Just as Paul adapted Greco-Roman epistolary conventions, we are free to adapt modern Western

sermonic conventions in the service of the gospel. In fact, that may be
the primary homiletical response to the genre: flex. Not every sermon
must have three points. Not every sermon must be entirely monologue. Not every sermon must arrive on a homiletical conveyor belt,
turned and polished like the thousand sermons before it, stamped and
labeled like the thousand that will come after it. Epistles have more
variety than that. We should too. Some of the suggestions below will
reinforce what you are probably doing already, and some may fall off
your conveyor belt.

Flex (by Paying Attention to Mood and Form)

If your text percolates with "inexpressible and glorious joy" (1 Peter
1:8), don't turn it into a rebuke: "You don't have that joy do you?" If
your text is a beautiful poem like 1 Corinthians 13, don't turn it into a
lecture: "The word 'love' was of considerable importance to the author.
This is indicated by its frequent repetition in the chapter, appearing
nine times, and by its position, being mentioned first and last."

When preaching on Romans 11:33–36, a glorious hymn inserted
abruptly into the flow of Paul's argument, Craddock attempts to capture the mood. Commenting on his own sermon, he states,

> Since the text is a doxology, a burst of praise in the midst of
> a theological discourse, so is the sermon. To have converted
> the text into a syllogism, or a polemic, or an exhortation, or
> a defense of a proposition would have been a literary, herme-
> neutical, aesthetic, and practical violation without excuse.
> Let doxologies be shared doxologically, narratives narratively,
> polemics polemically, and parables parabolically. In other
> words, biblical preaching ought to be biblical.[39]

F. W. Boreham's sermon on 1 Timothy 3:16, another ancient hymn,
is itself a virtual hymn about Jesus' humanity and divinity. With a
series of contrasts, the preacher captures the antiphonal form of the
text and prompts a sense of wonder at the mystery of God become
flesh:

> He was born a tiny babe in Bethlehem—He was as *human* as
> that! Yet angels filled the air with heavenly song—He was

as *divine* as that! He rested, tired and thirsty, on Samaria's well—He was as *human* as that! Yet He told the woman whom He found there that she had but to ask and He would give her the water of everlasting life—He was as *divine* as that! He slept, exhausted, in the bow of a boat—He was as *human* as that! Yet, when He rose and rebuked the angry waves, the[y] crouched like dogs at His feet—He was as *divine* as that! He wept with the sisters beside the tomb at Bethany—He was as *human* as that! Yet, He cried "Lazarus come forth!" and he that was dead left the sepulchre—He was as *divine* as that![40]

If your text uses word pictures, why not use word pictures, or even real pictures, so beneficial in our media-saturated culture? When I preached on the "sealing of the Holy Spirit" (2 Cor. 1:22), I used visuals to illustrate the rich metaphor: a seal is a mark of ownership, as with the stamp of my name I place on my books; it's a mark of authenticity, as the imprint on the bottom of a handmade Longaberger basket; it's a symbol of authority, not to be tampered with, as an imprint made with a signet in wax. When I expounded James 4:14, "Your life is a mist," I lit a candle, let it burn for a few seconds, then snuffed it out. The congregation watched in silence as the smoke briefly billowed and then faded.

Many studies have confirmed what we know intuitively, that the combination of visual with aural communication greatly enhances impact and retention.

Method	Recall 3 hours later (%)	Recall 3 days later (%)
Telling alone	70	10
Showing alone	72	22
Showing and telling	85	65

Fig. 8.3. Communication Methods and Recall[41]

If your text is autobiographical, as in Paul's defense of his apostleship in 2 Corinthians, why not present the sermon as a first-person monologue? If your text is one side of a debate, as when Paul contends that he, not the Judaizers, preaches the real gospel (Gal. 1:11–24), why not present your sermon as a debate? I did this, role-playing both sides of the debate. From one lectern I presented the Judaizers' arguments, and from another lectern, Paul answered their charges. If your text soars, let the sermon soar. If it marches, let it march. Let's not cage wild things.

Use Dialogue

The use of dialogue is appropriate in sermons from genres such as proverb, with its pedagogical tone, and parable, which invites discussion. I've reserved extended discussion of dialogue, however, until this chapter because of the dialogic nature of epistle. As you know, an epistle is one-half of a conversation, so preachers who want to borrow the rhetorical dynamics of the genre should consider using dialogue.[42]

I hope this doesn't raise red flags. The form is certainly biblical. Jesus modeled it constantly, with the Gospels recording 153 questions Jesus asked for the purpose of teaching:[43] "Who do men say that I am?" "Why do you call me good?" "Which one was neighbor to this man?" Jesus knew the power of dialogue, leading learners inductively but surely to the truth. Paul also knew the power. Acts uses the word *dialegomai* ten times to describe Paul's preaching, especially his evangelistic ministry (e.g., Acts 17:2; 17:17; and 19:8). The Greek term means "to reason, discuss, or argue." Its sense is captured in the English loan word *dialogue.* Paul's love of dialogue may have come from his immersion in the Old Testament. Some entire books take the form of dialogue, such as Habakkuk and Malachi. All of this is to say that dialogue has ample precedent, and we should feel free to use it, especially when preaching from epistles.[44] We must get over the myth that monologue to mutes is the only way to preach. Communication does not occur simply by telling people what they ought to do.

Try some of these techniques:

- *Question and answer* (from audience to preacher). This can be done in a follow-up session after the sermon, as when Bill Hybels stands in front of the stage to converse with all who come. This can also be done during the sermon if your church culture permits it and if you make people comfortable enough to voice their thoughts.

- *Question and answer* (from preacher to audience). These questions will usually be "closed" rather than "open"—that is, they will call for simple and direct answers—but even these questions engage listeners. Ask them, "What is the Great Commission? Say it with me"; or "In your opinion, which character in the Bible experienced the greatest trials?" I often ask such questions, even when I'm a guest preacher in an unfamiliar church. Sometimes the people looked stunned and confused, but I put them at ease by telling them, "It's okay. I'm a professor. You're allowed to talk to me." Find your own way of helping people talk, because when they talk, they think, and when they think there's no telling what might happen!
- *Rhetorical questions.* These questions simulate two-way communication, and they can be as effective as real dialogue. Engage the people mentally with open questions such as, "What place does prayer have in your struggle with materialism?" Haddon W. Robinson has asked, "I know that you believe God loves you, but do you think that he likes you?"
- *Interview.* Follow your sermon by dialoguing in public with an expert or with someone who has personal experience. The listeners will experience this as vicarious dialogue.
- *Dialogic structure.* The outline of your sermon can be question and answer. This is an excellent form for teaching because it voices the people's thoughts. I have a doctrinal sermon on baptism, the main points being four questions:
  1. What does "baptism" mean?
  2. Who should be baptized?
  3. What does baptism do?
  4. How should baptism be done?
- *Feedforward.* This is like feedback, but it comes before the sermon. Use a question box or survey the congregation to discover exigencies you may be unaware of. Run your sermon past your spouse or a focus group to hear their questions. I've tried all of these and have been pleased with the results.
- *Dialogic delivery.* Remember that your tone of voice, facial expression, eyes, and posture tell the audience, "I like you, I value you, I am interested in your ideas," or "Your opinions are

not welcome here. Shut up and listen." Consider your use of the pulpit.[45] If you want to prompt dialogue, should you come out from behind it or even remove it? In communication studies, the use of physical space is called "proxemics"—how location and proximity send silent messages. I'm not advocating one particular style of delivery. Rather, I'm just raising consciousness that the nonverbal channel influences the communication event, and since we have freedom of form, we should use proxemics purposefully.

- *"Dictate" to an imaginary secretary.* This creative and unusual form can be quite engaging in the right situation. By using hypothetical dialogue between, say, Paul and Timothy, a wealth of background commentary and application can be woven into the sermon. I did this with a message from Philippians 1, combining three homiletical forms: verse-by-verse commenting, set within a general narrative structure, punctuated by hypothetical dialogue between Paul and Timothy.

  The beginning of the sermon sets the scene: Timothy has returned to Paul from Philippi. They embrace, and Timothy displays the letter and gift of money from the beloved church. The next day Paul dictates a reply (Phil. 1) to Timothy. As he dictates he expounds his own words, explaining allusions and other material to Timothy the scribe. The verse-by-verse commenting allowed me to teach the passage in depth; the narrative helped me keep attention and provide background information; and the dialogue helped listeners enter the scene and have their own questions answered as Paul instructed Timothy.

Use Examples

As with the suggestions above, this suggestion is good medicine for nearly any sermon. Review the sections in this book on using case studies when preaching proverbs and on using concrete language when preaching poetry. I promote the idea again here because epistles suggest it; perhaps they even demand it.

To communicate with relevance the way epistles do, come down the ladder of abstraction. At the top of the ladder are abstract concepts like *justice* and *courage*. At the bottom are concrete examples. We can't measure a pound of *justice* or hear the voice of *courage*, but when I embody them in the person of abolitionist William Wilberforce, I communicate with power. To be sure, a sermon always needs some abstract statements, but good communicators range up and down the ladder, spending much time near the bottom. So speak about the Auca Indians and Deacon Smith and last week's headline.

Use hypothetical examples, as well as real ones. I've found that these serve just as well if they're realistic. Here's a passage from my sermon on 1 Thessalonians 4:1–8, in which the big idea is "Avoid sexual immorality."

> Here's a student who is invited to the prom. She wants to go. It's the highlight of her senior year. She likes the fellow who asked her, but before she decides, she considers this command: "Avoid sexual immorality." She asks herself, "Will saying yes to the prom help me say yes to that command?"
>
> Here's a man traveling on business. He's alone in his motel room. As he opens the doors of the armoire he sees a sign above the TV, "The title of the movie you rent will not appear on your statement." He decides to leave the TV off.
>
> Here's a pastor who has a strict policy: he doesn't counsel women alone in his office. When women come to him, he refers them to his copastor, a woman, or he sets up a meeting when his wife can be present. Some of the deacons question the policy. They imply that he's shirking his duty, so to help them understand where he's coming from, he takes out his Bible and turns to 1 Thessalonians 4, "Avoid sexual immorality."

When you exhort your people to pray, follow James's example and use an example: Elijah prayed, and it worked (5:17)! When you exhort your people to be patient, tell them to be like the farmer who "waits for the land to yield its valuable crop" (v. 7). When they are sick, do not tell them to "seek means of spiritual support." Instead, tell them to "call the elders of the church to pray . . . and anoint . . . with oil in the name of the Lord" (v. 14). Good communicators, like James, spend a lot of time near the bottom of the ladder of abstraction.

Remember That You Are Speaking, Not Writing

Once again, this suggestion is tonic and elixir to any sermon, but I mention it here because epistles were oral/aural events. The following techniques are crucial when communicating for the ear.

Repetition and Restatement

Oral communication is ephemeral. It lasts as long as an echo. Once words are spoken, they are swept away in the stream of time, and lost elements can never be recovered. Arnold states, "Oral rhetoric is time-bound, occasion-bound, and bound to a particular human relationship previsioned, instigated, and sustained within a particular set of circumstances that pass into history as utterance ends."[46] So gifted preachers use purposeful redundancy to fix ideas in the minds of their listeners.[47] We must master this technique if we want to make our communication as clear as a full moon in a cloudless sky.

In any given sermon, there will be about eight or ten key sentences that the audience must grasp if they are to comprehend the unity of the message. These sentences are like the pegs of my tie rack. Take away the pegs and you have only a colorful jumble. With the pegs, the ties hang straight and can be examined. The ten to fifteen key sentences are, in order of importance, the big idea, the key movements (or Roman numerals), structural phrases like transitions, and any other ideas you'd like to emphasize such as the conclusion or summary statement of an illustration.

While repetition duplicates exact language, restatement uses similar language. Here's an example that uses both:

> Jesus says that worry is a sin. He says that fretting and fussing is wrong. Our Lord tells us that anxiety over things we cannot control is not his way, not the way of disciples. Jesus says that worry is a sin. Why would he say such a thing?

The rhetorical effect of such redundancy is like pausing a video for a moment so that a single frame becomes a still life. The listeners will not be aware that you have pushed pause, but the idea will form in their minds, and they will comment later how clear your sermons are. As Bryan Chapell states,

Restatement uses the principles of focus and redundancy to make a point clear. Until the preacher restates . . . the words of the text tend to blend together in listeners' minds. . . . Such repetition would seem simplistic and redundant in a written document, but experienced preachers recognize that *repetition is one of the most powerful oral communication tools.* Since listeners (unlike readers) cannot review what has come before, repetition underlines what a preacher wants most to impress on their minds.[48]

Simplicity

The Greek dialect of the New Testament epistles is *koinē*, or "common," the language of the marketplace. It is not a sacred or particularly learned language. To be sure, the epistles range in style from literary (1 Peter) to routine (1, 2, 3 John), but in general, their language is straightforward and simple. One way to reproduce that style today is with short sentences. The average length of an Elizabethan sentence was forty-five words. The average length of a Victorian sentence was twenty-nine. By 1946, the sentence had shrunk to twenty words.[49] Today, in the era of sound bites and slogans, I'm sure the number is even lower.

Prepare Orally

To preach for the ear, we should prepare orally, yet most of our preparation is done in solitude with only books and computers for companions. Both of those aids are, of course, indispensable, but if we never come up for air, we may drown ourselves—and later our listeners—in a sea of words. So in your preparation, for sure read books, but also speak.[50] Like Paul and his team preparing drafts, submit your ideas to cross-examination. Seek feedforward. Like Peter dictating to Silas, listen to your words and imagine others listening. Because few people have the ability to write in an oral style—with short sentences, purposeful redundancy, contractions, sound values, personal pronouns, and all the normal syntactical breakup of normal speech—I recommend extemporaneous, not manuscript, delivery.[51] Just talk like you do in animated conversation, using your own *koinē*.

Ground the Imperative in the Indicative

As already seen, this is how the epistles argue. Their behavioral standards are extremely high, yet they always provide the motive and power to reach those standards. The motive is the love of Christ, which compels us (2 Cor. 5:14), and the grace of God, which teaches us to say no to ungodliness (Titus 2:12). The power is the resurrection of Christ, ours by virtue of union with him (Eph. 1:19–20; Phil. 3:10–11).

So challenge your people to lay aside every weight that hinders and every sin that entangles. Urge them to pray without ceasing and to obey the governing authorities. Charge them to stop complaining and to start thanking. But in your urging, move them by the deep, deep love of Jesus—vast, unmeasured, boundless, and free.

Join Kerygma and Didache

The epistles recognize that our audiences are, as Jesus foretold, always mixed. Weeds grow up with wheat. In nearly every congregation, listeners range from calloused unregenerate pew-warmers to fully devoted followers of Christ. The way to reach the whole congregation is by both announcing the good news and explaining its implications—kerygma and didache.[52] As James Thompson observes,

> Paul's preaching reminds us that, in preaching to those who have already heard, we are not forced to say something new each week. In speaking to one congregation, we speak to a variety of listeners. Some—especially in a post-Christian society—have not heard the Christian message before; others have heard, but they did not hear well. Others will forget the Christian message if their memories are not refreshed. The appeal to the memory will connect the community with its foundational story, reaffirm the liturgical expression by which the community responds to God, and recall the community's moral norms.[53]

A primary but overlooked function of preaching is simply reminding. Preaching should help us remember who we are, where we came from, and where we're going. Thus, we "should not have an aversion to stating what has been said before."[54]

Watch Your Ethos

This is one more homiletical truism, applicable when preaching any genre, but it deserves special mention here because the epistles highlight the speaker-audience relationship. Because preaching is truth through personality, we must not pretend that sermons are stand-alone events. Rather, our words and actions outside the pulpit greatly determine the efficacy of our words inside the pulpit. Aristotle reminds us of what we know intuitively: ethos may be "the most effective means of persuasion," and we "believe good men more fully and more readily than others."[55]

One of the most powerful ways to apply ethos is through judicious use of self-disclosure.[56] Immediately I see red flags rising, so let me assure you that I do not advocate turning the pulpit into a confessional booth or psychiatrist's couch. I know that self-disclosure can be done poorly, hindering the proclamation of the Word. But when it is done well, when it is done as Paul and the other epistolographers have done it, self-disclosure incarnates the truth, motivates action, creates a culture of authenticity, and glues the hearts of speaker and listener. Listen to Paul's words to the Thessalonians:

> You know how we lived among you for your sake. You became imitators of us and of the Lord. (1 Thess. 1:5–6)

> You know we never used flattery, nor did we put on a mask to cover up greed. . . . As apostles of Christ we could have been a burden to you, but we were gentle among you, like a mother caring for her little children. We loved you so much that we were delighted to share with you not only the gospel of God but our lives as well, because you had become so dear to us. Surely you remember, brothers, our toil and hardship; we worked night and day in order not to be a burden to anyone. . . . You are witnesses, and so is God, of how holy, righteous and blameless we were among you who believed. For you know that we dealt with each of you as a father deals with his own children, encouraging, comforting and urging you to live lives worthy of God. (1 Thess. 2:5–12)

To preach like the epistles preach, try judicious self-disclosure. And above all, watch your ethos. I wish I could give you a few tips for improving ethos. I suppose such tips would tell us to smile, be good listeners, and remember people's names, but our goal is higher than simply trying to win friends and influence people. We're trying to honor God and love the listeners in his stead. The only way to do that is by doing that. No amount of technique will substitute. But when the love of Christ compels us, foundations quake.

Chapter Checklist

- ❑ Exegete and respond to mood. Don't cage wild things.
- ❑ If your text uses word pictures, use word pictures.
- ❑ Or use real pictures. Light a candle.
- ❑ If your text is autobiography, tell a story.
- ❑ If your text is a debate, debate.
- ❑ If your text is a doxology, doxologize.
- ❑ Pay attention to ideas, paragraphs, and logical transitions.
- ❑ Use dialogue.
- ❑ Try question and answer.
- ❑ Try feedforward.
- ❑ Try feedback.
- ❑ Put the listeners at ease so they'll talk.
- ❑ Interview.
- ❑ Use rhetorical questions.
- ❑ Use question and answer for your main points.
- ❑ "Dictate" to a secretary.
- ❑ Use examples, lots of examples—real or hypothetical.
- ❑ When you climb the ladder of abstraction, come down quickly.
- ❑ Repeat, repeat, repeat.
- ❑ Use purposeful redundancy on eight to ten key statements in every sermon.
- ❑ Remember that you are not delivering an essay. Use *koinē*.
- ❑ Prepare out loud (as well as silently).
- ❑ Ground the imperative in the indicative.

❑   Join kerygma and didache, the gospel and catechesis.
❑   Try appropriate self-disclosure.
❑   Watch your ethos.

9

Apocalyptic Literature

VISION AND VICTORY

I confess *Apocalyptic Studies* are fittest for those Raised Souls, whose *Heart Strings* are made of a Little *Nicer* Clay than other men's.

> —Cotton Mather, quoted in McGinn, "Revelation"

Many good and faithful preachers rank preaching on apocalyptic texts alongside handling serpents; they have heard that people do it, but they have no desire to come anywhere near them.

> —Larry Paul Jones and Jerry L. Sumney,
> *Preaching Apocalyptic Texts*

[Revelation is] a curious record of the visions of a drug addict.

> —George Bernard Shaw, quoted in McGinn, "Revelation"

Logicians may reason about abstractions. But the great mass
of men must have images.

—Thomas Macaulay, quoted in Wiersbe,
Preaching and Teaching with Imagination

We come now to the most challenging genre to be addressed in
this book. I've saved for last the literature of visions and voices,
symbols and signs, demons and dragons, horns and toes—apocalyptic
literature.

Like a maze of high hedges with gold at the center, this genre does
not easily yield its treasure. The history of interpretation shows us
that humility is needed when handling the literature of visions. Many
predictions have shipwrecked on the reefs of hubris, as when John
Napier, in *A Pleine Discovery of the Whole Revelation of St. John*,
correlated the defeat of the Spanish Armada in 1588 with a "precise
a timetable [which] could be uncovered in Revelation, even down to
the determination that the seventh and last age of history had begun
in 1541 and would last until 1786."[1] Jerome might have been right in
saying that "Revelation has as many mysteries as it does words."[2]

Preaching this genre may feel like handling snakes, but let's remember that God has given it a major place in the canon. There is,
in fact, more of this genre than two of the other genres we've looked
at—proverb and parable. That alone is sufficient reason to preach it.
I hope that after reading this current chapter, though, you'll be motivated to preach it not only from a sense of duty but also with a sense
of joy and confidence, because the central message of apocalyptic
graphically encapsulates the faith: the Devil hates us, but he loses;
God loves us, and he wins; it isn't even close; it is permanent. That
will preach!

What *Is* Apocalyptic Literature?

The term *apocalyptic* is not used in the Bible to denote a genre,
although the Greek word *apocalypsis* is used to mean an "uncover-
ing, disclosure, revelation" (e.g., Rev. 1:1). As a term denoting a genre,
apocalyptic first appeared in biblical criticism at the beginning of the
nineteenth century to refer to visionary eschatological literature,

but the genre itself existed from the Babylonian exile (586 B.C.) to the destruction of Jerusalem (A.D. 135). That is, the form of literature with the characteristics I describe in this chapter existed for about seven hundred years, even though it did not have a name. Many of the books of the Pseudepigrapha and Apocrypha, the books of the intertestamental period, belong to this genre. To my knowledge, we have no instances of it today.

Apocalyptic is highly symbolic literature with a rough narrative framework designed to exhort and console oppressed believers by disclosing a transcendent vision of the future that God has prepared, which will overturn present earthly circumstances.[3] Apocalyptic is a hybrid genre, partaking of narrative, poetry, and prophecy. As narrative, it has rudiments of plot, character, setting, and point of view. As poetry, it uses figurative language (especially symbolism) and heightened emotion. As prophecy, it is eschatological and hortatory, but it differs from prophecy in its view of the world. Prophecy tells its recipients that if they repent, disaster can be avoided. The world is redeemable. Apocalyptic tells the faithful that the world is too far gone. Only the impending cataclysm will set things right, so hang on! As the noncanonical apocalypse, 2 Baruch states, "The pitcher is near to the cistern, and the ship to the port, and the course of the journey to the city, and life to its consummation" (85:10).

In the Bible, the following passages are often categorized as apocalyptic: Isaiah 24–27; Daniel 7–12; Zechariah 1–6; 9–14; Matthew 24–25; Mark 13; Luke 21; 1 Thessalonians 4:13–18; 2 Thessalonians 2:1–12; 2 Peter 3:1–13; and the book of Revelation. Because Revelation is the longest and "purest" apocalyptic literature in the Bible, most examples in this present chapter come from that book.

How the Text Communicates, What the Text Does

This unusual form warrants examination. Why did persuaders use it? If the president of the United States used smoke signals and tom-toms to communicate the State of the Union Address, we would ask why such a form. If you preached next week using grand opera, we would ask why. Why did the divine Author use surrealistic visions to encourage the oppressed?

The answer can be found in Lloyd Bitzer's concept of the "rhetorical situation," which is composed of an *exigence,* a need marked by urgency; an *audience* who is capable of removing or altering the exigence when skillful discourse moves them; and *constraints* or materials the persuader can use to move the audience.[4] Just as epistles are occasional documents, designed to address specific exigencies, so are apocalypses. They arise from urgent circumstances and alter those circumstances with rhetorical content and form.

Here's how it works: apocalyptic addresses believers who are in crisis. They are being persecuted by a corrupt society, and it appears that God is not in control. Apocalyptic literature arises from frightened, dispossessed people who yet hope in God. Daniel and his friends were strangers in a strange land. In Zechariah, little Israel was bullied by the heathen nations roundabout. The seven churches of Revelation cringed before Domitian (A.D. 81–96) who, toward the end of his reign, demanded to be addressed as "our lord and god." Earlier in the century, Jews had been exempted from Caesar-worship, but as Christianity became distinct from Judaism, no longer holding its meetings in synagogues, Rome's iron fist fell. Along with physical and social crisis came spiritual crisis. The old question arose: if God is just, powerful, and loving, why do the innocent suffer? Society is corrupt and hostile, and God seems blind. The rhetorical situation of crisis invites a "fitting response."

Apocalyptic provides that response by announcing a competing interpretation of reality, helping the audience change perspective. This kind of literature pulls back the curtain to reveal that God is certainly not blind; he sees his children surrounded by wolves. He is certainly not unfeeling; his pity and wrath gather like floodwaters. He is certainly not powerless; the shaft of judgment is ready to spring from his bow. This genre provides another instance of the rhetoric of transcendence, which we saw in the previous chapter on epistles. The writers lift the hearts of the faithful to visualize the world with eyes of faith. As Long states, "Apocalypse does not eliminate the suffering or wipe out the possibility of death. Indeed, Christian apocalyptic literature is quite candid about the fact that the saints will suffer and die. It does, however, make possible the shout, 'O death, where is your sting?'"[5]

Paul's words to the Thessalonians illustrate the rhetorical situation of apocalyptic:

> We boast about your perseverance and faith in all the persecutions and trials you are enduring. . . . God is just: He will pay back trouble to those who trouble you and give relief to those who are troubled. . . . This will happen when the Lord Jesus is revealed from heaven in blazing fire with his powerful angels. He will punish those who do not know God and do not obey the gospel of our Lord Jesus. They will be punished with everlasting destruction . . . on the day he comes to be glorified. (2 Thess. 1:4–10)

This genre consoles the persecuted faithful, but it also chastises the prosperous unfaithful. In the words of the old saw, it comforts the afflicted and afflicts the comfortable. Some recipients of apocalyptic literature, you see, had become friends with the world. Through compromise and accommodation, they gained a measure of security, but it was false security, for they had put their faith in jeopardy. Fear of man overshadowed fear of God. In this situation, apocalyptic literature's fitting response is a jangling wake-up call, opening eyes to the peril of compromise, lifting the curtain to reveal that the world, which looks so alluring, is a whore, aligned with the accuser of the brethren.

The seven churches of Revelation may say of themselves, "'I am rich; I have acquired wealth and do not need a thing.' But [they] do not realize that [they] are wretched, pitiful, poor, blind and naked" (3:17). God has "a few things against" them because they "tolerate that woman Jezebel" (2:14, 20). They need to repent or God "will fight against them with the sword of [his] mouth" (2:16). They are to "come out of her, . . . so that [they] will not share in her sins, so that [they] will not receive any of her plagues" (18:4). Thus, the "pastoral function of apocalyptic is twofold. It is both to bolster the faithful in their precarious situation and to hold their feet to the fire."[6]

This genre seeks to change the hearers' perspective by means of dazzling language. This kind of language goes beyond a merely referential function of language, whereby we talk about things, people, or ideas. Instead, apocalyptic uses the "expressive" and "evocative" functions of language. Like poetry it reveals and elicits attitudes and feelings. Ryken puts it this way:

> Visionary literature, with its arresting strangeness, breaks through our normal way of thinking and shocks us into seeing that things are not as they appear. Visionary writing attacks our ingrained patterns of deep-level thought in an effort to convince us of such things as that the world will not always continue as it now is, that there is something drastically wrong with the status quo, or that reality cannot be confined to the physical world that we perceive with our senses. Visionary literature is not cozy fireside reading. It gives us the shock treatment.[7]

Visionary literature expands vision. The first-century believers who heard Revelation may have walked the sturdy Roman roads and relaxed in the security of the Pax Romana, but all was not as it seemed. Those believers were actually looking at a beast who sought to tear and grind them with power granted by a dragon. Revelation reveals this, rouses emotion, and elicits response. With its symbolic trumpet blasts, hideous hybrid animals, and dire curses, Revelation conjures dread, disgust, resentment, and pity, as when a modern reader or movie-goer sees Aslan at the stone table. The harpies, ogres, wolves, and hags, symbols of evil, bind, shave, and torture the great lion, symbol of the Lord Christ. Our hearts are moved to see the truth represented through fiction, and we understand better what actually happened at the Place of the Skull. Apocalyptic literature may be surrealistic, but it captures the "deep magic" better than almost any other form of literature. Apocalyptic captures that magic perhaps *because* it is surrealistic.

The surrealism of apocalyptic functions through three literary-rhetorical features: its dualism, symbols, and hybridized narrative.

Dualism

After reading no more than a chapter of apocalyptic literature, you see dramatic dualism. This is not the dualism of Eastern religions with their yin and yang—two sides of one reality—but the dualism of an old-fashioned Western—the good guys and the bad guys. In Revelation,

the beast that comes up from the Abyss attacks and kills the two wit-
nesses (11:7), and the "mother of prostitutes" is "drunk with blood of
the saints" (17:5–6). In Daniel, the beast, "terrifying and frightening
and very powerful" with "large iron teeth; . . . crushed and devoured
its victims" (7:7). In Zechariah, Satan stands to accuse Joshua before
the angel of the Lord (3:1–2).

This agonistic mind-set is foreign to most of us. We drink from
the fountain of tolerance fed by the stream of relativism, and while
tolerance is certainly a virtue, Allan Bloom feels that it has trumped
traditional values like purity, humility, truthfulness, industry, and
courage.[8] Tolerance may be the last universal virtue of our society. As a
result, when we read of the judgment of God on Babylon, with plagues,
torment, doom, weeping, smoke, and ruin (Rev. 18:8–19), we squirm.
Our squirming turns to flinching when we read, "Hallelujah! . . . He
has condemned the great prostitute who has corrupted the earth by
her adulteries. He has avenged on her the blood of his servants. . . .
The smoke from her goes up for ever and ever" (19:1–3).

The rhetorical function of in-your-face dualism relates to tension.
For the faithful—the first group apocalyptic addresses—tension is reduced. For the second group, the lukewarm, tension is generated. The
first group already feels the tension of theodicy, but then they receive
assurance that God has not forgotten them. This reduces their doubts
and invigorates their faith. They can hold on, because they will soon
be rewarded. For the lukewarm, tension rises, because they see reality
in a new light. They must let go of their worldliness, for they now
recognize that they are in league with the synagogue of Satan (Rev.
3:9). In this literature, there is no place to hide. You are either for God
or against him. You wear either white robes or the mark of the beast.
This world will give way to the next, but your fate is determined by
how you act in this world. Your name is written either in the Book of
Life or in the books of judgment. The faithful may sigh in lament, but
they also sigh in relief, while the lukewarm sigh in regret.

Imagine that you are a devoted Christ-follower in the age of Domitian. You are harassed and marginalized, perhaps even imprisoned
and tortured. Why? Because you love Jesus and have offered yourself
to him as a living sacrifice. Imagine your feelings of vindication and
relief when the curtain rises to show you God, called Faithful and True,

who will soon strike down the nations (Rev. 19:11, 15). The tension of theodicy is resolved, and you determine to endure to the end. On the other hand, imagine that you are a "secret disciple" in that age. You hide your faith, spin the truth, and compromise to avoid persecution. Imagine discovering that you have crawled into bed with an ancient serpent and that the cowardly will take their place in the fiery lake of burning sulfur (Rev. 20:2; 21:8). Your tension rises. Dualism is a fitting response to the two audiences. It persuades both.

Symbols

The second rhetorical feature of the genre may be its most obvious—an overwhelming use of visionary symbols. When the curtain rises, we enter a mystical world of visions replete with symbols. This is not the world of the epistles with their flow of logic, or the worlds of narrative and parable with their feet planted in the soil of everyday life. It is closer to the world of poetry, but this is poetry amplified, at least in its use of symbols.

The symbols can be animate beings such as a red dragon (Rev. 12:3–4), living creatures with "six wings . . . covered with eyes all around" (Rev. 4:8), a warrior on a red horse (Rev. 6:4), or two flying women with wings like those of a stork (Zech. 5:9). The symbols can also be inanimate objects such as candlesticks, bowls, trumpets, swords, and crowns. In the world of visions, these inanimate objects can themselves become actors as when the earth helps the fleeing woman by swallowing a pursuing torrent (Rev. 12:13–16) and when the ram's horn grows to knock down stars (Dan. 8:9–10). Numbers are also highly symbolic in this genre. In Revelation there are seven letters, seals, trumpets, plagues, angels, and bowls. The foundation of the city is made of twelve precious stones, and twelve thousand servants of God from each tribe of Israel are "sealed."

Most of these symbols were familiar to Middle Eastern readers, just as modern Americans would recognize a political cartoon of a donkey and elephant playing tug-of-war. But even with the advantage of cultural immersion, Daniel cried, "I heard, but I did not understand" (Dan. 12:8).

The storehouse of symbols comes not only from Middle Eastern culture, but even more dominantly, in the case of Revelation, from the Old Testament. In particular, Ezekiel, Daniel, Zechariah, and parts of Isaiah contribute to the storehouse of symbols. Metzger has figured that of the 404 verses in Revelation, 278 contain one or more allusions to the Old Testament: "John had so thoroughly pondered the Old Testament that when it came to recording the import of his visions of God and of heaven, he expressed himself by using phrases borrowed from the prophets of Israel."[9]

Why would a biblical writer use potentially hermetic symbols? What is to be gained from fantasy that cannot be gained from realism? Visionary symbols are more than stylistic choices; they are powerful rhetoric.

Like a riddle, this literature prompts contemplation. Apocalyptic is parable-like where one thing stands for another. While some of the symbols may make us feel "like an illiterate with a crossword puzzle,"[10] many of the symbols are universal and accessible to modern readers. We know that thunder is the voice of God in judgment, that the lion is the king, and that the harvest is the time of judgment. We can be thankful that five symbols are interpreted for us in Revelation:

Text	Picture	Meaning
1:20	Seven stars	Angels of the seven churches (granted, this itself needs interpretation)
1:20	Seven lampstands	Churches
12:9	Dragon	Satan
17:9	Dragon	Hills on which the woman sits (again, this calls for interpretation)
17:18	Woman	The great city (Rome)

Fig. 9.1. Interpreted Symbols in Revelation

With visionary symbols, authors engage our minds and emotions as we discern what is meant by the grotesque beasts and shining stars. Think of how a modern symbol, the skull and crossbones, functions: we comprehend that the bottle contains poison, and we fear to touch it. The communication occurs in a flash, but that flash illumines what might take a hundred words of realistic prose to convey.

Narrative-like

The third aspect of form to consider is apocalyptic as hybridized narrative. Apocalyptic possesses the rudiments of narrative. There is character, plot, setting, and point of view, but those elements are modified. We encounter not only God, angels, and saints but also bizarre characters, such as composite beasts and the forces of nature. Similarly, some aspects of plot are "normal" as the story moves from conflict through resolution, but as Ryken observes, the plot of visions possesses "kaleidoscopic structure" with "brief units, always shifting and never in focus for very long."[11] Visionary plot is like a pageant or parade with jugglers, floats, animals, and bands passing before us without lingering. The procession moves forward steadily from beginning to end, but the flow is also fragmented and somewhat cyclical. Display follows display, band follows band, float follows float, and the impact overwhelms us. The settings of apocalyptic increase its fragmented yet overwhelming quality, for they transport us from earth to heaven, mountains to sea, and we stand before the holy city descending. In terms of point of view, apocalyptic uses panorama, the long shot. Epic, not lyric, captures the mood and mode of this genre. This is the grand opera of the Bible.

The rhetorical functions of hybridized narrative are similar to those of standard historical narrative. Plot creates suspense, but here we wonder *how* and *when* God will win, not *if* he will win. Character creates identification and dissociation as we side with the white-robed martyrs and recoil from the dragon and demons. Setting and point of view lift the curtain to show us the big picture. When you read apocalyptic, hang onto your hat. You're in for a wild ride.

How can we take our listeners on that ride? Some preachers feel that the ride spins too fast, climbs too high, and plunges too low. Of all the genres covered in this volume, apocalyptic may be the least amenable to preaching, but surely we can find some ways to reproduce its vision-expanding and faith-heartening rhetorical effects.

Try This

During Exegesis, Use Imagination

Because this genre communicates through images, we must imagine. We must engage the "willing suspension of disbelief."[12] This phase from the Romantic poet Coleridge reminds us that the authors of surrealistic literature purposefully use images and symbols to capture reality and produce results, so we must yield to their strategy by voluntarily entering the kaleidoscopic vision. If we do not do so, we reduce the effect God intends. You may want to review the suggestions in chapter 3 on the exegesis of poetry and the use of imagination.

Surface Tensions

Apocalyptic is a literature of extremes, and this produces tension. Don't shy away from it. For the faithful who are oppressed, surfacing tension is easy. They already feel it. The tension between what is and what should be and will be is daily experience. For the lukewarm, unaware of or hardened to their sin, surfacing tension is more difficult, but "the apocalyptic preacher states without equivocation that the surrounding culture not only is *not* Christian but also is *against* Christianity. . . . The apocalyptic preacher wants the church to have absolute certainty about whose it is and what it is, and, in order to meet this end, does not shirk from labeling the prevailing culture as dangerous, oppressive, and sinful."[13] Show the listeners, for example, how advertising and consumerism desiccate our souls. Show them Christian martyrdom in sub-Saharan Africa. Awaken them to the evils of pornography. My church sponsored a "Purity Weekend" to enlighten our minds and stir our hearts. To pull back the curtain on reality, we brought in experts who taught us how pervasive pornography is in America and how it ruins lives. It is not a "victimless crime." An apocalyptic preacher would say that it comes from the pit of hell.

Apocalyptic also raises tension on that most vexing of all issues: suffering. Why is human experience a long and winding road, sometimes smooth and pleasant, but other times broken and steep under the baking sun?[14] Here is a passage from one of my sermons that helps people connect emotionally to the conundrum:

> A few years ago I was teaching at a Bible College in the North-west. One of our students named Mark died in his sleep. His roommate tried to waken him in the morning, but he was dead. Mark was popular on campus. He was a spiritual leader and member of the basketball team. The whole campus mourned, and a few days after his death we held a memorial service. As I entered the service through the double doors into the back of the large auditorium, two groups of students were positioned on either side of me. On one side a group of basketball play-ers and cheerleaders were weeping and holding each other; and on the other side, not ten yards away, another group was laughing, hugging, and giving each other "high fives." One of their circle had just gotten engaged, and she was displaying her diamond ring.
>
> There I stood in the middle, suspended between grief and joy. It struck me that that experience was a parable of the human condition. Grief and joy. Pain and pleasure. Mingled toil, with peace and rest.

Besides the questions that arise from suffering, apocalyptic raises tension over other issues as well, especially for those who drink from the fountain of relativism and tolerance. For them, issues like the wrath of God and the everlasting punishment of the wicked brings discomfort. In his sermon on the seven bowls of the wrath of God (Rev. 16:1), Thomas Long addresses that discomfort:

> A faculty colleague and I were being introduced recently to a visitor to our campus, a minister from a small town in a neighboring state. "This is Bob so-and-so," we were told. "He's the pastor of the Lutheran Church of God's Love. . . ." [M]y colleague leaned over to me and whispered with a wink, "I wonder if across the street from Bob there's the Presbyterian Church of God's Wrath."
>
> That quip evoked a gentle chuckle; the very idea that the Presbyterians, or anybody else for that matter, would name a

church after something as somber as the wrath of God seemed laughable. . . .

[T]he wrath of God is not simply an unlikely name for a congregation, it is also a theological *idea* we probably feel that we can just as well do without. Jonathan Edwards may have roused and galvanized his hearers with his severe sermonic descriptions, . . . but today such dire messages seem fit only for the ragged tents of mill-village revivals and the hysterical Sunday-morning screamers who inhabit the right hand of the AM radio dial. . . .

What, then, can we make of this scene in the 15th and 16th chapters of Revelation? It is an account of the wrath of God in all of its sea-boiling, thunder-rolling, earthquake-rattling fury. Here we see the very kitchens of heaven serving up brimming bowlfuls of God's wrath to be poured by angels upon the face of the earth. And what we read is not just a *description* of the wrath of God; it is a hand-clapping, hallelujah-shouting *celebration* of its coming.[15]

Through inductive arrangement, Long sustains the tension deep into the message until finally he explains the doctrine:

The problem with our understanding of the wrath of God is not that we have made too much of it, but precisely that we have made too little of it. Or, to be more exact, we have conceived of God's wrath in ways that are too small, too intrapersonal, too psychological. We have pictured a wrathful God as a larger version of a wrathful *us*. . . . To the contrary, . . . God's wrath is that expression of God's love that will not allow victims to suffer everlastingly without hope, that will not forever abandon the helpless. . . . So if you hunger for righteousness, hear this word of the wrath of God poured out on all evil. If you cry out in hopeless pain, hear this word of the wrath of God poured out on all foul disease and cruelty. If you cannot read the newspaper without weeping for children who are abused and war widows who grieve without consolation and people who starve with knots of grass in their stomachs, hear this word of the wrath of God poured out upon injustice. And pray—pray to God that it's true. "Lord God the Almighty! Just and true are thy ways."[16]

Biblical apocalyptic, God's inspired Word, tackles hard questions. A faithful preacher does too, and biblical apocalyptic texts give us the venue and model for doing it.

Offer Hope

Tension is not an end in itself. In biblical literature it is a means, addressing rhetorically the situation of the recipients, to produce hope and praise. In apocalyptic, we "see through what is going on to what is really going on."[17] We see angels, mentioned sixty-seven times in Revelation. We see God's sovereignty, justice, and compassion. We see Jesus crucified, resurrected, and enthroned. The book of Revelation, in the midst of wrath and fire, sings sixteen hymns. In apocalyptic, weeping endures for a night, but joy comes in the morning. Although we see oppression and violence, we have been to the mountaintop, and we also see God's victory. You undoubtedly catch my allusion to Martin Luther King's final speech. He was in Memphis to support a strike by garbage workers. In that mundane setting, King pulled back the curtain so his audience could see a transcendent reality:

> The world is all messed up. The nation is sick. Trouble is in the land. Confusion is all around. . . . But I know, somehow, that only when it is dark enough, can you see the stars. And I see God working in this period of the twentieth century in a way that men, in some strange way, are responding—something is happening in our world.
>
> Well, I don't know what will happen now. We've got some difficult days ahead. But it doesn't matter with me now. Because I've been to the mountaintop. And I don't mind. Like anybody, I would like to live a long life. Longevity has its place. But I'm not concerned about that now. I just want to do God's will. And He's allowed me to go up to the mountain. And I've looked over. And I've seen the promised land. I may not get there with you. But I want you to know tonight, that we, as a

people will get to the promised land. And I'm happy, tonight.
I'm not worried about anything. I'm not fearing any man. Mine
eyes have seen the glory of the coming of the Lord.[18]

Apocalyptic is not a genre of logical argumentation; it is a genre of
eschatological vision. In Revelation, John witnesses, describes, and
reports (rather than argues), and in doing so, gives the readers hope.
In the same way, we can describe the glorious future to help listeners
see themselves in God's unfolding drama. Hope is raised and faith
is renewed when preachers announce that the Lamb who was slain
will be enthroned in the New Jerusalem. Help your listeners catch
that vision.

In Revelation we finally see Jesus unveiled: "the ruler of the kings
of the earth" (1:5), the "Alpha and the Omega" (1:8), "with a voice
like the sound of rushing waters" and his face "like the sun shining
in all its brilliance" (1:15–16). He stands on Mount Zion and sits on
clouds (14:1, 14). He wears a crown of gold (14:14) and rides a white
horse (19:11). He wields a sharp sword and rules with an iron scepter
(19:15). The Jesus we meet in Revelation, with his robe dipped in blood
(19:13), has come a long way from the Jesus we met in the Gospels,
where his glory occasionally flashed from behind the curtain. To be
sure, he is still the Lamb of God, but now the Lamb is also "the Lion
of the tribe of Judah, the Root of David, [and he] has triumphed" (5:5).
"Thousands upon thousands, and ten thousand times ten thousand"
angels sing in a loud voice, "Worthy is the Lamb, who was slain, to
receive power and wealth and wisdom and strength and honor and
glory and praise!" (5:12). He wipes away the tears of the faithful,
spreads his tent over them, and leads them to springs of living water
(7:17), but for the wicked, the hour of his wrath arrives as the kingdom
of this world becomes the kingdom of the Christ (11:18, 15). Ask God
to help you catch this vision, and ask him to help you convey it to
the listeners.

Require Discipleship

Apocalyptic dares us to be "identifiably different."[19] Preachers
should too. Apocalyptic rejects moral relativism. Preachers should too.
Preachers announce that history is predetermined, and the Lamb *will*
win, so we must decide now which side to follow. Our behavior now

determines our reward later. Preachers must not strip apocalyptic of this stringent and no-nonsense worldview. We are in a war.

> The Prince of Darkness grim,
> We trembled not for him;
> . . . .
> The body they may kill:
> God's truth abideth still,
> His kingdom is forever.[20]

Let us remind our listeners that "discipleship goes the way of the Cross, that God has not promised us freedom *from* suffering and death, but triumph *through* it."[21] Craddock puts it this way: "Churches which try to have Easter without Good Friday are symbolized by the plastic lily: It cannot die and hence it cannot bloom. Resurrection cannot be celebrated if no one is dead."[22]

Emphasizing discipleship means that we will deliberately preach on issues of culture and lifestyle. When the text warrants it, we will address with candor topics such as homosexuality. We will, of course, strive to understand our culture and its misunderstandings of the gospel, but we will not fail to emphasize the indissoluble relationship between works and faith. Revelation knows no dichotomy, so do not soften its message by downplaying obedience. In your ardor to maintain the cornerstone of the Reformation—justification by faith—do not embarrassedly mute the trumpet that calls us to repent and return to the works of our first love (Rev. 2:4–5). Notice how the messages to the seven churches of Revelation emphasize deeds (e.g., 2:2, 19; 3:1–2, 8, 15); then go and do likewise, for he will repay each of us, preachers included, according to our deeds (Rev. 2:23). Remember that requiring discipleship of others means that we first require it of ourselves. We are to be examples of speech, life, love, faith, and purity (1 Tim. 4:12).

Preach Big Themes in Big Ways

This suggestion is implicit in the previous points, but let me make it explicit here. Apocalyptic is not about hangnails. It is about the end of the age. Apocalyptic preachers will preach on big themes with forms congruous to that scope. We present God as *pantocratōr* ("ruler of all," see Rev. 1:8 and eight other times in the book).

One way to re-create the panoramic quality of visionary literature is with panoramic illustrations. In these sermons, suffering will not be presented as a fever and stuffy nose; it is Richard Wurmbrand tortured for his faith and imprisoned for fourteen years by the communists in Romania.[23] Save your illustrations of failing grades and traffic jams for another sermon from another genre because "they do not have Golgotha written on them; they are not analogies of cross bearing."[24] Let your people know that martyrdom is raging even in the twenty-first century. The government of North Korea, estimated to be the greatest persecutor of Christians today, is in league with the dragon.[25]

Another way to re-create grand scope is by using a slightly elevated style. Leave chattiness behind: "So, the other day, I was, you know, walking down the street, and I kinda tripped or something. I don't know. But anyway . . ." Instead, mirror this style: "Woe to the earth and the sea, because the devil has gone down to you! He is filled with fury, because he knows that his time is short" (Rev. 12:12). Of course, we have to be careful with such a lofty style; effective communicators do not call attention to themselves.

Listen to Allan Boesak speak about the evils of apartheid:

> The South African government's time is up. That we know. We are seeing the beginning of the end. But that does not stop them. Still they invent new weapons, which they display with great pride at the Arms Fair in Brazil. Still they announce newer, more refined anti-riot equipment: barbed wire fences falling out of the back of a truck like deadly vomit out of the mouth of a dragon. Still they legislate new powers for the Minister for Law and Order. . . . But oppressed people know what that means: the respectability of "law" for wanton destruction, unending streams of arrests, besieged townships, invaded communities and homes, fear-ridden streets, thousands of policemen and soldiers, grim and wild-eyed as they feverishly grip their guns—in a word: legalized murder.[26]

Another way to preach big themes in big ways is through the nonverbal channel. Although I haven't emphasized delivery in this book, remember that we communicate not only through what we say but also how we say it. Every genre and passage suggests a nonverbal mode, and apocalyptic is no exception. The literature of visions will call for your highest level of energy. I hesitate to suggest anything more specific than that because adopting a particular tone or manner, without an accompanying deeply felt conviction, will be perceived as it is, a sham. But when your heart soars by the vision of the Lamb who is also a Lion, let it soar!

Work in Concert with the Entire Service

You may remember this suggestion from chapter 3 on biblical poetry, but it is worth repeating here because apocalyptic, Revelation in particular, abounds in singing, confession, and prayer. Perhaps you could intersperse the sermon with other liturgical elements, thus mirroring the pageantlike quality of the text. In any case, the sermon need not be, indeed it should not be (since it cannot be), the only vehicle of worship in any given service. Craddock says it well:

> Let the whole liturgy bring Revelation to the congregation. The sermon is not alone the bearer of the Word of God. Anthems drawn either in spirit or in text from Revelation, hymns inspired by the Apocalypse, and healthy portions of Revelation well read but without comment do not simply serve as context for a sermon but, on their own, can say and do what the prophet John sought to say and do. In fact, given the highly liturgical nature of Revelation, this final suggestion to the preacher is weightier than an option; the book itself demands it.[27]

Group reading of apocalyptic Scripture is especially effective. Capture the antiphonal and climactic spirit of a doxology like Revelation 7:9–12. Here is an arrangement of that text for four readers and a choir:

READER 1:   I looked and there before me was a great multitude that no one could count, from every nation,

READER 2:   tribe,

READER 3:	people
READER 4:	and language,
READER 1:	standing before the throne and in front of the Lamb.
READER 2:	They were wearing white robes
READER 4:	and were holding palm branches in their hands.
READERS 1–4:	And they cried out in a loud voice:
CHOIR:	"Salvation belongs to our God, who sits on the throne, and to the Lamb."
READER 2:	All the angels were standing around the throne
READER 4:	and around the elders
READER 1:	and the four living creatures.
READER 3:	They fell down on their faces before the throne and worshiped God, saying:
READER 1:	"Amen!
READERS 1 & 4:	Praise and glory
READERS 1–4:	and wisdom and thanks and honor
READERS 1–4, TENORS, & ALTOS:	and power and strength
READERS 1–4 & CHOIR:	be to our God for ever and ever. Amen!"

Robert Coleman's book, *The Songs of Heaven*, is about the poetry in Revelation. Coleman's book models how to weave hymns and other music into the flow of a sermon. When preaching on the song of the martyrs, Coleman uses this moving World War I story. A group of soldiers had a final party before being shipped out, and at the end of the evening, the following events took place:

> A young officer rose to express appreciation for the entertainment. His remarks were cheerful, full of charm and humor. Then, suddenly as an afterthought before sitting down, . . . he said, "We are soon crossing to France. . . . and very possibly, of course, to death. Will any one of our friends here tell us how to die?" There was a stunned silence. It seemed that no one knew what to say. Finally, one of the singers who had taken part in the program . . . began to sing the great aria from Mendelssohn's *Elijah*:

> > O rest in the Lord, wait patiently for Him,
> > And He shall give thee thy heart's desires;
> > Commit they way unto Him, and trust in Him;
> > And fret not thyself because of evil-doers.
> > O rest in the Lord, wait patiently for Him,
> > And He shall give thee thy heart's desires.[28]

The story is moving when the words of the aria are simply quoted, but perhaps the aria could also be sung in conjunction with the sermon.

Following your sermon with a great hymn like Anne R. Cousin's "The Sands of Time Are Sinking" will inspire faith, hope, and endurance.

> The sands of time are sinking, the dawn of
> > Heaven breaks;
> The summer morn I've sighed for—the fair,
> > sweet morn awakes:
> Dark, dark hath been the midnight, but dayspring
> > is at hand,
> And glory, glory dwelleth in Immanuel's land.

I've wrestled on towards Heaven, against storm,
>   wind, and tide,
Now, like a weary traveler that leaneth on his guide,
Amid the shades of evening, while sinks life's
>   lingering sand,
I hail the glory dawning from Immanuel's land.

The king there in His beauty, without a veil is seen:
It were a well-spent journey, though seven deaths
>   lay between.
The Lamb with His fair army doth on Mount
>   Zion stand,
And glory, glory dwelleth in Immanuel's land.

The Bride eyes not her garment but her dear
>   Bridegroom's face;
I will not gaze at glory but on my King of grace.
Not at the crown He giveth but on His pierced hand;
The Lamb is all the glory of Immanuel's land.[29]

If you have gifted artists in your congregation, why not unleash them when preaching from apocalyptic? Discover the joy that comes from working with a team, and discover the power of proclaiming visionary literature with symbol and song.

Chapter Checklist

- ❑ Use imagination during exegesis.
- ❑ Challenge the lukewarm to repent.
- ❑ Offer hope.
- ❑ Describe, and report God's glorious future.
- ❑ Witness to God's faithfulness.
- ❑ Pull back the curtain.
- ❑ Describe apocalyptic parallels in our world (such as persecution in North Korea).
- ❑ Tackle hard questions (such as the problem of evil).
- ❑ Tackle hard issues (such as homosexuality).

- ❑ Tackle hard doctrines (such as wrath, judgment, and hell).
- ❑ Require discipleship.
- ❑ Require it of yourself, too.
- ❑ Don't preach about hangnails.
- ❑ Present God as pantocrator.
- ❑ Use panoramic illustrations.
- ❑ Use a slightly elevated style (but be yourself).
- ❑ Use slightly elevated delivery (but be yourself).
- ❑ Let your heart soar.
- ❑ Work in concert with the whole service, using music, creeds, readings, and prayers.
- ❑ Intersperse the sermon with liturgical elements.
- ❑ Try group readings.
- ❑ Unleash the artists.

Epilogue

The form of a text is not simply the husk surrounding the seed; it is the way authors manage their relationship with readers. Much of the authors' rhetorical intentions lie in the forms they choose. Poetry embodies and elicits emotion with its images, hyperbole, and self-disclosure. Narrative prompts identification as we walk in the shoes of biblical characters. Proverbs, brief and witty summaries of wisdom, require us to contemplate their meaning. Parables spark meditation by comparing the kingdom of God with the city of man. Epistles carry us along in a flow of logic, but they can also carry us up to the heights of delight with doxology and prayer. Apocalypse parades a dazzling pageant before the mind's eye to remind us that God wins, and it isn't even close.

Expository preachers pay attention to form. We consider not only *what* God has communicated but also *how* he has communicated. And because there is no such thing as *the* sermon form, we have freedom to use various communication methods to unleash the rhetorical force of the text. Just as our Lord and the prophets used rational and affective modes of communication—discourse and narrative, word and image, monologue and dialogue, prose and poetry—so can we. Give it a try! Your hearers may bless you, and your preaching may take on new life. Yield to the ideas and form of the text, and expect God to transform the listeners through the living and enduring Word of God (1 Peter 1:23), which is able to make us wise for salvation (2 Tim. 3:15).

Notes

Introduction: 9.5 Theses

1. Stott, *Between Two Worlds,* 137–38.

2. Samuel Butler contended that "definitions are a kind of scratching and generally leave a sore place more sore than it was before." Quoted in Wiersbe, *Preaching and Teaching with Imagination,* 378.

3. The following are a sample of definitions from homiletics texts:

   "An oral interpretation of God's Word to his gathered people, through which he speaks and acts upon their lives." E. Achtemeier, *Creative Preaching,* 86.

   "A message whose structure and thought are derived from a biblical text, that covers the scope of the text, and that explains the features and context of the text in order to disclose the enduring principles for faithful thinking, living, and worship intended by the Spirit, who inspired the text." Chapell, *Christ-Centered Preaching,* 31.

   "Expository preaching is 'Bible-centered preaching.' That is, it is handling the text 'in such a way that its real and essential meaning as it existed in the mind of the particular Biblical writer and as it exists in the light of the over-all context of Scripture is made plain and applied to the present-day needs of the hearers.'" Merrill Unger, *Principles of Expository Preaching* (Grand Rapids: Zondervan, 1955), 33, quoted in Greidanus, *Modern Preacher and Ancient Text,* 11.

"Preaching is theology coming through a man who is on fire."
Lloyd-Jones, *Preaching and Preachers,* 97.

"The following minimal elements identify expository
preaching:
1. The message finds its sole source in Scripture.
2. The message is extracted from Scripture through careful
   exegesis.
3. The message preparation correctly interprets Scripture in its
   normal sense and its context.
4. The message clearly explains the original God-intended meaning
   of Scripture.
5. The message applies the Scriptural meaning for today."
Mayhue, "Rediscovering Expository Preaching," 12–13.

"Expository preaching is the communication of a biblical concept,
derived from and transmitted through a historical, grammatical,
and literary study of a passage in its context, which the Holy Spirit
first applies to the personality and experience of the preacher, then
through the preacher, applies to the hearers." Robinson, *Biblical
Preaching,* 21.

"A form of human verbal communication that involves the organized explanation and application of biblical truth, presented in a
manner that is reasonable, imaginative, and intrinsic to the text."
Wiersbe, *Preaching and Teaching with Imagination,* 304–5.

4. Isocrates, *Antidosis* 2:239.
5. Quoted in E. Achtemeier, *Creative Preaching,* 37.
6. Piper, *The Supremacy of God in Preaching.*
7. For an interesting study of sermon form from a secular source,
    see McGee, "Thematic Reduplication." Having examined a broad
    sample of Christian sermons, McGee concludes that the distin-
    guishing characteristic of such rhetoric is simply "re-duplication"
    of the Bible's message. The content of preaching is already given.
    Heralds simply recommunicate that content.
8. Davies, quoted in Rice, "Shaping Sermons," 102.
9. Howard, *Creativity in Preaching,* 29.
10. When introducing form-sensitive sermons to a congregation,
    Mike Graves recommends the following tips: (1) educate the con-
    gregation about preaching through pastoral articles, small group

settings, and informal times—teach them that sermon form is culturally conditioned; (2) ease the congregation into new styles; (3) prepare the people ahead of time—for example, announce, "Next week's sermon will be different." *Sermon as Symphony*, 32–33.

11. E. Achtemeier, *Creative Preaching*, 11.

12. Howard, *Creativity in Preaching*, 36.

13. Spurgeon, *Lectures to My Students*, 136.

14. These figures are from a 1999 survey conducted by *Christianity Today* of 206 pastors and 2,223 church attenders nationwide. The published results of the survey can be found in Eric Reed, "The Preaching Report Card," *Leadership* 20, no. 3 (Summer 1999): 82–87. The statistics about number of sermons preached do not appear in the article, but can be found in the unpublished "Executive Summary," p. 3, prepared by the independent tabulating firm of Davison, Dietsch, and McCarthy.

Chapter 1: The Great Communicator

1. Calvin, *Institutes*, 1:61, 72, 341, quoted in Wiersbe, *Preaching and Teaching with Imagination*, 33.

2. "Amazon Research Expedition," Smithsonian National Zoological Park Web site, July 22–30, 2006, Smithsonian Institute, September 13, 2006 http://nationalzoo.si.edu/ActivitiesAndEvents/Travel/Eco-Explorers/Amazon.cfm>.

3. Hopkins, "Pied Beauty," 298–99.

4. R. L. Lewis and G. Lewis, *Inductive Preaching*, 147.

5. R. L. Lewis and G. Lewis, *Learning to Preach Like Jesus*, 29.

6. Ibid.

7. Ryken, *How to Read*, 9.

8. C. S. Lewis, *They Asked for a Paper: Papers and Addresses*, 49.

9. Ramm, *Protestant Biblical Interpretation*, 113.

10. This analogy is suggested by Graves, *Sermon as Symphony*, 9.

11. Burke, *Counter-Statement*, 31.

12. Ibid., 124.

13. One of Burke's examples is the murder scene from *Macbeth*. The gruesome quality of the scene creates a desire for comic relief, which Shakespeare, the expert rhetorician, supplies in the next

scene with buffoonery. Burke states, "If the author managed over a certain number of his pages to produce a feeling of sultriness, or oppression, in the reader, this would unconsciously awaken in the reader the desire for a cold, fresh northwind." Ibid., 39.

14. Burke, *A Rhetoric of Motives*, 58.
15. Ibid.
16. At this point, you may be thinking that rhetoric—those persuasive techniques designed to move an audience—is disreputable. It makes its home on Madison Avenue—or worse, Berlin in the 1930s and 1940s. This view of rhetoric is ancient and understandable, finding its great advocate in Plato. The early church also questioned the ethics of rhetoric, debating whether rhetorical training should be used for preaching because so many scoundrels used it for selfish ends. Augustine's answer is the perspective I follow in this book: rhetoric is a neutral instrument that serves the intentions of the user. Like a sharp knife in the hands of a murderer or a surgeon, it can be used to kill or to save. Churchill used it for good; Hitler for evil. See Augustine, *On Christian Doctrine*, bk. 4.
17. Craddock, *Preaching*, 173–74.
18. Lubeck, "Dusting Off the Old Testament," 33.

Chapter 2: Speaking Bantu to Channel Surfers

1. Quoted in Griffin, *Clive Staples Lewis*, 401.
2. C. S. Lewis, *God in the Dock*, 94.
3. Lloyd-Jones, *Christian Soldier*, 290–91.
4. Ong, *Presence of the Word*. Ong uses the term "sensorium" throughout the book. My reference is to the concept, not a particular passage. If you need a passage, use pp. 1–16.
5. Quicke, "Applying God's Word," 11.
6. Crouch, "Visualcy," 62.
7. RealVision, "Facts and Figures," http://www.tvturnoff.org/images/facts&figures/factsheets/FactsFigs.pdf.
8. Revere, *Boston Gazette*, quoted in Postman, *Amusing Ourselves to Death*, 59.
9. Guinness, *Fit Bodies, Fat Minds*, 81; Postman, *Amusing Ourselves to Death*, 126.
10. Lovejoy, "But I Did Such Good Exposition," 29–30.

11. Crouch, "Visualcy," 62. See also, Mitchell, *Visually Speaking*.
12. These facts and statements regarding the HCSB Light Speed Bible and the 100-Minute Bible are reported in Aucion, "The Need for Speed," D5.
13. Henry David Thoreau, *Walden* (Boston: Houghton Mifflin, 1957), 36, quoted in Postman, *Amusing Ourselves to Death*, 65.
14. For dozens of examples of society's shift toward participation, see Miller, *Experiential Storytelling*, 11–26.
15. Mayor, "Video Games," 19.
16. Quote taken from newsletter on *Preaching Now*, http://www.preachingnow.com. April 21, 2005.
17. Buttrick, *A Captive Voice*, 67.
18. Gregory, *Seven Laws of Teaching*, 37.
19. Ibid., 44.
20. For summaries of learning theories applied to preaching, see Cochran, "The Ear of the Listener," 7–10; Geoffrey Stevenson, "Conceptions of Learning in the Preacher's Progress"; Tornfelt, "Preaching and Learning Styles"; and Zink-Sawyer, "The Word Purely Preached and Heard," 342–57.
21. Myers and Briggs, *Gifts Differing*.
22. Hermann, "The Creative Brain," 10–16.
23. Gardner, *Multiple Intelligences*.
24. Tannen, *You Just Don't Understand*.
25. Pascal, *Pensées*, 277.
26. Macneile Dixon, *The Human Situation* (Darby, PA: Darby Books, republished 1981), quoted in Wiersbe, *Teaching and Preaching with Imagination*, 24.
27. Edwards, *First-Person Biblical Preaching*, 17.

Chapter 3: Psalms: The Sound of Music

1. Ciardi, *How Does a Poem Mean?*
2. Cummings, "in Just—," 347.
3. Alter, "Ancient Hebrew Poetry," 612.
4. C. S. Lewis, *Reflections on the Psalms*, 3.
5. See Alter, "Ancient Hebrew Poetry," 612. For the most thorough book-length study of parallelism, see Kugel, *Idea of Biblical Poetry*.
6. Alter, "Ancient Hebrew Poetry," 616.

7. Long, *Preaching and the Literary Forms,* 49.

8. Alter, "Ancient Hebrew Poetry," 615.

9. Ibid., 621.

10. Alter, "Ancient Hebrew Poetry," 620.

11. For definitions and examples of these and other poetic devices, see Soulen, *Handbook of Biblical Criticism.*

12. Ryken, *How to Read,* 17.

13. Ibid., 95.

14. Robert Frost, "Education in Poetry," in *The Norton Reader,* ed. Arthur M. Eastman (New York: W. W. Norton, 1980), 412, quoted in Ryken, *How to Read,* 92.

15. To go deep on figures of speech, consult Caird, *Language and Imagery of the Bible,* and Bullinger's monumental work, *Figures of Speech Used in the Bible.*

16. Fee and Stuart, *How to Read the Bible,* 171.

17. Ryken, *Literature of the Bible,* 124.

18. Henry Ward Beecher, n.p., quoted in Larsen, *Anatomy of a Sermon,* 108.

19. Besides the suggestions in this chapter on developing imagination, see Wiersbe, *Preaching and Teaching with Imagination,* 289–300.

20. Troeger, *Imagining a Sermon,* 53–58.

21. Robert Frost, n.p., quoted in Troeger, *Imagining a Sermon,* 70. Originally quoted in Lawrence Thompson and R. H. Winnick, *Robert Frost: A Biography* (New York: Holt, Rinehart and Winston, 1981), 172.

22. Ralph Waldo Emerson, n.p., quoted in Larsen, *Anatomy of Preaching,* 71.

23. Quintilian, *The Institutes of Oratory,* 427.

24. See Arthurs, "No Notes," 600–606.

25. C. H. Spurgeon, *Spurgeon's Sermons,* 20 vols. (New York: Funk and Wagnalls, n.d.), quoted in E. Achtemeier, *Creative Preaching,* 101. See also Adams, *Sense Appeal in the Sermons of Spurgeon.* Adams provides documentation on Spurgeon's sermons on pp. 20, 24, 25, 26.

26. Wiersbe, *Preaching and Teaching with Imagination,* 235.

27. Arthurs, "Long and Winding Road," *Preaching Today,* http://www.preachingtoday.com/27499.

28. Larsen, *Anatomy of Preaching,* 70.
29. From "Amen," 1981, sermon audio and transcript, Moody Public Relations.
30. For an illuminating commentary on Ecclesiastes, composed almost entirely of photographs, see Short, *A Time to Be Born.*
31. See Arthurs, "The Place of Pathos in Preaching."
32. Aggertt and Bowen, *Communicative Reading,* 146–50; and Lee and Gura, *Oral Interpretation,* 126–29.
33. T. Harwood Pattison, n.p., quoted in Larsen, *Anatomy of Preaching,* 82.

Chapter 4: Narrative, Part 1: Everyone Loves a Story

1. Barthes, *Image, Music, Text,* 79.
2. Crites, "The Narrative Quality of Experience," 291.
3. See Middleton and Walsh, *Truth Is Stranger Than It Used to Be,* 64.
4. Peters and Waterman, *In Search of Excellence,* 61. See also Simmon, *The Story Factor.*
5. E-mail correspondence with the author, November 28, 2001.
6. Cicero, *Brutus/Orator,* section 69, trans. G. L. Hendrickson and H. M. Hubbell, Loeb Classical Library (Cambridge, MA: Harvard University Press, 1952), referenced in Kennedy, *Classical Rhetoric,* 100.
7. Schaeffer, *The God Who Is There,* 16–65.
8. Kaiser, *Toward an Exegetical Theology,* 205.
9. C. S. Lewis, *An Experiment in Criticism,* 82–83.
10. Wright, "An Experiment in Biblical Criticism," 251–52.
11. C. S. Lewis, *They Asked for a Paper,* 49.
12. Auerbach, *Mimesis,* 14–15.
13. Sailhamer, *Introduction to Old Testament Theology,* 46–47.
14. Leading proponents of historical-redemptive preaching are Greidanus, *Preaching Christ from the Old Testament;* Goldsworthy, *Preaching the Whole Bible as Christian Scripture;* and Chapell, *Christ-Centered Preaching.* For historical survey of the debate over the purpose of Old Testament narrative, see Greidanus, *Sola Scriptura.*
15. Goldingay, "Preaching on the Stories in Scripture," 106.

16. On speech act theory, see Searle, *Speech Acts*; and Austin, *How to Do Things with Words.*

17. Fee and Stuart, *How to Read,* 74–75.

18. Goldingay, "Preaching on the Stories in Scripture," 106–9.

19. Pratt, *He Gave Us Stories,* 124.

20. Aristotle, *Rhetoric and the Poetics,* 1450a.

21. Ryken, "And It Came to Pass," 132.

22. Bar-Efrat, *Narrative Art in the Bible,* 93.

23. This partial list is from Ryken, *How to Read,* summarized in Mathewson, *Art of Preaching Old Testament Narrative,* 48. See also Alter, *Art of Biblical Narrative,* 47–62.

24. Burke, *Counter-Statement,* 124.

25. Bar-Efrat, *Narrative Art in the Bible,* 148.

26. Pratt, *He Gave Us Stories,* 138–39.

27. Berlin, *Poetics and Interpretation,* 36.

28. Borden, "Is There Really One Big Idea?" 75.

29. Mathewson, *Art of Preaching Old Testament Narrative,* 70.

30. Ryken, *How to Read,* 43.

31. Pratt, *He Gave Us Stories,* 147.

32. Kirkwood, "Storytelling and Self-Confrontation," 68.

33. Frye, *Great Code*; Sailhamer, *Introduction to Old Testament Theology.*

34. Frye, *Anatomy of Criticism,* 316.

35. Mathewson, *Art of Preaching Old Testament Narrative,* 73–74.

36. Pratt, *He Gave Us Stories,* 120.

37. Based on a figure from Camery-Hoggatt, *Speaking of God,* 55.

38. For major studies of irony in biblical narrative, see Good, *Irony in the Old Testament*; Duke, *Irony in the Fourth Gospel*; Camery-Hoggatt, *Irony in Mark's Gospel*; and Dawsey, *Lukan Voice.*

39. Booth, *Rhetoric of Irony,* 22.

40. Booth, "Pleasures and Pitfalls of Irony," 2.

41. These four steps are expounded in Booth, *Rhetoric of Irony,* 12–14.

42. Sunukjian, "A Night in Persia." See also, Carson, "Four Ironies of the Cross."

Chapter 5: Narrative, Part 2: Everyone Loves a Story

1. Sunukjian, "A Night in Persia."

2. Flannery O'Connor, n.p., quoted in Sally and Robert Fitzgerald, eds., *Mystery and Manners* (New York: Farrar, Straus and Giroux, 1957), 76, quoted in Ryken, *How to Read,* 59.
3. H. G. Davis, *Design for Preaching,* 157.
4. Aurandt, *Paul Harvey's The Rest of the Story;* idem, *More of Paul Harvey's The Rest of the Story;* and idem, *Destiny.*
5. Borden, "Is There Really One Big Idea?" 78.
6. Chapell, *Christ-Centered Preaching,* 48–55.
7. Haddon W. Robinson, unpublished lectures.
8. Borden, "Is There Really One Big Idea?" 79.
9. Greidanus, *Modern Preacher and the Ancient Text,* 225.
10. Robinson, *Biblical Preaching,* 130.
11. Since its inception in the 1930s, Monroe's "Motivated Sequence" has become standard doctrine in the field of public speaking. The textbook where it first appeared has become a classic, selling more than one million copies and evolving through more than a dozen editions. See McKerrow, Gronbeck, Ehninger, and Monroe, *Principles and Types of Speech Communication.*
12. Lowry, *Homiletical Plot.*
13. See Lowry, *How to Preach a Parable.* See also Goldingay, "Preaching on the Stories in Scripture," who draws principles of narrative organization from the structures of the four Gospels.
14. Corey, "Nehemiah 5," from an unpublished sermon.
15. Ibid.
16. Robinson, "Mid-Life Crisis," from an unpublished sermon.
17. Ibid.
18. For more information, see Arthurs, "Performing the Story."
19. Sunukjian, "A Night in Persia," 71.
20. H. W. Robinson, "Broken Heart of David Jessison," from an unpublished sermon.
21. E. K. Bailey, "My Name IS Hosea," *Preaching Today,* from an audio sermon; see bibliography.
22. Sunukjian, "The Cripple's Story," 156.
23. Buttry, *First-Person Preaching,* 48. For other sources on first-person preaching, see: H. W. Robinson and T. W. Robinson, *It's All in How You Tell It;* Rogne, *Tell It Like It Was;* R. Bailey and

Blevins, *Dramatic Monologues*; and Brown, *Dramatic Narrative in Preaching.*

24. Adams, "Sense Appeal and Storytelling," 350.
25. I have found the following helpful when studying cultural background: *The Zondervan Pictorial Encyclopedia of the Bible,* vols. 1–5 (Grand Rapids: Zondervan, 1975); *The Illustrated Bible Dictionary,* vols. 1–3 (Wheaton, IL: Tyndale, 1980).
26. Ayer, "The Art of Effective Preaching," 38.
27. Three excellent sources on using narrative with wisdom and balance are Chapell, *Using Illustrations to Preach with Power,* 177–92; Lischer, "The Limits of Story"; and J. W. Thompson, *Preaching Like Paul,* 1–19.
28. Lowry, *How to Preach a Parable,* 139.
29. Craddock, *Overhearing the Gospel,* 74.
30. Crites, "Narrative Quality of Experience," 308.
31. See Arthurs and Gurevich, "Theological and Rhetorical Perspectives," 215–26.
32. In Simmon, *Story Factor,* 7.

Chapter 6: Parables: Hidden Land Mines

1. R. L. Lewis and G. Lewis, *Learning to Preach Like Jesus,* 86.
2. More than fifteen hundred rabbinic parables survive from the years following Christ, but only 324 of them date before A.D. 200, and only three before Christ. They seem to have been used rarely in Jesus' time, although the fact that Jesus' listeners recognized the genre may suggest otherwise. Perhaps they were used in synagogue sermons that have not survived. (In contrast to the apparent scarcity in the Near East during the time of Christ, Aristotle's discussion of parables suggests that the genre was common in the Greek culture of the fourth century B.C. [see *Rhetoric and the Poetics,* 1393b]). In any case, Jesus' use of parables differed from the rabbis'. They used forms like fables and used them to illumine Torah, but Jesus spoke on his own authority, announcing the kingdom. Also, only Jesus seems to have used the "sample parable," a story without analogy that sets an example of good or bad behavior like the Good Samaritan and the Rich Fool. See Newman, "Rabbinic Parables."

3. Some others are the "Song of the Vineyard" (Isa. 5), "Israel as Bride" (Jer. 2), the "Marred Vessel" (Jer. 18), the "Trees and Thornbush" (Judg. 9), and the "Eagles and Vine" (Ezek. 17:2–10).

4. Buttrick, *Speaking Parables,* 4.

5. Wiersbe, *Preaching and Teaching with Imagination,* 164.

6. Dodd, *The Parables of the Kingdom,* 5.

7. Ryken, *How to Read,* 202.

8. K. Bailey, *Finding the Lost;* idem, *Jacob and the Prodigal;* and idem, *Poet and Peasant.*

9. K. Bailey, *Finding the Lost,* 61–92.

10. Ibid., 97–107.

11. K. Bailey, *Finding the Lost,* 100–101, gives details of first-century homes. For example, in the area of Capernaum the floors were made of black basalt. A small silver coin in the crack between black paving stones in a dim room would indeed be hard to find.

12. Kirkwood, "Storytelling and Self-Confrontation," 60.

13. Wilder, *Jesus' Parables and the War of Myths,* 92.

14. Ryken, Wilhoit, and Longmann, eds., "Parable," 623, n.a.

15. Horne, *Jesus—the Master Teacher,* 86.

16. Kirkwood, "Storytelling and Self-Confrontation," 68.

17. Wilder, *Early Christian Rhetoric,* 74.

18. Long, *Preaching and the Literary Forms,* 95–98. See also Snodgrass, "Parable," 591–93.

19. Summarized in Fee and Stuart, *How to Read,* 124.

20. Long, *Preaching and the Literary Forms,* 97.

21. Aristotle, *Rhetoric and the Poetics,* 1393b. See also, Kennedy, *Classical Rhetoric,* 70.

22. Buttrick, *Speaking Parables,* 18–19.

23. D. Stevenson, *In the Biblical Preacher's Workshop,* 107.

24. Barton, *Millionaire and the Scrublady,* 27–28.

25. Blomberg, *Preaching the Parables,* 22.

26. Graves, *Sermon as Symphony,* 51–52. See also Yancey who contemporizes the Prodigal Son in a similar way: *What's So Amazing About Grace?* 49–51.

27. Wells, "Prayer," 1465.

28. J. L. Bailey and Vander Broek, *Literary Forms in the New Testament,* 110.

29. For a hermeneutical and homiletical defense of point-making, see Blomberg's works (*Interpreting the Parables; Preaching the Parables*). He argues that individual parables can be placed on a spectrum of allegory by locating a dominant lesson (or point) with each main character. Most of Jesus' parables have three main characters, so a story like the Prodigal Son teaches something in regard to the natures of (1) repentance (the prodigal), (2) love (the father), and (3) jealousy (the brother) ("Preaching the Parables: Preserving Three Main Points," 31–41).

30. Dodd, *The Parables of the Kingdom,* 5.

31. Graves, *Sermon as Symphony,* 50.

32. From *Entertainment Weekly,* quoted by Rob Bell, "Subversive Preaching," from a live lecture given over satellite link sponsored by *Christianity Today* and *Leadership.*

33. TeSelle, *Speaking in Parables,* 23.

34. In Tolstoy, *Kreutzer Sonata and Other Short Stories,* 1–14. Subsequent quotations in the following paragraphs come from this short story.

35. Adapted from Faro, "Stories Near and Stories Far." Originally a folktale from Israel. Subsequent quotes in the following paragraphs come from Faro's parable.

36. Larsen, *Telling the Old, Old Story,* 152.

37. Adapted from Lucado, "It's Not Up to You," preached 6/23/04 at Willow Creek Comunity Church, South Barrington, IL. Available from http://www.willowcreek.org/seeds.asp # CO0426.

38. Blomberg, *Preaching the Parables,* 217.

39. Buttrick, *Speaking Parables,* 26.

40. Buzzell's entire sermon is in H. W. Robinson and T. W. Robinson, *It's All In How You Tell It,* 99–105.

41. Buttrick, *Speaking Parables,* 19.

Chapter 7: Proverbs: Short Sentences Long Remembered

1. Crossan, *In Fragments,* 330–41.

2. Guershoon, *Certain Aspects of Russian Proverbs,* 15.

3. Cervantes, n.p., quoted in Crenshaw, *Old Testament Wisdom,* 56.

4. Crenshaw, *Old Testament Wisdom,* 56.

5. Lord John Russell, n.p., quoted in Meider and Dundes, *The Wisdom of Many,* 61.

6. Garrett, *Proverbs,* 29.

7. Crenshaw, *Old Testament Wisdom,* 56.

8. Tolkien, *Fellowship of the Ring,* 193.

9. Norrick, *How Proverbs Mean,* 29.

10. Ibid., 28.

11. Aristotle, *Rhetoric and the Poetics,* 1376a–b, 77b.

12. Ong, *Presence of the Word,* 79–87. See also Aristotle, *Rhetoric and the Poetics,* 1394a–95b.

13. For a similar example see Kirshenblatt-Gimblett, "Toward a Theory of Proverb Meaning,"113–14.

14. Garrett, *Proverbs,* 46–47. See also Waltke, "Old Testament Interpretation," 41–52.

15. Ryken, *How to Read,* 127.

16. Norrick, *How Proverbs Mean,* 20–21.

17. Long, *Preaching and the Literary Forms,* 58.

18. Dundes, *Study of Folklore,* 279.

19. Arthurs, "Proverbs in Inspirational Literature." The entire article demonstrates how inspirational speakers show a fondness for proverbs. See specifically pages 1–16.

20. McKenzie, *Preaching Proverbs,* 35.

21. Ryken, *How to Read,* 124.

22. Ricoeur, "Biblical Hermeneutics," 113.

23. Ryken, *How to Read,* 124.

24. Long, *Preaching and the Literary Forms,* 55.

25. Barbara Herrnstein Smith, *Poetic Closure: A Study of How Poems End* (Chicago: University of Chicago Press, 1968), 208, quoted in Ryken, *How to Read,* 122.

26. Alter, *The Art of Biblical Poetry,* 164.

27. Long, *Preaching and the Literary Forms,* 59–60.

28. Fee and Stuart, *How to Read the Bible,* 196.

29. Williams, "Proverbs and Ecclesiastes," 273. This entire article is an outstanding explication of the aural qualities of Hebrew proverbs. See also, J. M. Thompson, *Form and Function of Proverbs,* 63–66.

30. Kirshenblatt-Gimblett, "Toward a Theory of Proverb Meaning," 111.

31. See Tannen, *You Just Don't Understand,* who characterizes women's communication as "rapport talk," and men's communication as "report talk," 74–95. Tannen also demonstrates that women use overlapping dialogue more than men do. To men this feels like an interruption, but for women, it is jointly constructing an utterance, 188–215.
32. McKenzie, *Preaching Proverbs,* 30.
33. Tisdale, *Preaching as Local Theology and Folk Art.*
34. Long, *Preaching and the Literary Forms,* 59.
35. Garrett, *Proverbs,* 29.
36. See Garrett, *Proverbs,* and the magnum opus of Old Testament scholar Bruce K. Waltke, *The Book of Proverbs, Chapters 1–14;* and idem, *The Book of Proverbs, Chapters 15–31.*
37. Ryken, *How to Read,* 128.
38. McKenzie, *Preaching Proverbs,* xvii–xviii.
39. Ibid., 20.
40. Long, *Preaching and the Literary Forms,* 65.
41. Summarized from Tan, *The Joy Luck Club,* 170–73. Subsequent quotations in the following paragraph come from Tan's novel.
42. See Willhite, "A Bullet Versus Buckshot," 20.
43. Piper, "Battling the Unbelief of Bitterness," from an audio sermon published by *Preaching Today* (see bibliography). Although this sermon is not an exposition of Proverbs, Piper displays the skills of a wordsmith and sage.
44. McKenzie, *Preaching Proverbs,* 94.
45. Ibid.
46. Ibid., 127–28.
47. Ibid., 80–81.
48. Ibid., 88.
49. MacDonald, *Gifts of the Christ Child,* 27.
50. Aristotle, *Rhetoric and the Poetics,* 1356b, 1394a.
51. Bitzer, "Aristotle's Enthymeme Revisited," 408.
52. For more help in using dialogue, see Arthurs and Gurevich, "Proclamation Through Conversation," 35–45.
53. See R. R. Howard, "Gender and Point of View." Howard surveyed a typical issue of *Pulpit Digest* and found that twenty out of twenty-

four illustrations were androcentric. Two presented women in active roles and two presented both men and women as principle actors.

Chapter 8: Epistles: One Side of a Conversation

1. The nonepistolary books are the Gospels, Acts, and Revelation. Hebrews and 1 John are hybrids, sharing many characteristics of epistles, but omitting an address to specific groups. Acts and Revelation contain embedded epistles as do some Old Testament historical books. See 2 Samuel 11:14–15; 1 Kings 21:8–10; 2 Kings 5:4–6; 10:1–3; Ezra 4:9–12, 17–22; and 6:3–12.
2. One communication scholar has even discerned the influence of Paul's epistles on Martin Luther King Jr.'s "Letter from Birmingham Jail." See Snow, "Martin Luther King's 'Letter from Birmingham Jail.'"
3. Booth, *Rhetoric of Fiction*, 441.
4. Deissmann, *Light from the Ancient East*, 227–44.
5. Osborne, *Hermeneutical Spiral*, 254.
6. Heikki Koskenniemi, *Studien zur Idee und Phraseologie des griechischen Briefes bis 440 n.Chr.* (Helsinki: Soumalaien Tiedeakatemie, 1956), quoted in Doty, *Letters in Primitive Christianity*, 11–12.
7. Du Toit, *New Testament Milieu*, 496–97.
8. Arnold, "Oral Rhetoric, Rhetoric, and Literature," 66–67.
9. Wilder, *Early Christian Rhetoric*, 15–16, 54–55.
10. In his handbook on epistolary style, Demetrius states that Artemon, the editor of Aristotle's letters, likened the letter to one-half of a dialogue (Demetrius, *On Style*, sec. 223, quoted in White, *Light from Ancient Letters*, 190).
11. Fee and Stuart, *How to Read the Bible*, 46.
12. Allen Verhey, *The Great Reversal: Ethics and the New Testament* (Grand Rapids: Eerdmans, 1984), 104–5; quoted in Greidanus, *Modern Preacher and the Ancient Text*, 326.
13. See Burke, *Rhetoric of Motives*, 76; Weaver, *Ethics of Rhetoric*, 55–58, 86–87; and Stewart, Smith, and Denton, *Persuasion and Social Movements*, 175–77.
14. See Thompson, *Preaching Like Paul*, 127–41.
15. Doty, *Letters in Primitive Christianity*, 12.

16. Aune, *New Testament in Its Literary Environment,* 162–64, 183; and O'Brien, "Letters, Letter Forms," 551–52.

17. Stirewalt, *Paul the Letter Writer,* 25.

18. P. Achtemeier, "Omne Verbum Sonat," 22.

19. Richards, *Paul and First-Century Letter Writing,* 132.

20. Bryant, "Rhetoric: Its Functions and Its Scope," 413.

21. Aune, *New Testament in Its Literary Environment,* 159; and Doty, *Letters in Primitive Christianity,* 49–63.

22. Greidanus, *Modern Preacher and the Ancient Text,* 323.

23. See Ong, *Presence of the Word,* 17–110.

24. Davids, *Epistle of James,* 50.

25. Ellis, *Making of the New Testament Documents,* 116.

26. Hafemann, "Preaching in the Epistles," 365.

27. Ong, *Orality and Literacy,* 115; Havelock, *Literate Revolution in Greece,* 29; Doty, *Letters in Primitive Christianity,* 7; and Webb, *Divine Voice,* 200.

28. Stirewalt, *Paul the Letter Writer,* 23.

29. See C. W. Davis, *Oral Biblical Criticism,* 80–90.

30. Richards, *Paul and First-Century Letter Writing,* 134.

31. Ibid., 161.

32. Ibid., 32–35, 64. The author of the letter was always held responsible for its contents even when the letter was prepared with the help of a secretary or team. See ibid., 84.

33. Ibid., 165–69.

34. Ibid., 26–31.

35. Stirewalt, *Paul the Letter Writer,* 20–22.

36. Lovejoy, "But I Did Such Good Exposition," 26.

37. C. W. Davis, *Oral Biblical Criticism,* 16.

38. Review chapter 6 on parables to see how Jesus likened himself to the responsible wife, strong shepherd, and loving father.

39. Craddock, *As One Without Authority,* 131.

40. Boreham, "The First Hymn," 88.

41. Francis M. Dwyer, *Strategies for Improving Visual Learning: A Handbook for the Effective Selection, Design, and Use of Visualized Materials* (State College, PA: Learning Services, 1978); quoted in Litfin, *Public Speaking,* 224.

42. For a fuller discussion of the material in this point, see Arthurs and Gurevich, "Proclamation Through Conversation," 35–45.

43. R. L. Lewis and G. Lewis, *Learning to Preach Like Jesus*, 28.

44. Much has been written about the use of dialogue. See Eggold, *Preaching Is Dialogue*; Freeman, *Variety in Biblical Preaching*, chaps. 8–10; Howe, *Miracle of Dialogue*; and Pagitt, *Preaching Re-Imagined.*

45. See Anderson, "The Place of the Pulpit."

46. Arnold, "Oral Rhetoric, Rhetoric, and Literature," 70.

47. See Sunukjian, "Skills of Oral Clarity."

48. Chapell, *Christ-Centered Preaching*, 122.

49. Rudolf Flesch, *The Art of Plain Talk* (New York: Harper and Bros., 1946), 147; quoted in Eggold, *Preaching Is Dialogue*, 87.

50. See McClellan, "Recovering a Sense of Orality."

51. See Arthurs, "No Notes."

52. As an exemplar, listen to the sermons of Timothy Keller, Pastor of Redeemer Presbyterian Church in New York City, http://www.redeemer3.com/store/index.cfm?fuseaction= category.display&category_id=11&CFID=189689&CFTOKEN= 90165877.

53. J. W. Thompson, *Preaching Like Paul*, 141.

54. Ibid.

55. Aristotle, *Rhetoric and the Poetics*, 1356a.

56. See Arthurs and Gurevich, "Theological and Rhetorical Perspectives," 215–26.

Chapter 9: Apocalyptic Literature: Vision and Victory

1. McGinn, "Revelation," 536.

2. Ibid., 523.

3. This definition is my own, influenced by J. J. Collins, "Introduction: Toward the Morphology of a Genre," 9; and A. Y. Collins, "Introduction: Early Christian Apocalypticism," 7; as well as the other articles in *Semeia*, nos. 14 and 36. See also Hanson, *Old Testament Apocalyptic*, 27–28; and J. J. Collins, *The Apocalyptic Imagination*, 2–11

4. Bitzer, "Rhetorical Situation," 6. See also, Fiorenza, "Followers of the Lamb," who uses Bitzer extensively.

5.   Long, "Preaching Apocalyptic Literature," 378.

6.   Charry, "Sharp Two-Edged Sword," 163.

7.   Ryken, *How to Read,* 169–70.

8.   Bloom, *Closing of the American Mind,* 25–43.

9.   Metzger, *Breaking the Code,* 13. Soulen has estimated that 70 percent of Revelation is from previously written sources such as hymns of the early church and the Old Testament, *Handbook of Biblical Criticism,* 18.

10. H. W. Robinson, *Biblical Sermons,* 255.

11. Ryken, *How to Read,* 170.

12. Coleridge, quoted in ibid., 169.

13. Jones and Sumney, *Preaching Apocalyptic Texts,* 27.

14. See Arthurs, "Long and Winding Road," http://www .preaching today.com/27499.

15. Long, "Praying for the Wrath of God," 133–34.

16. Ibid., 137–39.

17. Craddock, "Preaching the Book of Revelation," 278.

18. Martin Luther King Jr., from James Melvin White, ed., *Testament of Hope: The Essential Writings of Martin Luther King, Jr.* (San Francisco: Harper and Row, 1986), 280, 286, quoted in Jones and Sumney, *Preaching Apocalyptic Texts,* 30–31.

19. Ibid., 28.

20. Martin Luther, "A Mighty Fortress Is Our God," public domain.

21. Fee and Stuart, *How to Read the Bible,* 215.

22. Craddock, "Preaching the Book of Revelation," 275.

23. See http://home.pacbell.net/andrea/wurmbrandbio.html.

24. Ibid., 282.

25. See http://www.cswusa.com/Countries/NorthKorea.htm; and http://www.persecution.org/newsite/countryinfodetail .php?countrycode=29.

26. Allen Boesak, *Comfort and Protest: The Apocalypse from a South African Perspective* (Philadelphia: Westminster, 1987), 90, quoted in Long, "Preacher and the Beast," 18–19.

27. Craddock, "Preaching the Book of Revelation," 282.

28. Coleman, *Songs of Heaven,* 76.

29. This hymn is in the public domain. See http://www.simusic .com/worship/hymns/.

Bibliography

Achtemeier, Elizabeth. *Creative Preaching: Finding the Words.* Nashville: Abingdon, 1980.

Achtemeier, Paul. "Omne Verbum Sonat: The New Testament and the Oral Environment of Late Western Antiquity." *Journal of Biblical Literature* 109, no. 1 (1990): 3–27.

Adams, Jay E. "Sense Appeal and Storytelling." In *The Preacher and Preaching,* edited by Samuel T. Logan Jr., 350–66. Phillipsburg, NJ: Presbyterian and Reformed, 1986.

———. *Sense Appeal in the Sermons of Charles Haddon Spurgeon.* Phillipsburg, NJ: Presbyterian and Reformed, 1975.

Aggertt, Otis J., and Elbert R. Bowen. *Communicative Reading.* 2nd ed. New York: Macmillan, 1963.

Alter, Robert. *The Art of Biblical Narrative.* New York: Basic, 1981.

———. *The Art of Biblical Poetry.* New York: Basic, 1987.

———. "The Characteristics of Ancient Hebrew Poetry." In *The Literary Guide to the Bible,* edited by Robert Alter and Frank Kermode, 611–24. Cambridge, MA: Harvard University Press, 1987.

Anderson, Kenton C. "The Place of the Pulpit." *Preaching* 15, no. 1 (1999): 23–25.

Aristotle. *The Rhetoric and the Poetics of Aristotle.* Translated by W. Rhys Roberts. New York: Modern Library, 1984.

Arnold, Carroll C. "Oral Rhetoric, Rhetoric, and Literature." In *Contemporary Rhetoric: A Reader's Coursebook,* edited by

Douglas Ehninger, 60–73. Glenview, IL: Scott Foresman, 1972. Originally published in *Philosophy and Rhetoric* 11 (1968): 191–210.

Arthurs, Jeffrey D. "The Long and Winding Road," a five-part sermon series, *Preaching Today,* http://www.preachingtoday .com/27499.

———. "No Notes, Lots of Notes, Brief Notes." In *The Art and Craft of Biblical Preaching: A Comprehensive Resource for Today's Communicators,* edited by Haddon W. Robinson and Craig Brian Larson, 600–606. Grand Rapids: Zondervan, 2005.

———. "Performing the Story: How to Preach First-Person Narrative Sermons." *Preaching* 12, no. 5 (1997): 30–35.

———. "The Place of Pathos in Preaching." *Journal of the Evangelical Homiletics Society* 1, no. 1 (2001): 15–21.

———. "Proverbs in Inspirational Literature: Sanctioning the American Dream." *Journal of Communication and Religion* 17, no. 2 (1994): 1–16.

Arthurs, Jeffrey D., and Andrew Gurevich. "Proclamation Through Conversation: Dialogue as a Form for Preaching." *Journal of the American Academy of Ministry* 5 (Winter–Spring 1997): 35–45.

———. "Theological and Rhetorical Perspectives on Self-Disclosure in Preaching." *Bibliotheca Sacra* 157, no. 626 (2000): 215–26.

Aucion, Don. "The Need for Speed." *Boston Globe,* November 19, 2005, D1, D5.

Auerbach, Eric. *Mimesis: The Representation of Reality in Western Literature.* Translated by Willard Trask. Princeton, NJ: Princeton University Press, 1953.

Augustine. *On Christian Doctrine.* Translated by D. W. Robertson Jr. The Library of the Liberal Arts. Indianapolis: Bobbs-Merrill, 1958.

Aune, David E. *The New Testament in Its Literary Environment.* Philadelphia: Westminster, 1987.

Aurandt, Paul. *Destiny.* New York: Bantam, 1983.

———. *More of Paul Harvey's The Rest of the Story.* New York: Bantam, 1980.

————. *Paul Harvey's The Rest of the Story.* New York: Bantam, 1977.

Austin, John L. *How to Do Things with Words.* New York: Oxford University Press, 1970.

Ayer, William Ward. "The Art of Effective Preaching." *Bibliotheca Sacra* 124, no. 493 (1967): 30–41.

Bailey, E. K. "My Name Is Hosea." Audio CD from *Preaching Today,* vol. 224.

Bailey, James L., and Lyle D. Vander Broek. *Literary Forms in the New Testament: A Handbook.* Louisville: Westminster/John Knox, 1992.

Bailey, Kenneth. *Finding the Lost: Cultural Keys to Luke 15.* St. Louis: Concordia, 1992.

————. *Jacob and the Prodigal: How Jesus Retold Israel's Story.* Downers Grove, IL: InterVarsity Press, 2003.

————. *Poet and Peasant: A Literary-Cultural Approach to the Parables in Luke.* Grand Rapids: Eerdmans, 1976.

Bailey, Raymond. "Preaching in the Electronic Age." *Review and Expositor* 90, no. 3 (1993): 351–57.

Bailey, Raymond, and James L. Blevins. *Dramatic Monologues: Make the Bible Live.* Nashville: Broadman and Holman, 1990.

Bar-Efrat, Shimon. *Narrative Art in the Bible.* Sheffield: Almond, 1989.

Barthes, Roland. *Image, Music, Text.* Translated by Stephen Heath. New York: Hill and Wang, 1977.

Barton, William E. *The Millionaire and the Scrublady, and Other Parables.* Edited by Garth Rosell and Stan Flewelling. Grand Rapids: Zondervan, 1990.

Bell, Rob. "Subversive Preaching." From a live lecture delivered by satellite link June 3, 2004. Sponsored by *Christianity Today* and *Leadership.*

Berlin, Adele. *Poetics and Interpretation of Biblical Narrative.* Sheffield: Almond, 1983.

Bitzer, Lloyd F. "Aristotle's Enthymeme Revisited." *Quarterly Journal of Speech* 45, no. 4 (1959): 399–408.

————. "The Rhetorical Situation." *Philosophy and Rhetoric* 1, no. 1 (1968): 1–14.

Blomberg, Craig. *Interpreting the Parables.* Downers Grove, IL: InterVarsity Press, 1990.

————. *Preaching the Parables: From Responsible Interpretation to Powerful Proclamation.* Grand Rapids: Baker, 2004.

————. "Preaching the Parables: Preserving Three Main Points." *Perspectives in Religious Studies* 11, no. 1 (1984): 31–41.

Bloom, Allan. *The Closing of the American Mind.* New York: Simon and Schuster, 1987.

Booth, Wayne C. "The Pleasures and Pitfalls of Irony." In *Rhetoric, Philosophy, and Literature: An Exploration,* edited by Don M. Burks, 1–13. West Lafayette, IN: Purdue University Press, 1978.

————. *The Rhetoric of Fiction.* 2nd ed. Chicago: University of Chicago Press, 1983.

————. *A Rhetoric of Irony.* Chicago: University of Chicago Press, 1974.

Borden, Paul. "Is There Really One Big Idea in That Story?" In *The Big Idea of Biblical Preaching: Connecting the Bible to People,* edited by Keith Willhite and Scott M. Gibson, 67–80. Grand Rapids: Baker, 1998.

Boreham, F. W. "The First Hymn." *Journal of the Evangelical Homiletics Society* 5, no. 2 (2005): 83–89.

Botha, Pierta J. J. "The Verbal Art of the Pauline Letters: Rhetoric, Performance and Presence." In *Rhetoric and the New Testament: Essays from the 1992 Heidelberg Conference,* edited by Staley Porter and Thomas Olbricht, 409–28. Sheffield: JSOT Press, 1993.

Brown, David M. *Dramatic Narrative in Preaching.* Valley Forge, PA: Judson, 1981.

Bryant, Donald C. "Rhetoric: Its Functions and Its Scope." *Quarterly Journal of Speech* 39, no. 4 (1953): 401–24.

Bullinger, E. W. *Figures of Speech Used in the Bible.* 1898. Reprint, Grand Rapids: Baker, 1968.

Burke, Kenneth. *Counter-Statement.* 1931. Reprint, Berkeley: University of California Press, 1968.

———. *A Rhetoric of Motives*. 1950. Reprint, Berkeley: University of California Press, 1969.

Buttrick, David A. *A Captive Voice: The Liberation of Preaching*. Louisville: Westminster/John Knox, 1994.

———. *Homiletic: Moves and Structures*. Philadelphia: Fortress, 1987.

———. *Speaking Parables: A Homiletic Guide*. Louisville: John Knox, 2000.

Buttry, David L. *First-Person Preaching: Bringing New Life to Biblical Stories*. Valley Forge, PA: Judson, 1998.

Caird, G. B. *The Language and Imagery of the Bible*. Philadelphia: Westminster, 1980.

Camery-Hoggatt, Jerry. *Irony in Mark's Gospel*. Cambridge: Cambridge University Press, 1992.

———. *Speaking of God: Reading and Preaching the Word of God*. Peabody, MA: Hendrickson, 1995.

Carey, Greg, and Gregory L. Bloomquist, eds. *Vision and Persuasion: Rhetorical Dimensions of Apocalyptic Discourse*. St. Louis: Chalice Press, 1999.

Carson, D. A. "Four Ironies of the Cross." From an audio CD. *Preaching Today,* vol. 236.

Chapell, Bryan C. *Christ-Centered Preaching: Redeeming the Expository Sermon*. 2nd ed. Grand Rapids: Baker, 2005.

———. *Using Illustrations to Preach with Power*. Rev. ed. Wheaton, IL: Crossway, 2001.

Charry, Ellen T. "A Sharp Two-Edged Sword: Pastoral Implications of Apocalyptic." *Interpretation* 53, no. 2 (1999): 158–72.

Ciardi, John. *How Does a Poem Mean?* Boston: Houghton Mifflin, 1975.

Clines, David J. A. "Story and Poem: The Old Testament as Literature and as Scripture." *Interpretation* 34, no. 2 (1980): 115–27.

Cochran, Shelley E. "The Ear of the Listener." *Homiletic* 18, no. 1 (1993): 7–10.

Coleman, Robert E. *Songs of Heaven*. Old Tappan, NJ: Revell, 1980.

Collins, Adela Yarbro. *Crisis and Catharsis: The Power of the Apocalypse.* Philadelphia: Westminster, 1984.

———. "Introduction: Early Christian Apocalypticism." *Semeia* 36 (1986): 1–11.

Collins, John J. *The Apocalyptic Imagination: An Introduction to Jewish Apocalyptic Literature.* 2nd ed. Grand Rapids: Eerdmans, 1998.

———. "Introduction: Toward the Morphology of a Genre." *Semeia* 14 (1979): 1–20.

Corey, Barry. "Nehemiah 5." Live sermon given at Gordon-Conwell Theological Seminary, November 24, 2004.

Craddock, Fred B. *As One Without Authority.* 4th ed. St. Louis: Chalice, 2001.

———. *Overhearing the Gospel.* Rev. ed. St. Louis: Chalice, 2002.

———. *Preaching.* Nashville: Abingdon, 1985.

———. "Preaching the Book of Revelation." *Interpretation* 40, no. 3 (1986): 270–82.

Crenshaw, James L. *Old Testament Wisdom: An Introduction.* Rev. ed. Atlanta: John Knox, 1998.

Crites, Stephen. "The Narrative Quality of Experience." *Journal of the American Academy of Religion* 39, no. 3 (1971): 291–311.

Crossan, John Dominic. *In Fragments: The Aphorisms of Jesus.* San Francisco: Harper and Row, 1983.

Crouch, Andy. "Visualcy: Literacy Is Not the Only Necessity in a Visual Culture." *Christianity Today* 29, no. 6 (June 2005): 62.

Cummings, E. E. "in Just—" In *The Poem: An Anthology,* edited by Stanley B. Greenfield and A. Kingsley Weatherhead, 347. New York: Appleton-Century-Croft, 1968.

Davids, Peter H. *The Epistle of James: A Commentary on the Greek Text.* Grand Rapids: Eerdmans, 1982.

Davis, Casey Wayne. *Oral Biblical Criticism: The Influence of the Principles of Orality on the Literary Structure of Paul's Epistle to the Philippians.* Sheffield: Sheffield Academic Press, 1999.

Davis, H. Grady. *Design for Preaching.* Philadelphia: Fortress, 1958.

Dawsey, James. *The Lukan Voice: Confusion and Irony in the Gospel of Luke.* Macon, GA: Mercer University Press, 1986.

Deissmann, Adolf. *Light from the Ancient East.* 1911. 2nd ed. Translated by L. R. M. Stachan. New York: George H. Doran, 1927.

Dodd, C. H. *The Parables of the Kingdom.* 1936. Rev. ed. New York: Scribner's, 1961.

Doty, William G. *Letters in Primitive Christianity.* Philadelphia: Fortress, 1973.

Duke, Paul D. *Irony in the Fourth Gospel.* Atlanta: John Knox, 1985.

Dundes, Alan. *The Study of Folklore.* Englewood Cliffs, NJ: Prentice-Hall, 1965.

Du Toit, A. B., ed. *The New Testament Milieu.* Translated by D. Roy Briggs. Halfway House: Orion, 1998. Libronix Digital Library System CD-ROM.

Edwards, J. Kent. *Effective First-Person Biblical Preaching: The Steps from Text to Narrative Sermon.* Grand Rapids: Zondervan, 2005.

Eggold, Henry J. *Preaching Is Dialogue: A Concise Introduction to Homiletics.* Grand Rapids: Baker, 1980.

Elliot, Mark Barger. *Creative Styles of Preaching.* Louisville: Westminster/John Knox, 2000.

Ellis, E. E. *The Making of the New Testament Documents.* Leiden: Brill, 1999.

Faro, Pam. "Stories Near and Stories Far." Lafayette, CO: n.p., 1994. From an audio cassette.

Fee, Gordon D., and Douglas Stuart. *How to Read the Bible for All Its Worth: A Guide to Understanding the Bible.* Grand Rapids: Zondervan, 1982.

Fiorenza, Elisabeth Schüssler. "The Followers of the Lamb: Visionary Rhetoric and Socio-Political Situation." *Semeia* 36 (1986): 125–46.

Freeman, Harold. *Variety in Biblical Preaching: Innovative Techniques and Fresh Forms.* Waco, TX: Word, 1987.

Frye, Northrop. *Anatomy of Criticism.* Princeton, NJ: Princeton University Press, 1957.

———. *The Great Code: The Bible and Literature.* New York: Harcourt, Brace, and Jovanovich, 1982.

Frye, Northrop, Sheridan Baker, and George Perkins. *The Harper Handbook to Literature.* New York: Harper and Row, 1985.

Gardner, Howard. *Multiple Intelligences: The Theory in Practice.* New York: Basic, 1999.

Garrett, Duane A. *Proverbs, Ecclesiastes, Song of Solomon.* Nashville: Broadman and Holman, 1993.

Goldingay, John. "Preaching on the Stories in Scripture." *Anvil* 7, no. 2 (1990): 105–14.

Goldsworthy, Graeme. *Preaching the Whole Bible as Christian Scripture.* Grand Rapids: Eerdmans, 2000.

Good, Edwin M. *Irony in the Old Testament.* Philadelphia: Westminster, 1965.

Graves, Mike. *The Sermon as Symphony: Preaching the Literary Forms of the New Testament.* Valley Forge, PA: Judson, 1997.

Gregory, John Milton. *The Seven Laws of Teaching.* 1884. Rev. ed. Grand Rapids: Baker, 1988.

Greidanus, Sidney. *The Modern Preacher and the Ancient Text: Interpreting and Preaching Biblical Literature.* Grand Rapids: Eerdmans, 1988.

———. *Preaching Christ from the Old Testament.* Grand Rapids: Eerdmans, 1999.

———. *Sola Scriptura: Problems and Principles in Preaching Historical Texts.* Toronto: Wedge, 1970.

Griffin, William. *Clive Staples Lewis: A Dramatic Life.* New York: Harper and Row, 1968.

Guershoon, Andrew. *Certain Aspects of Russian Proverbs.* London: Frederick Muller, 1941.

Guinness, Os. *Fit Bodies, Fat Minds: Why Evangelicals Don't Think and What to Do About It.* Grand Rapids: Baker, 1994.

Hafemann, Scott. "Preaching in the Epistles." In *Handbook of Contemporary Preaching,* edited by Michael Duduit, 361–77. Nashville: Broadman and Holman, 1992.

Hanson, Paul D. *Old Testament Apocalyptic.* Nashville: Abingdon, 1987.

Havelock, Eric A. *The Literate Revolution in Greece and Its Cultural Consequences.* Princeton, NJ: Princeton University Press, 1982.

Hermann, Ned. "The Creative Brain." *Training and Development Journal* 35, no. 10 (1981): 10–16.

Holmgren, Frederick. "Barking Dogs Never Bite, Except Now and Then: Proverbs and Job." *Anglican Theological Review* 61, no. 3 (1979): 341–53.

Hopkins, Gerard Manly. "Pied Beauty." In *The Poem: An Anthology,* edited by Stanley B. Greenfield and A. Kingsley Weatherhead, 298–99. New York: Meridith, 1968.

Horne, Herman H. *Jesus—the Master Teacher.* 1920. Reprint, Grand Rapids: Kregel, 1964.

Howard, J. Grant. *Creativity in Preaching.* Grand Rapids: Zondervan, 1987.

Howard, Robert R. "Gender and Point of View in the Imagery of Preaching." *Homiletic* 24, no. 1 (1999): 1–12.

Howe, Reuel L. *The Miracle of Dialogue.* New York: Seabury, 1963.

Isocrates. *Antidosis.* Translated by George Norlin. London: William Heinemann, 1929.

Jacobsen, David Schnasa. *Preaching in the New Creation: The Promise of New Testament Apocalyptic Texts.* Louisville: Westminster/John Knox, 1999.

Jeter, Joseph R., and Ronald J. Allen. *One Gospel, Many Ears: Preaching for Different Listeners in the Congregation.* St. Louis: Chalice, 2002.

Jones, Larry Paul, and Jerry L. Sumney. *Preaching Apocalyptic Texts.* St. Louis: Chalice, 1999.

Kaiser, Walter C., Jr. *Toward an Exegetical Theology: Biblical Exegesis for Preaching and Teaching.* Grand Rapids: Baker, 1981.

Keller, Timothy. See note 52 on page 219.

Kennedy, George. *Classical Rhetoric and Its Christian and Secular Tradition from Ancient to Modern Times.* Chapel Hill, NC: University of North Carolina Press, 1980.

Kirkwood, William G. "Storytelling and Self-Confrontation: Parables as Communication Strategies." *Quarterly Journal of Speech* 69, no. 1 (1983): 58–74.

Kirshenblatt-Gimblett, Barbara. "Toward a Theory of Proverb Meaning." In *The Wisdom of Many,* edited by Wolfgang Meider and Alan Dundes, 111–21. New York: Garland, 1981.

Kooienga, William H. *Elements of Style for Preaching.* Grand Rapids: Zondervan, 1989.

Kugel, James L. *The Idea of Biblical Poetry: Parallelism and Its History.* New Haven: Yale University Press, 1981.

Larsen, David L. *The Anatomy of a Sermon: Identifying the Issues in Preaching Today.* Grand Rapids: Kregel, 1989.

———. *Telling the Old, Old Story: The Art of Narrative Preaching.* Grand Rapids: Kregel, 1995.

Lee, Charlotte I., and Timothy Gura. *Oral Interpretation.* 7th ed. Boston: Houghton Mifflin, 1987.

Lewis, C. S. *An Experiment in Criticism.* Cambridge: Cambridge University Press, 1961.

———. *God in the Dock: Essays on Theology and Ethics.* Grand Rapids: Eerdmans: 1970.

———. *Reflections on the Psalms.* New York: Harcourt, Brace, and Jovanovich, 1958.

———. *They Asked for a Paper: Papers and Addresses.* London: Geoffrey Bles, 1962.

Lewis, Ralph L., and Gregg Lewis. *Inductive Preaching: Helping People Listen.* Westchester, IL: Crossway, 1983.

———. *Learning to Preach Like Jesus.* Wheaton, IL: Crossway, 1989.

Lischer, Richard. "The Limits of Story." *Interpretation* 38, no. 1 (1984): 26–38.

Litfin, Duane. *Public Speaking: A Handbook for Christians.* 2nd ed. Grand Rapids: Baker, 1992.

Lloyd-Jones, D. Martyn. *The Christian Soldier: An Exposition of Ephesians* 6:10–20. Grand Rapids: Baker, 1978.

———. *Preaching and Preachers.* Grand Rapids: Zondervan, 1971.

Long, Thomas G. "Praying for the Wrath of God." In *Preaching Through the Apocalypse: Sermons from Revelation,* edited by Cornish R. Rogers and Joseph R. Jeter Jr., 133–39. St. Louis: Chalice, 1992.

———. "The Preacher and the Beast: From Apocalyptic Text to Sermon." In *Intersections: Post-Critical Studies in Preaching,* edited by Richard L. Eslinger, 1–22. Grand Rapids: Eerdmans, 1994.

———. *Preaching and the Literary Forms of the Bible.* Philadelphia: Fortress, 1989.

———. "Preaching Apocalyptic Literature." *Review and Expositor* 90, no. 3 (1993): 371–81.

Lovejoy, Grant. "'But I Did Such Good Exposition': Literate Preachers Confront Orality." *Journal of the Evangelical Homiletics Society* 1, no. 1 (2001): 22–32.

Lowry, Eugene L. *The Homiletical Plot: The Sermon as Narrative Art Form.* Atlanta: John Knox, 1980.

———. *How to Preach a Parable: Designs for Narrative Sermons.* Nashville: Abingdon, 1989.

Lubeck, Ray. "Dusting Off the Old Testament for a New Millennium." In *Preaching to a Shifting Culture: Twelve Perspectives on Communicating That Connects,* edited by Scott M. Gibson, 17–37. Grand Rapids: Baker, 2004.

Lucado, Max. "It's Not Up to You." Audio recording of a sermon at Willow Creek Community Church, South Barrington, IL, June 24, 2004, available from http://www.willowcreek .org/seeds.asp.

MacDonald, George. *The Gifts of the Christ Child: Fairy Tales and Stories for the Childlike.* Edited by Glenn Edward Sadler. Vol. 1. Grand Rapids: Eerdmans, 1973.

Mathews, Alice P. *Preaching That Speaks to Women.* Grand Rapids: Baker, 2003.

Mathewson, Steven D. *The Art of Preaching Old Testament Narrative.* Grand Rapids: Baker, 2002.

Mayhue, Richard L. "Rediscovering Expository Preaching." In *Expository Preaching: Balancing the Science and Art of Biblical*

Exposition, edited by John MacArthur Jr., 3–21. Dallas: Word, 1992.

Mayor, Tracy. "What Are Video Games Turning Us Into?" *Boston Globe Magazine,* February 20, 2005, 19–21, 32–37.

McClellan, Dave. "Recovering a Sense of Orality in Homiletics." *Journal of the Evangelical Homiletics Society* 6, no. 1 (March 2006): 4–22.

McGee, Michael C. "Thematic Reduplication in Christian Rhetoric." *Quarterly Journal of Speech* 56, no. 2 (1970): 196–204.

McGinn, Bernard. "Revelation." In *The Literary Guide to the Bible,* edited by Robert Alter and Frank Kermode, 523–41. Cambridge, MA: Harvard University Press, 1987.

McKenzie, Alyce M. *Preaching Proverbs: Wisdom for the Pulpit.* Louisville: Westminster/John Knox, 1996.

McKerrow, Raymie E., Bruce E. Gronbeck, Douglas Ehninger, and Alan H. Monroe. *Principles and Types of Speech Communication.* 12th ed. Boston: Allyn and Bacon, 1999.

Meider, Wolfgang, and Alan Dundes. *The Wisdom of Many.* New York: Garland, 1981.

Melick, Richard. "Preaching and Apocalyptic Literature." In *Handbook of Contemporary Preaching,* edited by Michael Duduit, 378–89. Nashville: Broadman and Holman, 1992.

Metzger, Bruce M. *Breaking the Code: Understanding the Book of Revelation.* Nashville: Abingdon, 1993.

Middleton, J. Richard, and Brian J. Walsh. *Truth Is Stranger Than It Used to Be: Biblical Faith in a Postmodern World.* Downers Grove, IL: InterVarsity Press, 1995.

Miller, Mark. *Experiential Storytelling: [Re]Discovering Narrative to Communicate God's Message.* Grand Rapids: Emergent YS, 2003.

Mitchell, Jolyon P. *Visually Speaking: Radio and the Renaissance of Preaching.* Louisville: Westminster/John Knox, 1999.

Morris, Leon. *Apocalyptic.* Grand Rapids: Eerdmans, 1972.

Myers, Isabel Briggs, and Peter B. Myers. *Gifts Differing.* Palo Alto, CA: Consulting Psychologists Press, 1980.

Newman, R. C. "Rabbinic Parables." In *Dictionary of New Testament Background,* edited by Craig A. Evans and Stanley E. Porter, 909–11. Downers Grove, IL: InterVarsity Press, 2000.

Norrick, Neal R. *How Proverbs Mean: Semantic Studies in English Proverbs.* New York: Moulton, 1985.

Nouwen, Henri. *The Return of the Prodigal Son.* New York: Doubleday, 1992.

O'Brien, P. T. "Letters, Letter Forms." In *Dictionary of Paul and His Letters,* edited by Gerald F. Hawthorne, Ralph P. Martin, and Daniel G. Reid, 550–53. Downers Grove, IL: InterVarsity Press, 1993.

Ong, Walter J. *Orality and Literacy: The Technologizing of the Word.* New York: Methuen, 1982.

———. *The Presence of the Word: Some Prolegomena for Cultural and Religious History.* 1967. Reprint, Minneapolis: University of Minnesota Press, 1981.

Osborne, Grant. *The Hermeneutical Spiral.* Downers Grove, IL: InterVarsity Press, 1991.

Pagitt, Doug. *Preaching Re-Imagined: The Role of the Sermon in Communities of Faith.* Grand Rapids: Zondervan, 2005.

Pascal. *Pensées.* New York: E. P. Dutton, 1958.

Peters, Thomas J., and Robert H. Waterman. *In Search of Excellence: Lessons from America's Best Run Companies.* New York: Harper, 1982.

Piper, John. "Battling the Unbelief of Bitterness." *Preaching Today,* vol. 249 (from an audio CD).

———. *The Supremacy of God in Preaching.* Grand Rapids: Baker, 1990.

Postman, Neil. *Amusing Ourselves to Death: Public Discourse in the Age of Show Business.* New York: Penguin, 1985.

Pratt, Richard L., Jr. *He Gave Us Stories: The Bible Student's Guide to Interpreting Old Testament Narratives.* Brentwood, TN: Wolgemuth and Hyatt, 1990.

Quicke, Michael. "Applying God's Word in a Secular Culture." *Preaching* 17, no. 4 (2002): 7–15.

Quintilian. *The Institutes of Oratory.* London: George Bell and Sons, 1987.

Ramm, Bernard. *Protestant Biblical Interpretation.* 3rd ed. Grand Rapids: Baker, 1985.

RealVision. "Facts and Figures About Our TV Habit." TV-Turnoff Network. http://www.tvturnoff.org/images/facts&figs/factsheets/FactsFigs.pdf.

Rice, Charles. "Shaping Sermons by the Interplay of Text and Metaphor." In *Preaching Biblically: Creating Sermons in the Shape of Scripture,* edited by Don M. Wardlaw, 101–20. Philadelphia: Westminster, 1983.

Richards, E. Randolph. *Paul and First-Century Letter Writing: Secretaries, Composition, and Collection.* Downers Grove, IL: InterVarsity Press, 2004.

Ricoeur, Paul. "Biblical Hermeneutics." *Semeia* 4 (1975): 29–148.

Robinson, Haddon W. *Biblical Preaching: The Development and Delivery of Expository Message.* 2nd ed. Grand Rapids: Baker, 2001.

———, ed. *Biblical Sermons: How Twelve Preachers Apply the Principles of Biblical Preaching.* Grand Rapids: Baker, 1989.

———. "The Broken Heart of David Jessison." Sermon given in Portland, OR, 1994 (from an unpublished copy of cassette).

———. "Mid-life Crisis, Problem Ancient and Modern." From a cassette copy of an unpublished sermon given in Portland, OR, 1994.

Robinson, Haddon W., and Torrey W. Robinson. *It's All in How You Tell It: Preaching First-Person Expository Messages.* Grand Rapids: Baker, 2003.

Rogers, Cornish R., and Joseph R. Jeter Jr., eds. *Preaching Through the Apocalypse: Sermons from Revelation.* St. Louis: Chalice, 1992.

Rogne, David G. *Tell It Like It Was: Preaching in the First Person.* Lima, OH: CSS, 2001.

Russell, D. S. *Prophecy and the Apocalyptic Dream: Discovering Modern Meaning in an Ancient Message.* Peabody, MA: Hendrickson, 1994.

Ryken, Leland. "And It Came to Pass: The Bible as God's Storybook." *Bibliotheca Sacra* 147, no. 586 (1990): 131–42.

————. *How to Read the Bible as Literature.* Grand Rapids: Zondervan, 1984.

————. *The Literature of the Bible.* Grand Rapids: Zondervan, 1974.

Ryken, Leland, James C. Wilhoit, and Tremper Longmann III, eds. "Parable." In *Dictionary of Biblical Imagery,* 623–24. Downers Grove, IL: InterVarsity Press, 1998.

Sailhamer, John. *Introduction to Old Testament Theology.* Grand Rapids: Zondervan, 1995.

Sample, Tex. *Ministry in an Oral Culture: Living with Will Rogers, Uncle Remus, and Minnie Pearl.* Louisville: Westminster/John Knox, 1994.

————. *Powerful Persuasion: Multimedia Witness in Christian Worship.* Nashville: Abingdon, 2005.

Schaeffer, Francis A. *The God Who Is There.* Vol. 1. of *The Complete Works of Francis A. Schaeffer.* 1968. Reprint, Wheaton, IL: Crossway, 1982.

Schultze, Quentin J. *High Tech Worship? Using Presentational Technologies Wisely.* Grand Rapids: Baker, 2004.

Scott, R. B. Y. *The Way of Wisdom in the Old Testament.* New York: Collier, 1971.

Searle, John R. *Speech Acts: An Essay in the Philosophy of Language.* Cambridge: Cambridge University Press, 1969.

Short, Robert. *A Time to Be Born—A Time to Die.* New York: Harper and Row, 1973.

Simmon, Annette. *The Story Factor: Secrets of Influence from the Art of Storytelling.* Cambridge, MA: Perseus, 2001.

Snodgrass, K. R. "Parable." In *Dictionary of Jesus and the Gospels,* edited by Joel B. Green, Scot McKnight, and I. Howard Marshall, 591–93. Downers Grove, IL: InterVarsity Press, 1992.

Snow, Malinda. "Martin Luther King's 'Letter from Birmingham Jail' as Pauline Epistle." *Quarterly Journal of Speech* 71, no. 3 (1985): 318–34.

Soulen, Richard N. *Handbook of Biblical Criticism.* Atlanta: John Knox, 1976.

Spurgeon, C. H. *Lectures to My Students*. 1875. Reprint, Grand Rapids: Baker, 1977.

Stevenson, Dwight E. *In the Biblical Preacher's Workshop*. Nashville: Abingdon, 1967.

Stevenson, Geoffrey. "Conceptions of Learning in the Preacher's Progress." Evangelical Homiletics Society. http://www.ehomiletics.com/members/papers/03/papers03.php.

Stevenson, Gregory. "Preaching Apocalyptically." *Restoration Quarterly* 42, no. 2 (2000): 233–44.

Stewart, Charles J., Craig Allen Smith, and Robert E. Denton Jr. *Persuasion and Social Movements*. 2nd ed. Prospect Heights, IL: Waveland, 1989.

Stirewalt, M. Luther, Jr. *Paul the Letter Writer*. Grand Rapids: Eerdmans, 2003.

Stott, John R. *Between Two Worlds: The Art of Preaching in the Twentieth Century*. Grand Rapids: Eerdmans, 1982.

Sunukjian, Donald. "The Cripple's Story." In *Effective First-Person Biblical Preaching*, edited by J. Kent Edwards, 156–61. Grand Rapids: Zondervan, 2005.

———. "A Night in Persia." In *Biblical Sermons: How Twelve Preachers Apply the Principles of Biblical Preaching*, edited by Haddon W. Robinson, 69–80. Grand Rapids: Baker, 1989.

———. "Skills of Oral Clarity." *Preaching Today*, vol. 226 (audio CD).

Tan, Amy. *The Joy Luck Club*. New York: Putnam's Sons, 1989.

Tannen, Deborah. *You Just Don't Understand: Men and Women in Conversation*. New York: Ballantine, 1990.

TeSelle, Sallie. *Speaking in Parables: A Study in Metaphor and Theology*. Philadelphia: Fortress, 1975.

Thompson, James W. *Preaching Like Paul: Homiletical Wisdom for Today*. Louisville: Westminster/John Knox, 2001.

Thompson, John M. *The Form and Function of Proverbs in Ancient Israel*. The Hague: Mouton, 1974.

Tisdale, Leona Tubbs. *Preaching as Local Theology and Folk Art*. Minneapolis: Fortress, 1996.

Tolkien, J. R. R. *The Fellowship of the Ring*. 1954. Reprint, New York: Ballantine, 1994.

Tolstoy, Leo. *The Kreutzer Sonata and Other Short Stories.* New York: Dover, 1993.

Tornfelt, John V. "Preaching and Learning Styles: How to Communicate So People Can Listen." Evangelical Homiletics Society. http://www.ehomiletics.com/membrs/papers/03/papres03.php.

Troeger, Thomas H. *Creating Fresh Images for Preaching: New Rungs for Jacob's Ladder.* Valley Forge, PA: Judson, 1982.

———. *Imagining a Sermon.* Nashville: Abingdon, 1990.

Waltke, Bruce K. *The Book of Proverbs, Chapters 1–14.* Grand Rapids: Eerdmans, 2004.

———. *The Book of Proverbs, Chapters 15–31.* Grand Rapids: Eerdmans, 2005.

———."Old Testament Interpretation Issues for Big Idea Preaching: Problematic Sources, Poetics, and Preaching the Old Testament." In *The Big Idea of Biblical Preaching: Connecting the Bible to People,* edited by Keith Willhite and Scott M. Gibson, 41–52. Grand Rapids: Baker, 1998.

Weaver, Richard. *The Ethics of Rhetoric.* South Bend, IN: Gateway, 1953.

Webb, Stephen H. *The Divine Voice: Christian Proclamation and the Theology of Sound.* Grand Rapids: Brazos, 2004.

Wells, David F. "Prayer: Rebelling Against the Status Quo." *Christianity Today* 23, no. 25 (1979): 1465–67.

White, John L. *Light from Ancient Letters.* Philadelphia: Fortress, 1986.

Wiersbe, Warren W. *Preaching and Teaching with Imagination: The Quest for Biblical Ministry.* Wheaton, IL: Victor, 1994.

Wilder, Amos N. *Early Christian Rhetoric.* Cambridge, MA: Harvard University Press, 1971.

———. *Jesus' Parables and the War of Myths.* Philadelphia: Fortress, 1982.

Willhite, Keith. "A Bullet Versus Buckshot: What Makes the Big Idea Work?" In *The Big Idea of Biblical Preaching: Connecting the Bible to People,* edited by Keith Willhite and Scott M. Gibson, 13–23. Grand Rapids: Baker, 1998.

Williams, James G. "Proverbs and Ecclesiastes." In *The Literary Guide to the Bible,* edited by Robert Alter and Frank Kermode, 263–82. Cambridge, MA: Harvard University Press, 1987.

―――. *Those Who Ponder Proverbs: Aphoristic Thinking and Biblical Literature.* Sheffield: Almond, 1981.

Wilson, Len, and Jason Moore. *Digital Storytellers: The Art of Communicating the Gospel in Worship.* Nashville: Abingdon, 2002.

Wright, Stephen I. "An Experiment in Biblical Criticism: Aesthetic Encounter in Reading and Preaching Scripture." In *Renewing Biblical Interpretation,* edited by Craig Bartholomew, Colin Greene, and Karl Möller, 240–67. Grand Rapids: Zondervan, 2000.

Yancey, Philip D. *What's So Amazing About Grace?* Grand Rapids: Zondervan, 1997.

Zink-Sawyer, Beverly. "The Word Purely Preached and Heard: The Listeners and the Homiletical Endeavor." *Interpretation* 51, no. 4 (1997): 342–57.